The Agile Manifesto*

Individuals and interactions	*over*	processes and tools
Working software	*over*	comprehensive documentation
Customer collaboration	*over*	contract negotiation
Responding to change	*over*	following a plan

That is, while there is value in the items on the right, we value the items on the left more.

The Agile Principles*

1. Our highest priority is to satisfy the customer through early and continuous delivery of valuable software.

2. Welcome changing requirements, even late in development. Agile processes harness change for the customer's competitive advantage.

3. Deliver working software frequently, from a couple of weeks to a couple of months, with a preference to the shorter time scale.

4. Business people and developers must work together daily throughout the project.

5. Build projects around motivated individuals. Give them the environment and support they need, and trust them to get the job done.

6. The most efficient and effective method of conveying information to and within a development team is face-to-face conversation.

7. Working software is the primary measure of progress.

8. Agile processes promote sustainable development.

9. The sponsors, developers, and users should be able to maintain a constant pace indefinitely.

10. Continuous attention to technical excellence and good design enhances agility.

11. Simplicity—the art of maximizing the amount of work not done—is essential.

12. The best architectures, requirements, and designs emerge from self-organizing teams.

13. At regular intervals, the team reflects on how to become more effective, then tunes and adjusts its behavior accordingly.

* From the Agile Alliance. www.agilealliance.com

Agile and Iterative Development

The Agile Software Development Series

Alistair Cockburn and Jim Highsmith, Series Editors

Agile software development centers on four values identified in the Agile Alliance's Manifesto:

- Individuals and interactions over processes and tools
- Working software over comprehensive documentation
- Customer collaboration over contract negotiation
- Responding to change over following a plan

The development of Agile software requires innovation and responsiveness, based on generating and sharing knowledge within a development team and with the customer. Agile software developers draw on the strengths of customers, users, and developers, finding just enough process to balance quality and agility.

The books in The Agile Software Development Series focus on sharing the experiences of such Agile developers. Individual books address individual techniques (such as Use Cases), group techniques (such as collaborative decision making), and proven solutions to different problems from a variety of organizational cultures. The result is a core of Agile best practices that will enrich your experience and improve your work.

Titles in the Series:

Steve Adolph, Paul Bramble, Alistair Cockburn, and Andy Pols; *Patterns for Effective Use Cases;* 0201721848

Alistair Cockburn; *Agile Software Development, Second Edition;* 0321482751

Alistair Cockburn; *Crystal Clear;* 0201699478

Alistair Cockburn; *Surviving Object-Oriented Projects;* 0201498340

Alistair Cockburn; *Writing Effective Use Cases;* 0201702258

Anne Mette Jonassen Hass; *Configuration Management Principles and Practice;* 0321117662

Jim Highsmith; *Agile Software Development Ecosystems;* 0201760436

Jim Highsmith; *Agile Project Management;* 0321219775

Craig Larman; *Agile and Iterative Development;* 0131111558

Dean Leffingwell; *Scaling Software Agility*; 0321458192

Mary Poppendieck and Tom Poppendieck; *Lean Software Development;* 0321150783

Jean Tabaka; *Collaboration Explained;* 0321268776

Kevin Tate; *Sustainable Software Development;* 0321286081

Agile and Iterative Development

A Manager's Guide

Craig Larman

✦✦Addison-Wesley

Boston • San Francisco • New York • Toronto • Montreal
London • Munich • Paris • Madrid
Capetown • Sydney • Tokyo • Singapore • Mexico City

The publisher offers discounts on this book when ordered in quantity for bulk purchases and special sales. For more information, please contact:

U.S. Corporate and Government Sales
(800) 382-3419
corpsales@pearsontechgroup.com

For sales outside of the U.S., please contact:

International Sales
(317) 581-3793
international@pearsontechgroup.com

Visit Addison-Wesley on the Web: www.awprofessional.com

Library of Congress Cataloging-in-Publication Data

Larman, Craig.
    Agile and iterative development : a manager's guide / Craig Larman.
       p. cm. -- (Agile software development series)
    Includes bibliographical references and index.
    ISBN 0-13-111155-8 (pbk.)
    1. Computer Software--Development. I. Title. II. Series.

  QA76.76.D47L39 2003
  005.1--dc22
2003058266

ISBN 0-13-111155-8

Text printed in the United States on recycled paper at Courier Westford in Westford, Massachusetts.

10th Printing   October 2008

For Julie, Haley, and Hannah

with love and thanks

CONTENTS AT A GLANCE

TABLE OF CONTENTS

PREFACE

Thank you for reading this book! My sincere aim is that it is useful—quality information, quickly understood.

Some related articles and pointers are at www.craiglarman.com. Please contact me with questions at craig@craiglarman.com.

Typographic Conventions

This is a basic *point of emphasis*. Book titles are also italicized.

This is a ***noticeable point of emphasis*** I wish to make easy for you to see. Usually, so you can skim pages and pick out key ideas.

This is a **new term** in a sentence.

This is a reference [Bob67] in the bibliography.

About the Author

Craig Larman serves as Chief Scientist for Valtech, an international consulting and skills transfer company with divisions in Europe, Asia, and North America. He also works globally as an independent consultant, coach, and speaker.

Craig is the author of *Applying UML and Patterns: An Introduction to Object-Oriented Analysis and Design*, the world's best-selling text on OOA/D and iterative development, translated to many languages and used worldwide in industry and colleges.

After a failed career as a wandering street musician, he built systems in APL, PL/I, and 4GLs in the 1970s. Starting in the early 1980s—after a full recovery—he became interested in artificial intelligence (having little of his own) and knowledge representation, and built knowledge systems with Lisp machines, Lisp, Prolog, and Smalltalk. He has played bad lead guitar in his very part-time band, the *Changing Requirements* (it used to be called the *Requirements*, but some band members changed...).

Craig has a B.S. and M.S. in computer science from beautiful Simon Fraser University in Vancouver, Canada.

Acknowledgments

A special thanks to my friends and colleagues at Valtech, world-class iterative developers, especially Tim Snyder.

Many thanks to the reviewers, including Alistair Cockburn, Claudia Frers, Tom Gilb, Jim Highsmith, Ron Jeffries, Philippe Kruchten, Niels Maloteaux, Gary Pollice, Ken Schwaber, and Jeff Sutherland.

Thanks to Paul Petralia and Patti Guerrieri for shepherding.

INTRODUCTION

Logic is the art of going wrong with confidence.
—Joseph Wood Krutch

What value will you get from studying this book, an introduction to iterative and agile methods?

First, you will know the key practices of four noteworthy methods, **Scrum**, **Extreme Programming** (**XP**), the **Unified Process** (**UP**), and **Evo** (one of the original iterative methods). This is a "Cliffs Notes" summary, each chapter has something useful to you as a manager, developer, or student of development methods.

Scrum p. 109
XP p. 137
UP p. 173
Evo p. 211

Second, your learning curve will be shortened, as this is a distilled learning aid. The four method chapters have the same structure, to speed comprehension and compare-contrast. There's a FAQ chapter, a "tips" chapter of common practices, and plenty of margin pointers to related pages—paper hyperlinks.

FAQ p. 297
tips p. 247

Third, you will know motivation and evidence. Some organizations accept the value of iterative development, but others are still reluctant. If you need to make a case for an iterative project experiment, you will find in this book the key reasons, research, examples of large projects, standards-body acceptance, a business case, and promotion by well-known thought leaders through the

motivation p. 49
evidence p. 63

decades. The research and history sections are also of value to students of software engineering methods.

> Note that agile methods are a subset
> of iterative methods; this book covers both types.

The chapters may be read in any order; the big picture is this:

1. Introduction, and predictable vs. inventive development.

2. Basic iterative and evolutionary method practices.

3. Summary of agile principles and methods.

4. An agile project story to pull some ideas together.

5–6. Motivation and evidence chapters for iterative and agile methods; useful for some.

7–10. Four method summaries on Scrum, XP, UP, and Evo. Note: practices can be mixed.

11. A tips chapter that expands on some of the method practices, plus others.

12. A frequently asked questions (FAQ) chapter.

Finally, *people trump process*. Every process book should probably include this standard disclaimer:

Process is only a second-order effect.[1] The unique people, their feelings, qualities, and communication are more influential.

Some problems are just hard, some people are just difficult. These methods are not salvation.

---

1. A quote from the agile methodologist Alistair Cockburn.

SOFTWARE IS NEW PRODUCT DEVELOPMENT

Consider building mobile phones on an assembly line: It *is* possible to unambiguously define the specifications and construction steps. After building some phones and measuring things, it is possible to reliably estimate and schedule the building of future phones.

A different problem: Build a custom house. The owner wants to use new environmentally friendly materials and methods, but isn't exactly sure what they want, and is going to change or clarify their decisions as they see the house, costs, and weeks unfold.

At one end of the spectrum, such as manufacturing phones, there are problems with low degrees of novelty or change, and high rates of repeated identical or near-identical creation—*mass manufacturing* or *predictable manufacturing*.

At the other end, there are problems with high degrees of novelty, creativity, and change, and no previous identical cases from which to derive estimates or schedules. This is the realm of *new product development* or *inventive projects*.

The development process, management values, planning and estimation models appropriately associated with these two domains are different (Table 1.1).

Table 1.1 predictable vs. inventive projects

Predictable Manufacturing	New Product Development
It is possible to first complete specifications, and then build.	Rarely possible to create up-front unchanging and detailed specs.

Predictable Manufacturing	New Product Development
Near the start, one can reliably estimate effort and cost.	Near the beginning, it is not possible. As empirical data emerge, it becomes increasingly possible to plan and estimate.
It is possible to identify, define, schedule, and order all the detailed activities.	Near the beginning, it is not possible. Adaptive steps driven by build–feedback cycles are required.
Adaptation to unpredictable change is not the norm, and change-rates are relatively low.	Creative adaptation to unpredictable change is the norm. Change rates are high.

Of course, the point is,

> *Most software is not a predictable or mass manufacturing problem. Software development is new product development.*

Plus, many projects use new and buggy technologies that exacerbate the degree of novelty and unpredictability. Note also it is a new product for the inexperienced even if it has been done before.

Since predictable manufacturing is the wrong paradigm for software, practices and values rooted in it are not helpful.

This mismatch lies at the heart of many of the challenges associated with traditional approaches to running a software project.

A "waterfall" lifecycle, big up-front specifications, estimates, and speculative plans applicable to predictable manufacturing have been misapplied to software projects, a domain of inventive, high-change, high-novelty work.

Factors [CP86] preventing reliable up-front specifications include:

❑ The clients or users are not sure what they want.

❑ They have difficulty stating all they want and know.

❑ Many details of what they want will only be revealed during development.

❑ The details are overwhelmingly complex for people.

❑ As they see the product develop, they change their minds.

❑ External forces (such as a competitor's product or service) lead to changes or enhancements in requests.

This deep appreciation—that building software is complex, new product development with high change rates, and not predictable manufacturing—is at the heart of the motivation for agile and iterative methods.

Certainly, another driving force is the desire to compete and win. Iterative and agile methods foster flexibility and maneuverability—a competitive advantage. In *Agile Competitors and Virtual Organizations* [GNP97] the authors examine the limitations of the mass manufacturing model and the need for agility:

> *Agility [...] is about succeeding and about winning: about succeeding in emerging competitive arenas, and about winning profits, market share, and customers in the very center of the competitive storms many companies now fear.*

WHAT'S NEXT?

The next two chapters summarize basic practices and ideas of iterative, evolutionary, and agile methods. After that, a story chapter illustrates these practices with a concrete scenario.

WEB RESOURCES

Related book or journal article suggestions are given in their respective chapters. Web resource suggestions include:

Broad Link or Article Sites

❑ **www.agilealliance.com** — Collects many articles specifically related to agile methods, plus links.

❑ **www.cetus-links.org** — The Cetus Links site has specialized for years in object technology (OT). Under "OO Project Management—OOA/D Methods" it has many links to iterative and agile methods, even though they are not directly related to OT.

❑ **www.bradapp.net** — Brad Appleton maintains a large collection of links on software engineering, including iterative methods.

❑ **www.iturls.com** — The Chinese front page links to an English version, with a search engine referencing iterative and agile articles.

More Specific Sites

❑ **c2.com/cgi/wiki?FindPage** — This important, vast Wiki site was the home ground where many of the agile leaders (and design pattern leaders) held their original discussions on XP and other agile methods.

❑ **www.extremeprogramming.org** — Don Wells' (an early XP leader) introduction to XP.

❑ **www.xprogramming.com** — Ron Jeffries' (an early XP leader) introduction to XP.

❑ **www.agilemodeling.com** — Scott Ambler's site contains many articles related to agile modeling practices.

- **sunset.usc.edu** — Associated with the work of Dr. Barry Boehm, a long-time researcher into iterative (e.g., Spiral) methods. Articles related to iterative methods.

- **www.cutter.com** — Cutter's site has an Agile Project Management specialty area.

- **www.martinfowler.com** — Martin Fowler is an early agile methods thought leader (XP method). Articles and links.

- **www.jimhighsmith.com** — Jim Highsmith is an early agile methods thought leader (Adaptive Software Development method). Articles and links.

- **alistair.cockburn.us** — Alistair Cockburn is an early agile methods thought leader (Crystal methods). Articles and links.

- **www.controlchaos.com** — Ken Schwaber is an early agile methods thought leader (Scrum method). Articles and links.

- **jeffsutherland.com** — Jeff Sutherland is an early agile methods thought leader (Scrum method). Articles and links.

- **www.gilb.com** — Tom Gilb is one of the very earliest iterative and evolutionary thought leaders (Evo method). Articles and links.

- **www.craiglarman.com** — My site. Articles and links.

- **www.objectmentor.com** — Company led by Robert C. Martin, an early agile thought leader (XP related). Articles and links.

- **www.nebulon.com** — Company led by Jeff De Luca, an early agile thought leader (Feature-Driven Development method). Articles and links.

- **www.dsdm.org** — Official site for the DSDM method.

- **www.rational.com** — Official site for the Rational Unified Process (RUP) iterative method.

❏ **name.case.unibz.it** — Network for Agile Methodologies Experience (NAME). A European site that describes research into agile methods, and with links to other sites.

Iterative & Evolutionary

Experience is that marvelous thing that enables you
to recognize a mistake when you make it again.
—F. P. Jones

Overview

❑ Basic practices of iterative and evolutionary methods, including timeboxing and adaptive planning.

❑ A common mistake adopting iterative methods.

❑ Specific iterative and evolutionary methods, including Evo and UP.

Iterative and evolutionary development is a foundation not only of modern software methods, but—as the history section of the "Evidence" chapter shows—of methods used as far back as the 1960s. Agile methods are a subset of iterative and evolutionary methods. This chapter summarizes key practices:

history p. 79

iterative development *evolutionary development*

risk-driven and client-driven *evolutionary requirements*

timeboxing *adaptive planning*

Iterative Development

Iterative development is an approach to building software (or anything) in which the overall lifecycle is composed of several iterations in sequence. Each **iteration** is a self-contained mini-project

iterative planning tips
start on p. 248

composed of activities such as requirements analysis, design, programming, and test. The goal for the end of an iteration is an **iteration release**, a stable, integrated and tested *partially* complete system. To be clear: *All* the software across all the teams is integrated into a release each iteration. Most iteration releases are *internal*, a baseline primarily for the benefit of the development team—they are not released externally. The final iteration release is the complete product, released to the market or clients. See Figure 2.1.

Figure 2.1 iterative and
incremental development

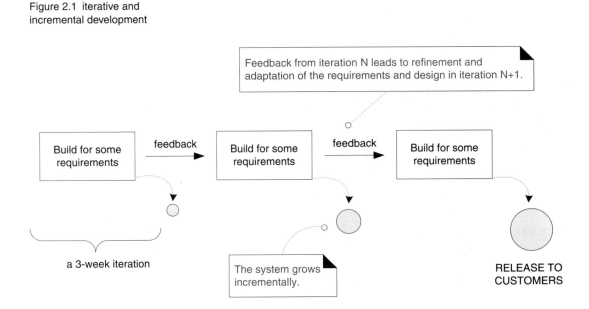

Feedback from iteration N leads to refinement and adaptation of the requirements and design in iteration N+1.

Build for some requirements
feedback
Build for some requirements
feedback
Build for some requirements

a 3-week iteration

The system grows incrementally.

RELEASE TO CUSTOMERS

Although an iteration can in theory be only for clean-up or performance tuning, usually the partial system grows incrementally with new features, iteration by iteration; in other words, **incremental development**. The concept of growing a system via iterations has been called **iterative and incremental development (IID)**, although simply "iterative development" is common. Some older process literature [Wong84] used the term "incremental development" to mean a combination of frozen up-front specifications followed by iterative development of the features, but there is no widespread agreement on usage. In this era, most development methods are IID methods. And, IID is at the core of all the agile methods, including Scrum and XP.

Most projects have at least three iterations before a final public release; I've seen a two-year Valtech project composed of close to 20 iterations averaging around four weeks each, and I know of at least one long project with 45 iterations.

> In modern iterative methods, the recommended
> length of one iteration is between one and six weeks.

Each iteration includes production-quality programming, not just requirements analysis, for example. And the software resulting from each iteration is not a prototype or proof of concept, but a subset of the final system.

Figure 2.2 disciplines across iterations

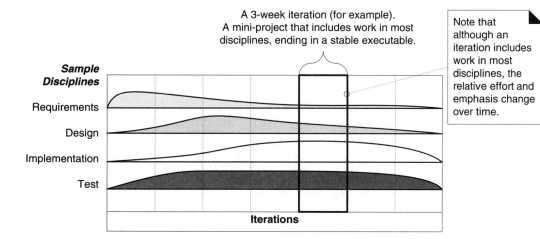

A 3-week iteration (for example).
A mini-project that includes work in most
disciplines, ending in a stable executable.

Note that although an iteration includes work in most disciplines, the relative effort and emphasis change over time.

Sample
Disciplines

Requirements

Design

Implementation

Test

Iterations

More broadly, viewing an iteration as a self-contained mini-project, activities in many disciplines (requirements analysis, testing, and so on) occur within an iteration (see Figure 2.2).

RISK-DRIVEN AND CLIENT-DRIVEN ITERATIVE PLANNING

risk-driven p. 263

ranking risks p. 273

first iteration p. 268

use cases and iteration planning p. 269

What to do in the next three-week iteration? IID methods promote a combination of risk-driven and client-driven[1] priorities. **Risk-driven iterative development** chooses the riskiest, most difficult elements for the early iterations. For example, maybe the client says "I want the Web pages to be green and the system to handle 5,000 simultaneous transactions." Green can wait. In this way, the highest risks are surfaced and mitigated early rather than late. Risk is a broad concept—maybe you are making a new 3D modeling tool and market research shows that what will capture market interest is a novel, much easier user interface metaphor. The high risk is not getting the UI right.

adaptive and client-driven planning p. 253

Client-driven iterative development implies that the choice of features for the next iteration comes from the client—whatever they perceive as the highest business value to them. In this way, the client steers the project, iteration by iteration, requesting the features that they *currently* think are most valuable. Note that the customer **adaptively plans** the choice for the next iteration, shortly before it starts, based on their latest insight, rather than speculatively at the start of the project. The customer has ongoing control and choice, as fresh information arises.

mixing and ranking iteration goals p. 265

Apply both schemes. Clients do not always appreciate what is technically hard or risky. Developers do not always appreciate what has high business value.

---

1. Throughout this book, *client* or *customer* could mean a proxy, such as a marketing or product manager for a consumer software product, true end-users for an internal application, etc.

TIMEBOXED ITERATIVE DEVELOPMENT

Iteration **timeboxing** is the practice of fixing the iteration end date and not allowing it to change. An overall project may be timeboxed as well. If it eventually appears that the chosen requests (the scope) for the iteration can't be met within the timebox, then rather than slip the iteration end date, the scope is reduced (placing lower priority requests back on the wish-list), so that the partial, growing system always ends in a stable and tested state on the original planned iteration end date. See Figure 2.3.

multi-site timeboxed iterations p. 248

overlapping activities across timeboxes p. 251

It is important that timeboxing is not used to pressure developers to work longer hours to meet the soon-coming deadline. If the normal pace of work is insufficient, do less.

In most IID methods, not all timebox lengths need be equal. The first iteration may be four weeks, the second iteration three weeks, and so forth. On the other hand, the Scrum method recommends that each timebox be exactly 30 calendar days. As mentioned, most IID methods recommend an iteration timebox between one and six weeks.

iteration length p. 267

what day to end a timebox? p. 258

A three-month or six-month timeboxed "iteration" is extraordinarily long and usually misses the point and value; research shows that shorter steps have lower complexity and risk, better feedback, and higher productivity and success rates. That said, there are extreme cases of projects with hundreds of developers where a three-month iteration is useful because of the overhead.

All the modern IID methods (including Scrum, XP, and so forth) either require or strongly advise timeboxing the iterations.

Figure 2.3 timeboxing

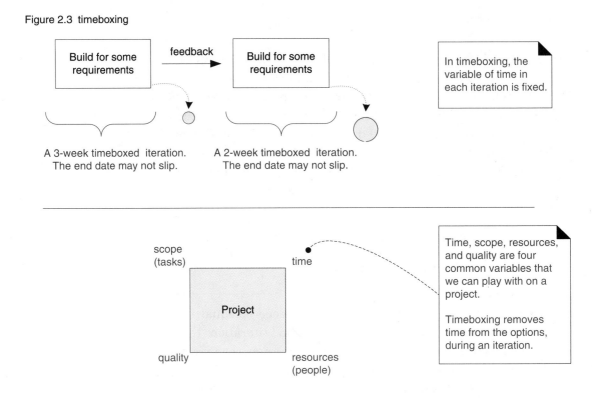

| Build for some requirements | feedback → | Build for some requirements |

A 3-week timeboxed iteration.
The end date may not slip.

A 2-week timeboxed iteration.
The end date may not slip.

In timeboxing, the variable of time in each iteration is fixed.

scope (tasks)

time

Project

quality

resources (people)

Time, scope, resources, and quality are four common variables that we can play with on a project.

Timeboxing removes time from the options, during an iteration.

DURING THE ITERATION, NO CHANGES FROM EXTERNAL STAKEHOLDERS

Iterative and agile methods embrace change, but not chaos. In a sea of constant change, a point of stability is necessary. In IID methods this is achieved with the rule:

Once the requests for an iteration have been chosen and it is underway, no external stakeholders may change the work.

scope reduction: primary and secondary iteration goals p. 270

One week into a three-week iteration, the product manager should not come along, and ask, "Can you do this too?" They wait for the next iteration. However, the team itself can reduce the scope of an iteration if the timebox deadline cannot otherwise be met.

EVOLUTIONARY AND ADAPTIVE DEVELOPMENT

Evolutionary iterative development implies that the requirements, plan, estimates, and solution evolve or are refined over the course of the iterations, rather than fully defined and "frozen" in a major up-front specification effort before the development iterations begin. Evolutionary methods are consistent with the pattern of unpredictable discovery and change in new product development.

evolutionary requirements p. 15

adaptive planning p. 17

Adaptive development is a related term. It implies that elements adapt in response to feedback from prior work—feedback from users, tests, developers, and so on. The intent is the same as evolutionary development, but the name suggests more strongly the feedback-response mechanism in evolution.

Some methods or methodologists emphasize the term "iterative" while others use "evolutionary" or "adaptive." The ideas and intent are similar, although strictly speaking, evolutionary and adaptive development does not require the use of timeboxed iterations.

EVOLUTIONARY REQUIREMENTS ANALYSIS

In evolutionary and adaptive development, it is *not* the case that the requirements are forever unbounded or always changing at a high rate. Rather, most requirements discovery and refinement usually occurs during early iterations, and the earliest attention is given to understanding the most architecturally significant or high-business-value requirements. For example, on an ultimately 20-iteration project, it is likely that most requirements will be discovered and refined within the first three or four iterations (that include, in parallel, early software development).

evolutionary requirements tips start on p. 281

Figure 2.4 evolutionary
and iterative requirements

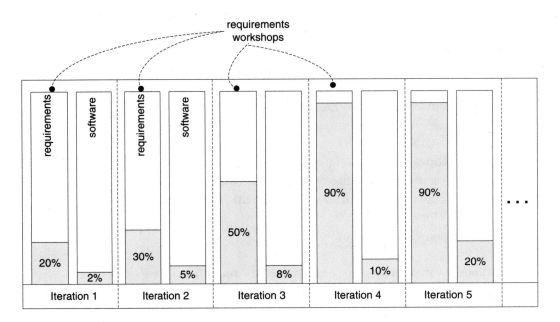

Imagine this will ultimately be a 20-iteration project.

In evolutionary iterative development, the requirements evolve over a set of the early iterations, through a series of requirements workshops (for example). Perhaps after four iterations and workshops, 90% of the requirements are defined and refined. Nevertheless, only 10% of the software is built.

workshops p. 284

In each iteration, there is a one- or two-day requirements workshop in which the specifications expand and refine, in response to further analysis and feedback from the system under development. See Figure 2.4. For example, the first workshop focuses on detailed analysis of 20% of the most architecturally significant and risky requirements; this gives the software architect enough meaningful input to start development and test in short cycles.

Note as a design comment, that it is not true that 100% of the *functional* requirements need be known to start building an excellent core architecture. The architect needs to know most nonfunctional or quality requirements (e.g., load, internationalization) and a much smaller representative subset of functional requirements.

EARLY "TOP TEN" HIGH-LEVEL REQUIREMENTS AND SKILLFUL ANALYSIS

It is a misunderstanding to equate evolutionary requirements analysis with "no early requirements" or sloppy requirements practices. Modern IID methods encourage the early creation and baselining of vision statements, "top ten" *high-level* requirements lists, and early analysis of architecturally influential factors, such as load, usability, and internationalization. Further, these methods encourage many skillful analysis techniques during early iterations, such as a series of requirements workshops involving both target users and developers, writing use cases, and much more.

vision boxes p. 282

product sheets p. 284

use cases p. 287

various elicitation methods start on p. 289

EVOLUTIONARY AND ADAPTIVE PLANNING

As with evolutionary requirements, with evolutionary and adaptive planning it is not the case that estimates and schedules are forever unbounded or unknown. Yet, due to early requirements change and other factors, there is an initial phase of high uncertainty, which drops as time passes and information accumulates. This has been called the **cone of uncertainty** (Figure 2.5) [McConnell98].

adaptive planning and related tips start on p. 253

The iterative response to this uncertainty is to defer an expectation of semi-reliable estimates for cost, effort or schedule until a few iterations have passed. Perhaps 10% to 20% into a project.

This is consistent with management practice in other new product development domains, where an initial exploratory phase is common. Further, the practice of **adaptive planning** is encouraged

adaptive and predictive planning p. 253

rather than **predictive planning**. That is, a detailed schedule is not created beyond a relatively short time horizon, so that the level of detail and commitment is commensurate with the quality of information.

Figure 2.5 cone of uncertainty

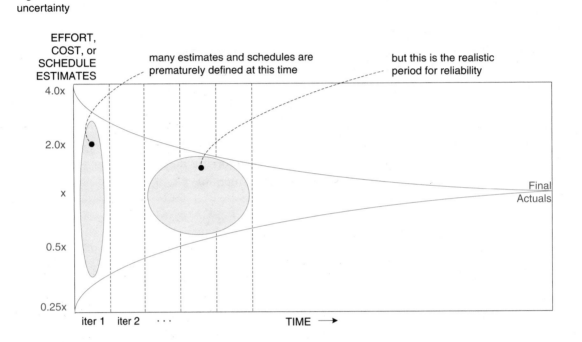

Fixed-Price Contracts

With respect to fixed-price bidding and evolutionary estimates, some IID methods (such as the UP) recommend running projects in two contract phases, each of multiple timeboxed iterations.

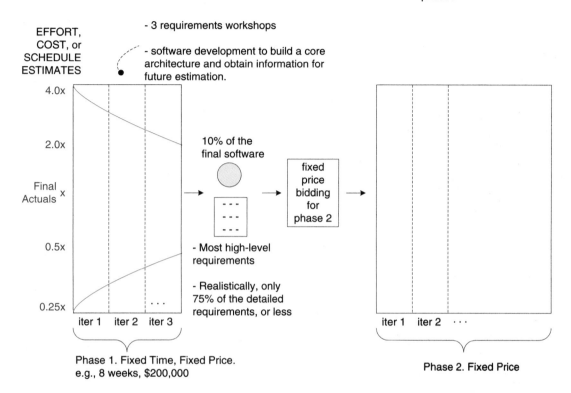

Figure 2.6 two contract phases

Phase 1. Fixed Time, Fixed Price. e.g., 8 weeks, $200,000

Phase 2. Fixed Price

The first phase, a relatively short fixed-time and fixed-price contract, has the goal of completing a few iterations, doing early but partial software development and evolutionary requirements analysis. Note the key point that partial software is produced, not merely documents.

The outputs of phase one—including the software base—are then shared with bidders for a phase two fixed-price contract. The evolutionary refinement of specifications and code in phase one provides higher quality data for phase two estimators, and advances the software for the project (Figure 2.6).

INCREMENTAL DELIVERY

Incremental delivery is the practice of repeatedly delivering a system into production (or the marketplace) in a series of expanding capabilities (Figure 2.7). The practice is promoted by IID and agile methods. Incremental deliveries are often between three and twelve months.

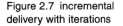

Figure 2.7 incremental delivery with iterations

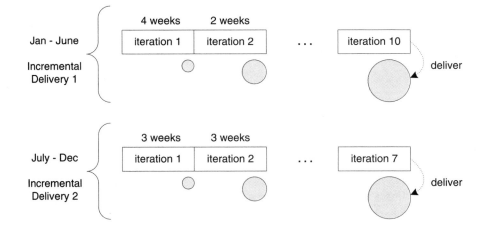

Incremental delivery is often confused with iterative development. A six-month delivery cycle could be composed of 10 short iterations. The results of each iteration are not delivered to the marketplace, but the results of an incremental delivery are.

EVOLUTIONARY DELIVERY

The Evo method and evolutionary delivery p. 212

Evolutionary delivery is a refinement of the practice of incremental delivery in which there is a vigorous attempt to capture feedback regarding the installed product, and use this to guide the next delivery. Naturally, the evolutionary goal is to best meet some difficult-to-predict need, such as the most frequently requested new features. Uniquely, the Evo method promotes—when possible—very short evolutionary delivery cycles of one or two weeks, so that each iteration delivers something useful to stakeholders.

To contrast "pure" incremental delivery with evolutionary delivery, in the former a plan is defined of several future deliveries—feedback is not driving the delivery plan. In evolutionary delivery, there is no plan (or at least no fixed plan) of future deliveries; each is dynamically created based on emerging information. In practice, a marriage of some future prediction and feedback is obvious and common, and the two terms are used interchangeably.

THE MOST COMMON MISTAKE?

Iterative and agile process coaches often see scenarios like this:

Jill: Sure, we don't apply the waterfall—everyone knows it doesn't work. We've adopted <iterative method X> and are into our first project. We've been at it for two months and have the use case analysis nearly finished, and the plan and schedule of what we'll be doing in each iteration. After review and approval of the final requirements set and iteration schedule, we'll start programming.

This profound misunderstanding, still superimposing waterfall-inspired, big up-front analysis and planning (predictable manufacturing) values onto iterative methods, is one of the most common mistakes that new iterative and agile method adopters make.

SPECIFIC ITERATIVE & EVOLUTIONARY METHODS

Specific *agile* methods are summarized in the next chapter. This section mentions some *iterative* methods (Evo and UP) that predate most agile methods; they may or may not be considered agile.

Of all the methods mentioned in this book (Scrum, XP, Evo, UP, OPEN, DSDM, ...) the UP or its variation the Rational Unified Process (RUP) is perhaps the most widely used. It is found in thousands or tens of thousands of development organizations worldwide. This does not mean it is well applied or well understood.

Evo

Evo details p. 211

Evo was perhaps the first iterative and evolutionary method, starting in the 1960s. Evo recommends short 1–2 week iterations, and uniquely, evolutionary *delivery* each iteration. Evo adaptively plans iterations by highest value-to-cost ratio, and strongly promotes the unambiguous definition of quality requirements (such as load) with quantified and measurable statements.

Unified Process

UP details p. 173

The UP or RUP, first developed in the mid-1990s, brings together the knowledge of many experienced large-system architects and process-leaders at Rational Corp., and their customers, into a well-defined IID method. One key UP theme is risk-driven development in the early iterations, focusing on creation of the core architecture and driving down the high risks. The UP also includes the definition of common project workproducts, such as the *Vision*, *Software Architecture Document*, and *Risk List*.

Other Methods

In addition to UP and Evo, other IID methods include:

❏ The **Microsoft Solutions Framework** process, available from Microsoft Education. It is a description of best practices used by Microsoft.

❏ The **OPEN** process from Henderson-Sellers, Firesmith, and Graham [FH01].

❏ **WinWin Spiral Model** and **MBASE Spiral Model** from Barry Boehm (creator in the 1980s of the well-known iterative Spiral Model) and colleagues [BEKPSM98], [BP01].

WHAT'S NEXT?

The next chapter summarizes agile method practices and values. After that, a story chapter illustrates these practices with a concrete scenario.

RECOMMENDED READINGS

❏ *Rapid Development*, by Steve McConnell. Examines variations of iterative development, citing plenty of research data.

❏ *The Mythical Man-Month*, by Frederick Brooks. The silver-anniversary edition of this classic discusses the advantages of IID, in addition to many timeless lessons.

AGILE

Health is merely the slowest possible rate at which one can die.
—anonymous

OVERVIEW

- ❑ Basic ideas and principles of agile methods.
- ❑ Classification of methods.
- ❑ Agile hype?
- ❑ Specific agile methods, including Scrum and XP.

AGILE DEVELOPMENT

Agile development methods apply timeboxed iterative and evolutionary development, adaptive planning, promote evolutionary delivery, and include other values and practices that encourage *agility*—rapid and flexible response to change. If agile methods have a motto, it is *embrace change*.[1] If agile methods have a strategic point, it is *maneuverability*.

It is not possible to exactly define **agile methods**, as specific practices vary. However, short timeboxed iterations with adaptive, evolutionary refinement of plans and goals is a basic practice various methods share. Thus, the book title and opening material includes *iterative development*, which lies at the heart of agile methods.

iterative development
p. 9

---

1. The subtitle of the first book on XP, *Extreme Programming Explained: Embrace Change*, by Kent Beck.

agile principles p. 27
In addition, they promote practices and principles that reflect an agile sensibility of simplicity, lightness, communication, self-directed teams, programming over documenting, and more.

Scrum practices p. 116

XP practices p. 146
Example practices from Scrum include working in a *common project room* and *self-directed teams* that coordinate through a daily stand-up meeting with special questions each member answers. Example practices from XP include using terse notes on paper *story cards* to summarize requirements, *programming in pairs*, and working in a common project room with *full-time participation by requirement donors* so that detailed written requirements can be replaced with ongoing verbal explanations.

As a distinct software process concept, agile is newer than iterative. Most older IID methods (such as Evo and UP) were not strongly agile in their original definition, although many methods can be applied in an agile spirit with the right understanding.

Although it is possible to imagine truly un-agile IID methods, as a practical matter they are rare or are quickly adopting agile values and practices—it is hard to find someone promoting *un-agility*!

CLASSIFICATION OF METHODS

other classification schemes p. 36
Having raised the issue of variations in methods, one classification is their degree of **ceremony**—the amount of **method weight** in terms of documentation, formal steps, review, and so forth. Another classification is their **cycles**—the number and length of iterations. For example, single-pass waterfall has no iterations; at the other end, an Evo project could have very many—one iteration per week. Figure 3.1 illustrates four methods categorized by this scheme.

Figure 3.1 methods by
ceremony and cycles

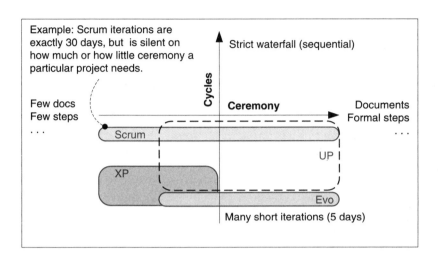

As hinted in Figure 3.1, XP recommends 1–4 weeks, and the UP
2–6 weeks. Some would say the lower left quadrant (many short
iterations, low ceremony) describes the agile methods, but this is
not quite accurate. For example, Scrum is silent on the question of
ceremony—or more precisely leaves the question to the discretion
of the team. A better way to describe agile methods in terms of ceremony is their promotion of *barely sufficient* ceremony. That could
be high in some case, such as for a USA Food and Drug Administration (FDA) regulated device.

THE AGILE MANIFESTO AND PRINCIPLES

In 2001 a group interested in iterative and agile methods (coining
the term) met to find common ground. Out of this came the Agile
Alliance (www.agilealliance.com) with a manifesto and statement
of principles. Worth study! Most of the many concrete practices
described throughout this book reflect these principles. Agile
project management is guided by these principles.

The Agile Manifesto

Individuals and interactions   *over processes and tools*
Working software   *over comprehensive documentation*
Customer collaboration   *over contract negotiation*
Responding to change   *over following a plan*

That is, while there is value in the items on the right, we value the items on the left more.

The Agile Principles

1. Our highest priority is to satisfy the customer through early and continuous delivery of valuable software.

2. Welcome changing requirements, even late in development. Agile processes harness change for the customer's competitive advantage.

3. Deliver working software frequently, from a couple of weeks to a couple of months, with a preference to the shorter time scale.

4. Business people and developers must work together daily throughout the project.

5. Build projects around motivated individuals. Give them the environment and support they need, and trust them to get the job done.

6. The most efficient and effective method of conveying information to and within a development team is face-to-face conversation.

7. Working software is the primary measure of progress.

8. Agile processes promote sustainable development.

9. The sponsors, developers, and users should be able to maintain a constant pace indefinitely.

10. Continuous attention to technical excellence and good design enhances agility.

11. Simplicity—the art of maximizing the amount of work not done—is essential.

12. The best architectures, requirements, and designs emerge from self-organizing teams.

13. At regular intervals, the team reflects on how to become more effective, then tunes and adjusts its behavior accordingly.

AGILE PROJECT MANAGEMENT

The Scrum and XP chapters include specific **agile project management** practices for those methods. Other authors present generalizations with common themes: manager promotes the vision, more communication, avoid command-control, and so on. This section summarizes two well-known descriptions.

Scrum practices p. 116

XP practices p. 146

Jim Highsmith, an Agile Alliance founder and creator of the Adaptive Software Development method, summarizes nine principles for the agile project manager [Highsmith02]:

1. Deliver something useful to the client; check what they value.

2. Cultivate committed stakeholders.

3. Employ a leadership-collaboration style.

4. Build competent, collaborative teams.

5. Enable team decision making.

6. Use short timeboxed iterations to quickly deliver features.

7. Encourage adaptability.

8. Champion technical excellence.

9. Focus on delivery activities, not process-compliance activities.

Augustine and Woodcock, two managers with experience in XP-oriented projects, recommend six practices [AW02]:

1. **Guiding Vision** – Establish a guiding vision for the project and continuously reinforce it through words and actions.

2. **Teamwork & Collaboration** – Facilitate collaboration and teamwork through relationships and community.

3. **Simple Rules** – Establish and support the team's set of guiding practices, such as Scrum or XP.

4. **Open Information** – Provide visible and open access to project management and other information.

5. **Light Touch** – Apply just enough control to foster emergent behavior in a self-directed team.

6. **Agile Vigilance** – Reinforce the vision, follow or adapt the rules, listen to the people.

A theme of agile project management in Scrum and XP is the devolution of both control and planning to the entire team, not the manager. The manager does not create a work breakdown structure, schedule, or estimates; this is done as a team. The manager does not (usually) tell people what to do. The manager does not define and assign many detailed team roles and responsibilities.

Rather, the project manager role emphasizes coaching, servant-leadership, providing resources, maintaining the vision, removing impediments, promoting agile principles, etc. Thus, managers more used to control and rule-based methods or project management have some challenge adopting agile methods.

EMBRACE COMMUNICATION AND FEEDBACK

daily Scrum p. 120

If the agile Prime Directive is *embrace change*, a close second is *embrace communication and feedback*. The manifesto and principles, and agile methods have a theme of working to increase communication, especially face-to-face conversation. This is illustrated in practices such as the daily Scrum meeting and XP's requirement to have onsite customers sitting full-time in the common project room.

Agile methods are adaptive, requiring feedback to guide direction. Beyond just conversation, they seek out early and frequent feedback through early testing, early demos, and much more.

PROGRAMMING AS IF PEOPLE MATTERED

People are more important than any process. Good people with a good process will outperform good people with no process every time. — Grady Booch [Booch96]

The first value in the Agile Manifesto is *Individuals and interactions over processes and tools*. It reminds us that programming is a human activity. For example, XP champions the importance of happy developers for sustainable development. Mindful of the impact of overwork on the ability to program well or maintain a healthy social or family life, XP has the rule of *sustainable pace*—avoiding working overtime. Agile Principle 8 states, *Agile processes promote sustainable development*.

Also, research shows that individual developer contributions vary enormously, with studies illustrating 10 times more productive from best to worst [Boehm81]. This does not imply promotion of (unsustainable) heroic individual programming, but the right knowledge and work habits play a significant productivity role— thus the value of ongoing education and mentoring for developers. XP encourages deep skills transfer through the practice of *pair programming*.

pair programming p. 149

The primacy of people and interactions over process is also promoted in agile methods by their emphasis on communication, especially face-to-face conversations. Scrum's *daily meeting* and *common project room,* and XP's *pair programming* and *whole team together* are examples.

daily Scrum p. 120

SIMPLE PRACTICES AND PROJECT TOOLS

Agile Principle 11 is *Simplicity is essential*. Most agile methods embrace *do the simplest thing that could possibly work*—an XP aphorism. This applies not only to software design, but to all project practices. Can requirements and tasks be tracked with paper cards in different piles (not done, done)? And so forth.

Most agile methods promote a "low-tech, high-touch" approach to project and management tools. Of course, low-tech is relative: If the simplest thing that could possibly work is a Web tool, then so be it.

> It is a misunderstanding to equate agile methods with sloppiness. Simplicity and lightness does not imply lack of skill or self-discipline. A project applying all the XP practices has plenty of structure and discipline. But—and this is perhaps a key point in agile methods—the "disciplined" practices are very delivery-oriented or quality-code-oriented. Developers quickly see benefit.

EMPIRICAL VS. DEFINED & PRESCRIPTIVE PROCESS

In general, agile methods promote empirical rather than defined processes, a categorization used by industrial process experts [OR94]. A **defined process** (also known as a **prescriptive process**) has many predefined and ordered activities to be followed during development. Defined processes are suitable for predictable manufacturing domains. **Empirical processes** are used for high-change and unstable domains; rather than many sequenced activities, they are based on frequent measurement and dynamic response to variable events. This approach is reflected in Agile Principles 12 and 13.

agile principles p. 28

For example, Scrum is silent on the activities of an iteration, other than the daily Scrum meeting as the measurement and response mechanism. The UP, on the other hand, strikes a middle way; it lists common activities (e.g., *Write Release Notes*), but the team is welcome to ignore or do them in any order.

Agile methodologists understand that the degree of "method weight" and predefinition of ordered activities are functions of the project type. An agile method or project lies on a continuum of more or less empirical, driven by need. A medical device under FDA approval requires more formal, predefined activities.

PRINCIPLE-BASED VERSUS RULE-BASED

Similar to empirical versus prescriptive methods, a related way to describe agile methods is as more principle-based than rule-based. Rather than a predefined set of rules regarding the many roles, team organization, responsibilities, relationships, and activities, the team and manager are primarily guided by the principles embodied in the Agile Manifesto and Principles. Agile project management is more than a set of practices—it is a mindset.

SUSTAINABLE DISCIPLINE: THE HUMAN TOUCH

There is no shortage of stories on attempts to adopt methods requiring significant discipline and effort, only to find compliance drop off dramatically shortly after its introduction. The psychological and social factors necessary for sustained adoption are missing. The agile methodologist Alistair Cockburn asks people and teams, "Would you do these practices again?" This is arguably a more important question than the inherent value of the practice.

The creators of a few agile methods (e.g., XP and Crystal) recognized that human factors such as enjoyment, simplicity, short-term reward, peer pressure, and lots of gain for the pain are important ingredients to create fertile soil for sustainable self-discipline with practices. Not surprisingly, XP practices rate well in response to Cockburn's question [Cockburn02].

For example, test-driven development reveals its payoff quickly to those who try it; developers enjoy the small win of making a test pass and the design clarification that comes from writing the tests before writing the code to be tested.

test-driven development p. 292

TEAM AS A COMPLEX ADAPTIVE SYSTEM

Some agile methods (including Scrum and Adaptive Software Development) speak of a healthy development team as a **complex adaptive system** (CAS). A classic CAS example is a flock of birds. Each bird has relatively local and simple rules of behavior, yet at the macro-scale the flock exhibits order and a collective **emergent behavior**. It is as though there is an overlaying flock-level plan, but there isn't. This is in contrast to a command-control management system where team and individual activities are decided and directed by higher-level managers.

agile principles p. 28

The agile methods promote the value that, for creative inventive projects, a CAS-inspired culture of self-organizing teams is more valuable than control or planning by managers. This is reflected in Agile Principle 12. For example, Scrum teams are self-organizing (no management assignment of roles or tasks); team-level organization and adaptation is enabled by the daily Scrum meeting with its special questions that provide each member with the information to make collective decisions.

Scrum meeting questions p. 120

AGILE HYPE?

"Be adaptable, collaborative, delivery driven, people oriented, customer focused, guided by a vision; develop in short iterations; manager is coach" and most other "agile" messages are hardly new. And iterative development had replaced the waterfall on major projects by the 1970s. So is this just hype—recycling old ideas? Yes and no. Many so-called agile messages are repetition from trends of prior decades.

early iterative projects p. 79

But, viewing *as a whole* all the principles and practices of Scrum or XP (for example), these methods have a fresh flavor; they push the envelope of embracing changing requirements, communication, self-organizing teams, adaptive planning, and so forth.

adaptive planning p. 17

Plus, some practices—such as test-driven development and continuous integration—are relatively new.

test-driven p. 292
continuous integration p. 275

Agile Methods Did Not Invent Iterative Development

There is misinformation stating that what is revolutionary about XP and other agile methods is their abandonment of the waterfall model and invention of iterative and evolutionary development. Not true—iterative and evolutionary methods that eschewed the waterfall and applied short iterations with adapting plans and specifications have been around since the 1960s.

early methods p. 82

SPECIFIC AGILE METHODS

Scrum and XP are widely applied agile methods—the two most common, according to at least one survey [Shine03]. However, there is anecdotal evidence indicating some "XP" adoption is misunderstood as simply "not the waterfall" and the teams are merely practicing iterative and evolutionary development or "programming without documentation" and calling this XP.

see misunderstanding XP: p. 157

Scrum

Scrum's distinctive emphasis among the methods is its strong promotion of self-organizing teams, daily team measurement, and avoidance of following predefined steps. Some key practices include a daily stand-up meeting (the Scrum meeting) with special questions, 30-calendar-day iterations, and a demo to external stakeholders at the end of each iteration.

Scrum details p. 109

XP

XP is probably the most well known agile method; it emphasizes collaboration, quick and early software creation, and skillful

XP details p. 137

development practices. It is founded on four values: communication, simplicity, feedback, and courage. It includes 12 core practices, including the whole team working together in a common room, pair programming, constant refactoring, and test-driven development.

Crystal Methods

The Crystal family of agile methods were developed by Alistair Cockburn [Cockburn02]. While acknowledging the necessity of an iterative lifecycle, in this group of methods Cockburn stresses the primacy of "peopleware" issues over process: communication, education, and so on. His definition of software development shows this emphasis: "...a cooperative game of invention and communication."

Figure 3.2 Cockburn scale

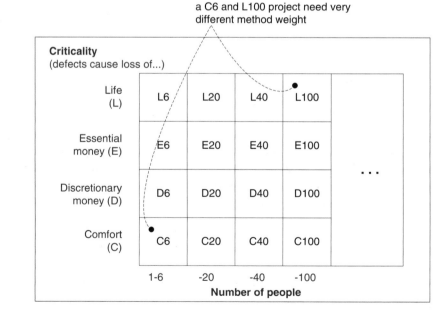

Different versions of Crystal (Clear, Yellow, ...) contain increasing **method weight** (or **process ceremony** in terms of defined and ordered steps, documents, reviews, etc.) as a function of staff size, criticality, and project priority. You choose size and criticality, and this maps to a particular version of Crystal with a recommended method weight. Cockburn has created a scale to illustrate matching method configurations to these factors (Figure 3.2). For example, E6 means a project of 1–6 people, where the worst that can happen from a system failure is loss of essential money. Subsequent chapters refer to this classification model, to classify Scrum, XP, UP, and Evo.

Agile Modeling

Agile Modeling is not a complete process or agile method, but a set of principles and practices for modeling and requirements analysis that complement most any IID method [Ambler02]. Scott Ambler summarizes best practices (Figure 3.3) that skilled iterative modelers apply. Briefly, Agile Modeling promotes the collaborative "low-tech, high-touch" creation of barely good enough, disposable models to aid understanding and communication. Practices encourage speed, simplicity, and creative flow.

Scenario

The project room walls are exposed (no furniture against them) and covered in whiteboards and static-cling-sheet whiteboard material. It's Monday, at the start of a three-week iteration. The team of eight developers has decided to spend two or three hours at the walls to better understand and communicate some ideas. Afterwards, they will start programming. They split into groups. Group 1 explores the object design for the main scenario. On one half of one wall, they sketch UML sequence diagrams. It isn't perfect UML; liberties are taken for sketching. After 15 minutes, they move to the other half of the wall, and sketch a class diagram that complements the sequence diagram. Over three hours, they move back and forth, developing two complementary diagrams. Finally, they take pictures, print them, and erase the boards. When programming later, the printouts provide some inspiration—some design ideas in code are inspired by the prior thought, and some not.

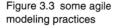

Figure 3.3 some agile modeling practices

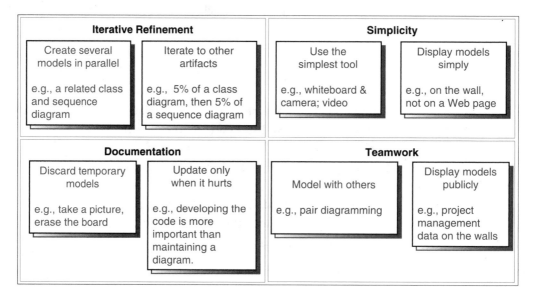

Other Methods and Practices

In addition to Scrum, XP, and the Crystal methods, there are now a host of other agile-oriented practices or methods in use or publication:

❑ **Adaptive Software Development (ASD)** from Jim Highsmith [Highsmith00]; inspired by the complex adaptive systems viewpoint, Rapid Application Development methods, and more.

❏ **Dynamic Solutions Delivery Model (DSDM)** from a group of 16 Rapid Application Development (RAD) experts [Stapleton97] (originally called Dynamic Systems Development Method). It continues to be refined by a member consortium.

❏ **Feature-Driven Development (FDD)** primarily from Jeff De Luca, with contributions by Peter Coad [PF02].

❏ **Lean Development** from Mary and Tom Poppendieck [Poppendieck03].

❏ **Pragmatic Programming** from Andy Hunt and Dave Thomas is not a complete method, but contains development practices sympathetic to an agile development approach. See www.pragmaticprogrammer.com.

WHAT'S NEXT?

The next chapter illustrates iterative and agile practices with a concrete story. After that, two related chapters on motivation and evidence. Then, four related chapters on well-known methods: Scrum, XP, UP, and Evo.

RECOMMENDED READINGS

❏ *Peopleware*, by DeMarco and Lister. Discusses critical people-side issues in development, a key concern of agile methods.

❏ *Agile Software Development*, by Alistair Cockburn. Emphasizes the principles and theory underlying agile methods, with a special focus on communication.

❏ *Agile Software Development Ecosystems*, by Jim Highsmith. Includes interesting interviews with several agile method founders, in addition to a survey of several methods and key principles.

STORY

I find that the harder I work, the more luck I seem to have.
—Thomas Jefferson

OVERVIEW

❑ Story of an agile project to relate some practices. This example illustrates a variety of Scrum, XP, UP, and Evo principles and practices.

It is Monday, January 2. The government Border Information Group (BIG) needs a biometrics tracking system for non-citizens entering the country, the Biometric Recording Or Tracking Hazardous External Radicals (BROTHER). BIG has a long list of requests, and Martin, the development manager, has convinced BIG management to use timeboxed iterative development and timeboxed evolutionary delivery. Thus, they will deliver the high-

evolutionary delivery
p. 20

est priority features possible by October 1. There is a wish list of features for the first release, and everyone has agreed it may vary, but the release date will not vary.

The plan is that after one or two months in operation at two low-volume airports, feedback from the border guards and travelers will be used to help decide refinements and features for the second release six months later, with a wider rollout.

Scrum demo p. 117

Following a Scrum practice, Martin and his team of seven developers also commit to demo to the Minister of BIG "running, integrated and tested software every three or four weeks, starting next week."

The project will use a combination of practices from Scrum, XP, and UP that Martin and the developers have decided make sense for the team. They organize their physical space: Rather than separate offices or cubicles with dividers, they take over a large room at one of the test airports, FooBarKhan International, near the border guards' office area. Four cubicles are set up near the project room that people can use when they need private time. The common project room is a Scrum and XP practice.

XP whole team together p. 147

caves and common room p. 279

All furniture against the walls is removed. Tables for computers are placed near the center. The walls are covered in giant whiteboards, and whiteboard-like static-cling sheets are used as wallpaper elsewhere. This will support the practice of Agile Modeling.

Agile Modeling p. 37

The responsible BIG manager, Domina, moves into the project room, along with Itchy, a long-time border guard. Itchy will be dedicated full-time to the BROTHER project, and Domina agrees to be around "most mornings." This is the XP practice of onsite clients.

onsite customer p. 147

On Thursday, January 5, they get together and hold a two-day requirements and planning workshop, a UP practice. In addition to receiving a 20-page wish list from senior BIG management, many "agile requirement analysis" techniques are applied the first morning. After lunch (beer and cake, FooBarKhan's national foods), Martin poses this request: *From the high-level requirements we've generated, choose the 20% most architecturally significant, risky, and valuable items.* They use dot-voting to prioritize the items.

workshop p. 284

agile requirements tips p. 281

dot voting p. 265

They spend the remaining afternoon and Friday morning analyzing the 20% items in detail. For functional requirements, they apply the UP practice of writing a few use cases, in the Cockburn style. For the nonfunctional quality requirements, they apply the Evo practice of clearly quantified and measurable goals; the vague "fast response" and "easy to use" goals in the original BIG wish list were not acceptable.

Evo specifications p. 233

On Friday after lunch, Martin moves the team on to planning, even though some of the team want to spend more time detailing and clarifying specifications. Martin poses this challenge to the group: "*We start developing next Monday, January 9. By Thursday, January 26, in 13 working days, we need to have a partial running system hooked up to at least one of the biometric readers. There will be a demo that morning to the BIG minister. What should we realistically do in the next 13 days from the 20% list we explored in detail? And, no overtime.*" No overtime or "sustainable pace" is an XP practice.

XP sustainable pace p. 150

scenarios and
iterations p. 269

The group picks a common "happy path" scenario from one of the use cases that will force them to touch on many architectural factors and components (a UP practice), some other features, and spends the afternoon analyzing and estimating the related fine-grained tasks in an XP-style Planning Game. Note that the manager does not create the work breakdown structure, schedule or estimates; the team does this. Eventually, they discover that their first set of goals is too much work, so they scale back some of the features until the estimates match their available Ideal Engineering Hours budget (an XP practice). They wrap the meeting. Martin enters the task items into a Scrum Sprint Backlog spreadsheet.

Planning Game p. 148

Ideal Engineering
Hours p. 154

Sprint Backlog p. 124

On Monday, January 9, the first iteration starts.

Scrum meeting p. 120

On Monday morning at 9:30, and all subsequent mornings, they hold a 20-minute daily stand-up Scrum meeting. Martin reminds the team of the overall vision, and the specific goals of the iteration. They are standing beside the whiteboard where all the iteration tasks are written. After the Scrum questions, team members start volunteering for tasks, writing their name beside them.

Afterwards, the entire group listens to a presentation by Rebecca, the chief architect. Having a chief architect is recommended in UP. Rebecca spent the prior week investigating and considering architectural issues and designs, given the basic information she had. She lays out her vision of the big pieces and problems, to provide a starting point for decomposition of work by large components. Group discussion refines the ideas. Mid-morning, three subgroups head for the walls, doing Agile Modeling for different subcomponents, reviewing the written use case. The team

Agile Modeling p. 37

reserved all of Monday as creative "wall time" to explore and coordinate design ideas during this "fuzzy front end" exploratory phase. Rebecca spends time rotating through all the groups, building a synergy of ideas. Digital snapshots of all the wall notes and UML-ish sketches are taken.

On Tuesday, January 10, teamwork starts at 9:30 with the Scrum meeting. New tasks and impediments are written on the adjacent whiteboard. Martin reminds the team of the vision and iteration goals. More tasks are volunteered for. As previously agreed, they will start programming this morning, even though many design points and coordination issues are fuzzy.

Most of the developers decided they didn't want to try pair programming, so that XP practice was bypassed, although Martin encouraged pairing by anyone who wanted to try it. However, they all agree to the XP practices of test-driven development and continuous integration. The team is using an IDE with great refactoring tools, and Martin frequently encourages the team to not just cut code, but keep it clean and simple by regularly applying refactorings, another XP practice. The developers occasionally look at the wall sketches or printouts of the snapshots for some inspiration. Some developers head for the walls for 30 minutes to UML-sketch some design ideas, then back to their development stations.

test-driven development p. 292

continuous integration p. 275

As the day progresses, questions about the features and happy path scenario arise, and Domina and Itchy talk with the developers to clarify and decide the requirements. These two also work with the developer Girija to create acceptance tests—an XP practice.

acceptance testing p. 147

As developers complete their classes, they check them and their unit tests in to the version control server. Girija checks in completed acceptance tests. A separate build machine is running these tests within a continuous integration service 24/7, every 15 minutes. Thus, bugs and integration problems are quickly surfaced and resolved. Continuous integration is an XP practice.

daily tracker p. 154

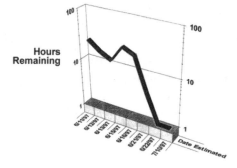

Estimated Hours Remaining by Date

Girija also volunteers to be daily tracker, another XP practice. So, each morning, she takes a few minutes to sit with each developer to learn the remaining estimate of effort on their

Sprint Backlog p. 124

tasks. She updates the Scrum Sprint Backlog spreadsheet with these estimates, and crosses out completed tasks on the whiteboard.

The first few days are rough and confusing. But, by being forced early to develop a very small amount of code and integrate it with the other developers coordination emerges and a small seed of the overall system starts to take shape and be integrated. Hour by hour, more unit and acceptance tests and production code are added to the build.

ending iterations on Wednesday p. 258

Fast forward to mid-iteration, Wednesday January 18. The team meets in a sanity check to discuss if they can really meet their original goals by the end of the following Wednesday (in preparation for the Thursday morning demo), or if they need to scale back. Following the timeboxing practices of UP, XP and Scrum, they won't extend the deadline or work longer hours to meet the deadline, but may defer work until a future iteration. However, things have gone well and the Sprint Backlog shows the total remaining effort estimate is within budget. So, no changes.

Next week on Thursday morning, January 26, the BIG minister shows up for the end-of-iteration demo, a Scrum practice. The iris scan demo doesn't do very much, but it runs and doesn't crash. The minister has never seen an iterative project before and is impressed that three weeks into a new project, the team has some software to show. She's used to waiting six months. In addition to encouraging the team with future efforts, the minister shares this: *I just attended a cabinet meeting where the Prime Minister enthused about a TV report she saw on automated face recognition in crowds, being used in Grepland. She wants it, as soon as possible! This is a matter of national pride; we FooBarKhans can't be outdone by the Greplanders!*

Thursday afternoon and Friday are reserved for a second requirements workshop and iteration 2 planning session. Multiple requirements workshops across early iterations is a UP practice. Since the team is applying the Evo, Scrum, and XP practice of adaptive planning, they had not previously decided what to do in iteration 2, although they had some likely ideas based on the iteration 1 planning session. Rather, they deferred the decision until this time, using their latest information to decide what would be most valuable. With the unexpected overhead and novelty of buying, learning, and integrating a third-party face recognition system, the team decides the next iteration needs more slack and should be four weeks rather than three. The team is very clear what should happen at the iteration 2 demo.

adaptive planning p. 253

WHAT'S NEXT?

The next two chapters present motivation for adopting iterative and agile methods and evidence. The evidence chapter is a relatively large summary of the research, history, case studies, and more.

Then, four related chapters describe Scrum, XP, UP, and Evo. The book concludes with a chapter on some detailed practice tips and a FAQ chapter.

MOTIVATION

If you are going through hell, keep going.
—Sir Winston Churchill

OVERVIEW

- ❏ The facts of change on software projects.

- ❏ Key reasons to adopt iterative and agile development.

- ❏ Meeting the requirements challenge iteratively.

- ❏ Problems with the waterfall.

Some have no need to justify iterative development. Others need to make a case; this information can help.

If It Ain't Broke, Don't Fix It

If your organization is applying a waterfall-oriented (or any other) process and has high success rates, productivity, and so forth, don't change. Adopting an iterative or agile method should be motivated by a challenge, not *method-du-jour* fads.

The average case within organizations is relatively high failure rates and other undesirable project qualities [Standish00]; it is in this context that IID methods are worth considering.

failure research p. 74, p. 100

Failure has several meanings. For example, at Symantec (now adopting XP on some projects), the company was attempting a waterfall model. Tight project management resulted in delivering a product on time and in budget, but it was the wrong product

[Bowers02]. They adopted XP, which led to a better targeted product; productivity and defect rates also improved.

> Project failure can mean not only a cancelled or very late project, but one in which the product did not hit the mark.

THE FACTS OF CHANGE ON SOFTWARE PROJECTS

The **Uncertainty Principle** in software [ZR97]: *Uncertainty is inherent and inevitable in software projects and processes.*

The data summarized in Figure 5.1, based on a large study of software projects [Jones97], illustrates that software development is a domain of inventive high-change projects.

Figure 5.1 rates of change on software projects

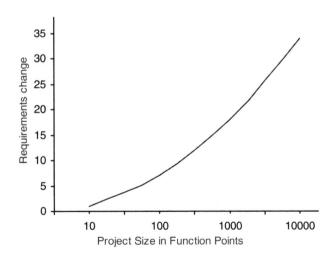

function points
see www.ifpug.org

The X axis plots project size in **function points**, a language-independent measure of system complexity. The Y axis plots the estimate of overall change or creep in requirements.

Even medium sized projects have change rates around 25%; on very large projects it is 35% or more.

> These are high change rates and are at the
> heart of the motivation for agile and iterative methods.

Further, this data is consistent with another study by Boehm and Papaccio showing that a typical software project experienced a 25% change in requirements [BP88].

> This data illustrates that a process, management practice, or value based on the assumption of low change and stability—including "reliable" up-front specifications, estimates, and schedules—is inconsistent with the nature of software projects.

KEY MOTIVATIONS FOR ITERATIVE DEVELOPMENT

Iterative development is lower risk; the waterfall is higher risk. Most practically, the motivation to adopt an iterative lifecycle rather than the waterfall is that research now shows the former is associated with lower risk and better success, productivity, and defect rates. It is these results that have led large and experienced software procurement organizations such as the USA Department of Defense (DoD) to promote the use of IID methods rather than the waterfall.

research p. 65

DoD evidence p. 87

Early risk mitigation and discovery. Risk-driven iterative development forces tackling the hardest, riskiest problems first, such as architecture, integration, and so on. And, early *development* iterations exercise and reveal the true nature of the team and individual skills, the tools, and third-party software. Finally, the truth of the risks emerges: Perceived risks prove not to be, and unsuspected issues are forced into the open.

Accommodates and provokes early change; consistent with new product development. IID methods work with rather than fight against the high-change nature of software projects.

size research p. 70

Manageable complexity. Failure rates are higher and productivity lower with high complexity software projects. Iterative development decomposes complex projects or phases into small and bounded mini-projects of manageable complexity.

Confidence and satisfaction from early, repeated success. Short iterations lead to a quick and repeating sense of completion, competency, and closure. These psychological factors are important for *individual satisfaction* and building *team confidence*. This also builds *customer confidence in the team*—they see early visible progress in the direction they care about.

Early partial product. Not only does early visible progress with an integrated and tested partial product increase client confidence, it provides new business opportunities. Earlier demos are possible. And for whatever reason, the product can ship sooner—with fewer features.

tracking p. 271

agile principles p. 28

Relevant progress tracking; better predictability. Following the waterfall can give a false sense of progress during the early, easier phases, but with low reliability in predicting later phase schedules, which vary widely. A more meaningful progress indicator—tested software—is provided each iteration when using IID methods. That's Agile Principle 7. Further, since work in each iteration exercises most disciplines and each iteration is a similar mini-project, there is earlier and more representative progress data useful for future extrapolation and estimation.

Higher quality; less defects. IID methods require testing early, *defect research p. 78* often, and realistically, in all possible dimensions: load, performance, usability, and so forth. And the tests themselves can be evaluated and refined over the iterations.

Final product better matches true client desires. Through early evaluation and feedback from clients or prospective users, the product is more likely to hit the mark. This is a refinement of "higher quality."

Early and regular process improvement. A common practice in IID methods is a per-iteration assessment—for example, a 15-minute discussion to discover a couple of concrete actions to take in the next iteration to address a problem or improve the living process. Broad-spectrum process improvement is enabled by IID, since work in many disciplines (programming, requirements, test, etc.) occurs each iteration.

Communication and engagement required. Failure research *failure research p. 56* reveals that lack of client or end-user engagement is a major factor in software project failure. Likewise with lack of coordination and collaboration between members or sub-teams. Developing in iterations forces early integration, coordination, and communication between development team members. A per-iteration demo that requires the presence and feedback of clients increases their engagement, as does their participation in a per-iteration planning meeting in which they contribute to the choice of requirements for the next iteration.

IKIWISI required. There's a well-known human-nature related problem in software specifications, especially user-interface oriented: IKIWISI, or I'll Know It When I See It. The complexity, many degrees of freedom in solutions, and intangibility of software seem to demand concrete and cyclic feedback from people evaluating prototypes or partially built systems to clarify and refine their vision.

Timeboxing Benefits

Research shows that timeboxing itself brings benefits in terms of increased productivity. One reason is **focus**. Steve McConnell summed it up best in his book *Rapid Development*, "It's amazing how much you can get done the day before a vacation." The psychological focus promoted by a fixed end date only three weeks away is very different than if the team's next visible milestone is three months away. Timeboxing may be viewed as an antidote to **Parkinson's Law**: "Work expands so as to fill the time available for its completion" [Parkinson58].

Another value in timeboxing, both of iterations and of the entire project, is a quirk of human nature: ***People remember slipped dates, not slipped features***. Delay a project three months from its original end date to include 100% of the desired feature set, and the "failure" will be remembered. Deliver on time with 75% of the most important features, and it's a success.

Another reason is being ***forced to tackle small levels of complexity***. With a short two-week timeboxed iteration, the team takes on manageable complexity, gets realistic about what they can do, and has the ability to reduce the scope if it appears the deadline can't be met. Data shows that lower-complexity steps are done more productively.

productivity research p. 76

A more subtle benefit of timeboxing is its effect on ***early forcing of difficult decisions and trade-offs***. For example, on a Scrum project, you have just committed to a 30-day timeboxed iteration. During the iteration planning meeting, the team has to be very realistic about what gets done and what gets deferred. Since the demo to the client is definitely in 30 days, there is no latitude to be fuzzy about the short-term goals and priorities. Stakeholders are forced to seriously consider priorities, early.

MEETING THE REQUIREMENTS CHALLENGE ITERATIVELY

Some interesting statistics:

- ❏ In a study of over 8,000 projects [Standish94], 37% of the factors on challenged projects were related to requirements (see Figure 5.2).

- ❏ A study of defects by category [SKTYBE92] found that the largest category was in requirements — 41%.

- ❏ Boehm [BP88] showed that the cost of fixing a requirement defect increased non-linearly from early to late in the project.

- ❏ *Requirements change 25% or more* [Jones97, BP88].

Thus, we have the requirements challenge,

We want the requirements to be stable, but they aren't.

Attempts to face this challenge by early detailed requirements analysis and freeze can rarely succeed, given the high rates of change. In a study of failure factors on over 1,000 software projects [Thomas01], such practices were associated with the largest contributing factor for failure, being cited in 82% of the projects as the number one problem.

It is also instructive to learn how valuable early specified features really are: As mentioned previously, research of many projects [Johnson02] showed that 45% of features were not used—with an additional 19% rarely used (Figure 5.3).

Even so, some waterfall requirements advocates have used the above-mentioned cost-of-change research by Boehm [BP88] to continue justifying the practice. It is noteworthy that the creator of this cost data, Boehm himself, was an early and active advocate of evolutionary IID methods, rather than the waterfall, to solve this problem [Boehm85, Boehm96].

Figure 5.2 factors on
challenged projects

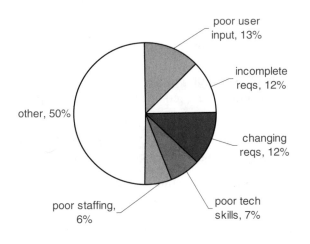

Thus, another approach, evolutionary requirements, is now recommended to meet the requirements challenge.

> The heart of why IID with evolutionary requirements works:
>
> *It **provokes** the inevitable change early.*
>
> Since requirements will change, IID provokes more of the change early on via early development iterations with feedback and practices such as multiple requirements workshops.

The reality of how people handle the requirements challenge is indeed becoming more iterative. In a study of 107 projects [CM95] only 18% of the projects tried to complete the requirements in a single early step; 32% used two cycles of requirements refinement (with programming in between); and in 50% of the projects the requirements analysis was completed over three or more iterations.

Figure 5.3 actual use of
requested features

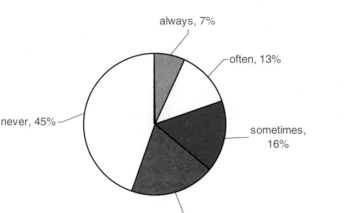

PROBLEMS WITH THE WATERFALL

Although the original description is more iterative than many know (see p. 102), in common usage the waterfall or sequential lifecycle model meant the following development steps:

1. Define up front, in detail, the requirements.

2. Define the "design" (text and diagrammatic descriptions of the software and hardware elements).

3. Implement the system (programming, and so forth).

4. Integrate and test the components.

In the 1970s this was taught as the ideal approach to software development, in response to ad hoc code-and-fix programming in the 1960s. Many books, consulting companies, and teachers promoted the method as ideal, unaware of the accumulating evidence of its problems. Research now shows it is associated with higher risk, failure, and lower productivity.

evidence p. 65

Royce p. 102

The underlying reason for the difficulties of the waterfall is that it requires a low-change, low-novelty, and low-complexity problem. It is unsuitable for complex or inventive projects. Interestingly—and unknown to many—the author of a key waterfall paper (Winston Royce) said the idea was only applicable for the most straightforward un-novel projects; and most interesting, he was himself a proponent of iterative and evolutionary development.

The waterfall lifecycle pushes many high-risk and difficult elements toward the end of a project, while IID methods, run by risk-driven iterations, surface and resolve the hardest and riskiest elements early (Figure 5.4). For example, programming and testing the core architecture, integrating its major components and clarifying the interfaces, is tackled in the earliest iterations.

Figure 5.4 risk profile: waterfall

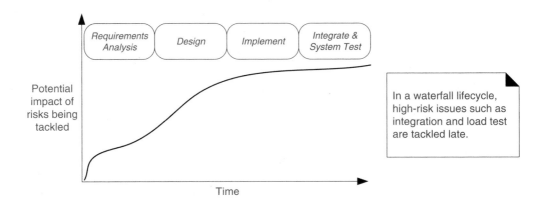

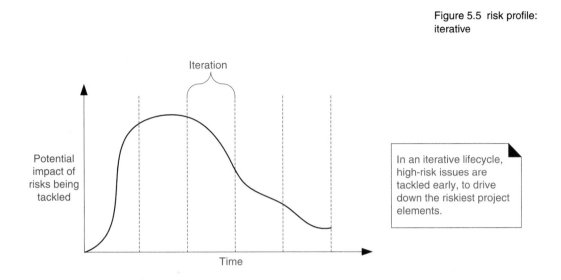

Figure 5.5 risk profile: iterative

Iteration

Potential impact of risks being tackled

Time

In an iterative lifecycle, high-risk issues are tackled early, to drive down the riskiest project elements.

The waterfall also aggravates complexity overload and **analysis paralysis**. Large steps with overwhelming degrees of complexity are attempted.

At some level, we need to know specifications before programming. On the scale of three or six weeks (an iteration or short project), the waterfall works. The breakdown occurs as complexity grows, change rates increase, and feedback is delayed; it works less and less well as a single step stretches from weeks to months to years.

As a historical footnote, in the 1970s and 1980s the DoD promoted the waterfall. In 1994, in response to failure and evidence of its unsuitability for software projects, the DoD changed its standards to remove the waterfall bias, and promote iterative and evolutionary development.

DoD standards p. 87

Senior executives within software organizations often received their software engineering and management education in the 1970s or 1980s, when the waterfall model was usually taught as "ideal." Therefore, it is understandable and common for some to be unaware of more recent evidence that this was not true.

> Thus, sometimes the challenge in moving an organization to adopt IID methods is the reluctance of leadership that still believes in the waterfall.

Other problems with the waterfall and the misapplication of its values on IID projects include the following points:

Problem: "Complete" Up-front Specifications with Sign-off

It isn't that IID proponents wouldn't like correct and detailed up-front specifications that do not need to change—if they could be successfully and efficiently created, very good. Yet, research shows it is rarely possible [CM95], and interestingly, a large study showed that 45% of features created from early specifications were never used—with an additional 19% "rarely" used [Johnson02]. A different approach—evolutionary requirements—is needed.

Problem: Late Integration and Test

I recall working with a defense contractor in the mid-1990s; a large project failure had just wound down. The prime reason? After two years of distributed multi-site development involving over 200 developers, the last stage of the project was to integrate all the software components and do system testing. Characteristically, the integration effort overwhelmingly failed; fundamental misunderstandings and wrong assumptions in the communications, components, and how they would collaborate did not surface until this late stage. The problem was so intractable that the project was cancelled.

Problem: "Reliable" Up-front Schedules and Estimates

When adopting an iterative or agile method, at the start of a project before programming and the first iteration, do not attempt to create a reliable plan or schedule that lays out all the iterations, what will happen in each and when, or all the *detailed* activities sequenced in a PERT chart. Similarly, do not attempt (at the start) to reliably estimate the overall cost or effort, or milestones of intermediate completion points, or the end date.

Such early attempts at **predictive planning** are more successful on repetitive manufacturing projects of low change and complexity, but not on inventive projects—where the full requirements and risks are not reliably known at the start, and high rates of change are the norm. As with up-front specifications, it isn't that IID practitioners wouldn't welcome reliable up-front estimates and schedules. But in domains of high change, complexity, and novelty, it is premature, risky, and unrealistic. Adaptive risk-driven or client-driven planning implies the scheduling of goals to iterations can and should change as better information and new priorities arise.

predictive planning p. 253

risk- and client-driven planning p. 12

Still, the demand for premature up-front commitments happens all the time. This doesn't invalidate applying an iterative or agile approach—it's just not ideal. Early estimates can be improved with the iterative estimation technique of **Wideband Delphi**. The iterative and agile practice of early visible progress and client-driven iterations can win the customer's confidence so that they eventually appreciate their dynamic steering control, and adopt **adaptive planning**, ceasing to care if the team is doing, week by week, what they were originally forced to speculate and schedule.

Wideband Delphi p. 260

adaptive planning p. 253

By developing in risk-driven iterations, the team will earlier discover the depth of their predicament and can react with mitigating actions, such as hiring specialists.

The waterfall has been called a *fail-late* lifecycle; one can have the illusion of an accurate schedule during the early, easier phases. This is because the hard and risky elements (like integration and test) are pushed towards the end. Then, halfway through the schedule—as the real complexity and difficult elements surface—pow! The schedule falls apart. It's like the story of the guy who fell off the cliff:

> *As he was hurtling down, someone yelled, "How are you doing?" The guy replied, "So far, so good!"*

Problem: "Plan the Work, Work the Plan" Values

The old management maxim of "plan the work, work the plan" is suitable advice—for predictable manufacturing. For high-change, novel, inventive domains such as software development, it has limited value except at the highest level of very coarse-grained activities or milestones. The maxim is associated with the values of waterfall development, predictive planning, command-control management, up-front specifications, and so forth. This is inconsistent with the agile method principles of adaptive planning, self-organizing and self-directed teams, and evolutionary development.

Of course, this does not imply that agile methods avoid planning or preparation. But the degree of detail, and commitment to plan are more light and flexible. Plus, the devolution of decision making and task assignment to the team itself rather than the manager changes the tone and goals of management planning.

WHAT'S NEXT?

The next chapter presents evidence illustrating problems with the waterfall, advantages of iterative development, case studies, thought leader advice, and more. Then, four related chapters discuss noteworthy IID methods: Scrum, XP, UP, and Evo.

EVIDENCE

Q: What are the most exciting, promising software engineering ideas or techniques on the horizon?

A: I don't think that the most promising ideas are on the horizon. They are already here and have been for years, but are not being used properly.

—David L. Parnas

OVERVIEW

❑ Research, historical, and other evidence related to IID.

❑ Evidence of waterfall risks.

❑ Business case for skills transfer to adopt IID.

Some have no need to justify iterative development. Others need to make a case; this material can help.

For students of software engineering methods or those needing to motivate an iterative experiment, this chapter provides some data, in several categories:

research evidence　　　　　*expert thought leader advice*

early large projects　　　　*business case*

standards-body advice　　　*waterfall problems*

IID practices have been entrenched for years in some development markets, yet some government standards still promote single-pass, document-driven, waterfall development, as do some larger

IT and consulting organizations, government and military service suppliers, engineering curriculums, and many requirements texts. For example, the Call For Papers in the 2002 *Time-Constrained Requirements Engineering* workshop stated:

> *In general, requirements engineering literature has been working with the assumption that a system should be clearly specified before its design and implementation can start.*

SUMMARY

p. 65   **Research evidence**—Data shows that iterative and evolutionary development is correlated with lower risk, higher productivity, and lower defect rates than waterfall projects.

p. 79   **Early large project evidence**—Major and life-critical systems have been developed iteratively rather than using the waterfall. Examples include the USA Space Shuttle flight control software, developed in 17 iterations, and the new Canadian air traffic control system. In the 1970s, the IBM Federal Systems Division conceived and widely applied the method *Integration Engineering*, an iterative lifecycle process.

p. 87   **Standards-body evidence**—In the 1980s the USA Department of Defense promoted a waterfall lifecycle in DOD-STD-2167. It was associated with high failure rates. In 1987 a recommendation was made to prefer iterative and evolutionary methods. This occurred in 1994 with the adoption of MIL-STD-498. NATO, the FDA, and other bodies have similar stories.

p. 93   **Expert thought leader evidence**—Many prominent software engineering thought leaders have recommended avoiding the waterfall and adopting iterative development, including Harlan Mills, Frederick Brooks, Barry Boehm, James Martin, Tom DeMarco, Ed Yourdon, and more.

Business case—Iterative development is correlated with lower failure rates; the opposite is true of the waterfall. Each year, 23% of projects, averaging $1.1 million USD, fail. A two-year ROI analysis of investing $100,000 in iterative skills transfer could show an NPV of $700,000 with IRR of 200%.

p. 100

Waterfall problems—The original "waterfall paper" was misinterpreted and seldom read, its author actually endorsed iterative and evolutionary development, the waterfall was associated with high risks, and the creator of the waterfall DOD-STD-2167 standard retrospectively says he would have promoted an iterative rather than waterfall lifecycle.

p. 102

Why still waterfall promotion?—There are at least seven reasons why the waterfall continued to be promoted, including lack of awareness of the growing evidence that it was not ideal, its simple definition, and the allure of simple progress tracking (such as "requirements complete").

p. 105

The remainder of the chapter is detail behind the summaries.

Exhaustive data can make for exhausting reading :-)
This chapter is probably best spot-read as a reference.

RESEARCH EVIDENCE

Iterative and Evolutionary Research

Evidence on the question of IID and evolutionary delivery comes from several studies by Alan MacCormack and others at Harvard Business School. In the first study [MacCormack01, MVI01] the question, "Does evolutionary development, rather than the waterfall model, result in better success?" was explored in a two-year in-depth analysis of projects. The report's conclusion?

Tom Gilb's Evo.
p. 211

> *Now there is proof that the evolutionary approach to software development results in a speedier process and higher-quality products. ... The iterative process is best captured in the evolutionary delivery model proposed by Tom Gilb.*

And specifically on evolutionary feedback-based requirements and design,

> *... our research suggests a clear agenda for managers: Get a low-functionality version of the product into customers' hands at the earliest possible stage and thereafter adopt an iterative approach to adding functionality.*

> *... projects in which most of the functionality was developed and tested prior to releasing a beta version performed uniformly **poorly**. In contrast, the projects that performed **best** were those in which a low-functionality version of the product was distributed to customers at an early stage. [emphasis added]*

The study identified four practices that were statistically correlated with the most successful projects:

1. An iterative lifecycle with early release of the evolving product to stakeholders for review and feedback.

2. Daily incorporation of new software and rapid feedback on design changes (daily builds with regression testing).

3. A team with broad-based experience of shipping multiple projects.

4. Early attention to an overall architecture of modular and loosely coupled components.

architecture in UP
p. 188

Practices 1 and 2 are associated with all modern IID methods. Practice 4 is a key element in the UP.

In a follow-up study [MKCC03], MacCormack and colleagues examined the effect of eight practices on productivity and defects (reported by customers), including IID and releasing a partial system early for evaluation and evolutionary design. The projects ranged from application software to embedded systems, with median values of nine developers and a 14-month duration; 75% used iterative and evolutionary development, 25% the waterfall. A key conclusion of the study:

> *In this study, we find that releasing [the result of an iteration] at an earlier stage of development appears to contribute to both a lower defect rate and higher productivity.*

> *Given this measure consistently predicts several different dimensions of performance across different samples of projects we conclude that it represents a software development "best" practice.*

In contrast, early detailed design specifications were not particularly valuable:

> *We find a weak relationship (p = 0.0781) between the completeness of the detailed design specification and a lower defect rate.*

And detailed design specs did not improve productivity. However, design reviews with peers did significantly reduce defect rates.

In the multivariate model of defect factors, the following iterative-related practices and their magnitude of impact were significant:

❑ Releasing a partial system (for evaluation, not operation) when 20% of the functionality is complete as opposed to waiting until 40% (the sample median) is associated with a decrease in the defect rate of 10.

by "10" is meant 10 defects per month per million lines of code

❑ Integration and regression testing at code check-in (the XP practice of continuous integration) is associated with a reduction in the defect rate of 13.

Similarly, in the model of productivity factors, over 50% of the variation in productivity was related to just two factors, both related to iterative practices:

by "8" is meant 8 more lines of source code per person-day

❏ Releasing the partial product earlier with *less* functionality (early iteration internal release for review) was better than waiting for more functionality. An increase in productivity of eight occurred when released at the 20% rather than 40% complete level.

❏ The use of daily builds with integration and regression testing is associated with a productivity improvement of 17.

In a study of productive software organizations [HC96], researchers at Bell Labs found a consistent pattern on highly successful projects:

❏ Iterative development with customer evaluation and feedback each iteration.

❏ Simple organizational structure; fewer roles than average.

❏ Even distribution of communication among people, more direct involvement of developers with other stakeholders, and more overall communication sharing.

A study published in 2001 summarized the results of research into over 400 projects spanning 15 years [CLW01]. Less than 5% of the code was actually useful or used. This high "software pollution" rate (reflecting un-useful requirements and over-engineering within a waterfall lifecycle) was significantly reduced by adopting iterative, short evolutionary delivery cycles—as in the Evo method—reducing releases from about six months on average to about two weeks.

In a survey of agile method results [Shine03], 88% of organizations cited improved productivity, and 84% improved quality. The most frequently used agile methods were Scrum and XP. Regarding cost of development, 46% stated no change and 49% stated it was less expensive with agile methods. One of the more interesting results—predictable in terms of agile method claims—was the increase in business satisfaction with the new software: Overall 83% claimed higher satisfaction and 26% overall claimed "significantly better satisfaction." The most frequently cited positive feature of agile methods (48%) was "respond to change rather than follow a predefined plan."

Another large study [Standish98] illustrating the value of iterative-related practices is the Standish Group's CHAOS study of project failure and success factors, analyzing 23,000 projects in the 1998 version. In the CHAOS TEN list of the top ten factors for success, at least four of the top five factors are strongly related to IID practices (Table 6.1).

Success Factor	Weight of Influence
User involvement	20
Executive support	15
Clear business objectives	15
Experienced project manager	15
Small milestones	10

Table 6.1 top five project success factors

High user involvement is central to IID methods; short iterations with demos, reviews, evolutionary requirements refinement, and client-driven iterations are key practices.

Executive support is promoted by these practices and especially through the demonstration of early, tangible results; people like to be associated with projects that show quick value and progress.

client-driven planning
p. 12

Clear business objectives is supported by adaptive client-driven iteration planning. By asking each iteration "What is most valuable?" and building it, the business objectives are clarified and realized, and the project aligned with them.

Of course, **small milestones** are at the heart of iterative methods.

To quote the study,

> *We have long been convinced that shorter time frames, with delivery of software components early and often, increase the success rate. Shorter time frames foster an iterative process of design, prototype, develop, test, and deploy small elements. "Growing" (instead of "developing") software engages the user earlier and confers ownership.*

Size Research

There is significant size research indicating smaller (and thus, less complex) projects are more successful and productive. This is not direct proof of the value of iterative development, but is very relevant to the IID practice of decomposing large projects into a series of small, short sub-project iterations.

A large study [Thomas01] of failure and success factors in over 1,000 UK IT projects found that 90% of the successful projects were less than 12 months duration; indeed, that 47% were less than 6 months. To quote,

> *This is not to say that projects over 12 months should not be started but that they should be broken into smaller projects within a programme of change whenever possible.*

The trend that the larger the project, the more likely it will fail, has been corroborated in a number of other studies. For example, in a study [Jones96] large sample set data show 48% of 10,000 function point (FP) projects are cancelled, as are 65% of 100,000 FP ones.

Going back to early, fundamental size issues, exploration of general systems theory in the 1950s by von Bertalanfy, Bateson, and others led to this fundamental conclusion [Bertalanfy68]:

The larger the system the harder it is to predict its behavior.

More straightforward evidence that small is beautiful comes from a 23,000 project study [Standish98]. For example, project success versus duration, see Figure 6.1.

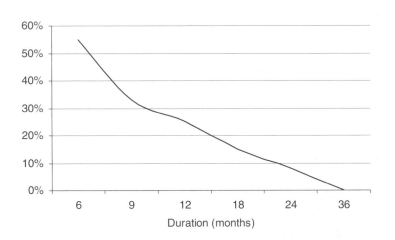

Project Success. 23,000 projects

Duration (months)

Figure 6.1 success vs. duration

Success was defined as "The project is completed on time and on budget, with all features and functions as originally specified."

This trend was confirmed in a follow-up study spanning 35,000 projects [Standish00], regarding cost (another size measure) versus success (Table 6.2).

Table 6.2 success vs. cost

Cost (USD)	< $0.5M	0.5M-3M	3M-6M	6M-10M	> 10M
Success	68%	22%	9%	1%	0%

And, to reiterate a portion of the Standish conclusion,

> ... *shorter time frames, with delivery of software components early and often, increase the success rate.*

Another interesting research note on size in the Standish research was the declining project failure rates, from 31% in the 1994 study to 23% in the 2000 study. This was correlated with smaller, shorter projects and smaller teams.

Direct smaller-size and evolutionary delivery evidence was presented in a previously cited study [CLW01]. The percentage of developed code that was ultimately found to be useful increased when the delivery cycle was reduced from around six months to about two weeks, as recommended in Evo.

Change Research

> *For cohesion, this section summarizes and repeats research introduced in an earlier chapter.*

A study by Boehm and Papaccio showed that a typical software project experienced a 25% change in requirements [BP88]. This trend is corroborated in another large study; as illustrated in Figure 6.2 [Jones97], software development is a domain of inventive high-change projects.

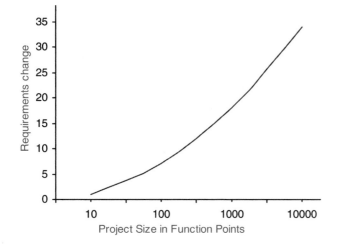

Figure 6.2 rates of change
on software projects

Another measure of change is to investigate how much use is actually made of implemented features defined in early specifications. A large study [Johnson02] showed that 45% of features were never used (Figure 6.3).

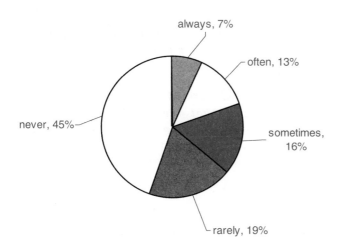

Figure 6.3 actual use of
requested features

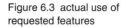

Evolutionary requirements to address change is becoming more widespread. A study of 107 projects [CM95] showed that only 18%

of the projects tried to complete the requirements in a single early step; 32% used two cycles of requirements refinement (with programming in between); and in 50% of the projects the requirements analysis was completed over three or more iterations.

The data in this section demonstrates that software development is a high-change domain. Practices or values that encourage early "complete" specifications or schedules are incongruous. Iterative and evolutionary practices that emphasize adaptability and steps to provoke early change are consistent with this research.

Waterfall Failure Research

In a study of failure factors on 1,027 IT projects in the UK [Thomas01] (only 13% didn't fail), scope management related to attempting waterfall practices (including detailed up-front requirements) was the single largest contributing factor for failure, being cited in 82% of the projects as the number one problem, with an overall weighted failure influence of 25%. To quote the study's conclusion,

> This suggests that … the approach of full requirements definition followed by a long gap before those requirements are delivered is no longer appropriate.

> The high ranking of changing business requirements suggests that any assumption that there will be little significant change to requirements once they have been documented is fundamentally flawed, and that spending significant time and effort defining them to the maximum level is inappropriate.

See "Standards-Body Evidence" on p. 87.

Other significant evidence of failure applying the waterfall comes from one of its most frequent users in the past, the USA Department of Defense (DoD). Most DoD projects were required—by the standard DOD-STD-2167—to follow a waterfall lifecycle. A report on failure rates in a sample of earlier 2167-era DoD projects concluded that 75% of the projects failed or were never used [Jarzombek99]. Consequently, a task force was convened, chaired by Dr. Frederick Brooks, the well-known software engineering expert. The report recommended replacing the waterfall with IID [DSB87]:

DOD-STD-2167 likewise needs a radical overhaul to reflect modern best practice. ... In the decade since the waterfall model was developed, our discipline has come to recognize that [development] requires iteration between the designers and users.

Evolutionary development is best technically, and it saves time and money.

In another study of 6,700 projects, it was found that four out of the five key factors contributing to project failure were associated with and aggravated by the waterfall model [Jones95], including inability to deal with changing requirements, and problems with late integration.

In 1996 Barry Boehm published a well-known paper summarizing failures of the waterfall [Boehm96], with advice to use a risk-reducing IID approach combined with three milestone anchor points around which to plan and control; this advice was eventually adopted in the UP.

UP phases p. 180

There are several studies (covering thousands of projects) that shed light on the value of large, up-front specifications in a waterfall-oriented lifecycle.

One study [Jarzombek99] cited a 1995 DoD software project study (of over $37 billion USD worth of projects) showing that 46% of the systems so egregiously did not meet the *real* needs (although they met the specifications) that they were never successfully used, and another 20% required extensive rework to meet the true needs (rather than the specifications) before they could be used.

As mentioned earlier, another study [Johnson02] showed that 45% of features were never used—with an additional 19% rarely used.

In the previously cited study of over 400 waterfall-oriented projects [CLW01] averaging six-month cycles, only 10% of the developed code was actually deployed, and of that, only 20% was used. The prime reasons included:

❑ Users couldn't provide much feedback before delivery.

❑ Changes in the business since the requirements phase.

❑ Requirements and business operations were misunderstood.

Productivity Research

There is a productivity motivation to apply short iterations, even if there were up-front requirements.

A study [Solon02] against a sample set (43,700 projects) showed the following productivity differences between IID and waterfall:

Rigorous IID or Evolutionary Prototyping	Rigorous Waterfall
570 function points per full-time equivalent developer	480

Interestingly, the same study showed that among the waterfall projects, those that applied it only "loosely" were significantly *more* productive than those that applied it "rigorously," indicating the negative effect that it has on productivity.

Another relevant study [Jones00] showed that as the size of project decreases (measured in language-independent function points), the monthly productivity of staff increases (Figure 6.4).

This data illustrates the motivation of organizing a project into small mini-project iterations with low function points per iteration, as the most dramatic productivity drop occurs in the lower function point range (under 1,000).

Figure 6.4 productivity vs. size

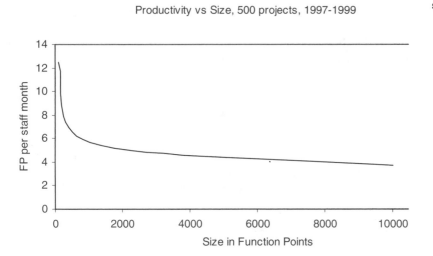

Productivity vs Size, 500 projects, 1997-1999

Timeboxing by itself has been shown to have a productivity effect. Dupont, one of the earliest timebox pioneers, found developer productivity around 80 function points per month with timeboxed iterations, but only 15 to 25 function points for other methods [Martin91].

Note the rate of 80 function points per month at Dupont compared to a high of 12 function points per month in Figure 6.4. This suggests that the combination of a low-complexity step *with* timeboxing has a higher productivity impact than simply a small step without timeboxing.

productivity was measured in function points per person-month

In another study [Jones00], 47 factors that increase or decrease productivity were identified, including project complexity:

Low complexity	High complexity
+ 13% in productivity	− 35%

This indicates a productivity advantage by organizing projects in low-complexity mini-project iterations.

To reiterate the results of a study on productivity and iterative development [MKCC03], their conclusion was,

> *In this study, we find that releasing [the result of an iteration] at an earlier stage of development appears to contribute to both a lower defect rate and higher productivity.*

Quality and Defect Research

Broadly, defect reduction comes from avoiding defects before they occur (Deming's Total Quality Management principle) and from feedback (tests, evaluations, and so forth). IID methods can address both. For example, several methods promote a per-iteration simple process assessment or reflection by the team, to encourage regular process improvement and defect avoidance. Feedback is enabled by the emphasis on early development of the riskiest elements, per-iteration demos, and a test-early, test-often approach. The association of lower defect rates with iterative development is consistent with Deming's predictions, as IID illustrates the Deming/Shewhart Plan-Do-Study-Act (PDSA) cycle, and supports a culture of continuous improvement by measuring, reflecting, and adjusting each iteration.

Specifically, the study [MKCC03] showed that IID was correlated with lower defects. In other research [MVI01], it was shown that as the time lag between coding and testing decreased, defect rates likewise decreased. A study by Deck [Deck94] also shows a statistically significant reduction in defects using an iterative method. Large case-study research [Jones00] showed that defect rates increase non-linearly as project size grows (Figure 6.5).

Although not statistically reliable, there are several single-case study reports of lower defect densities associated with iterative methods (e.g., [Manzo02]).

Figure 6.5 defects vs. size

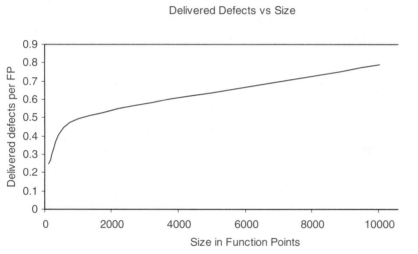

Delivered Defects vs Size

EARLY HISTORICAL PROJECT EVIDENCE[1]

The usual citation style is replaced with inline citations in this section, as a goal is showing the references in context.

This section emphasizes a history of *early* published iterative projects; there were surely many hundreds or thousands more that applied IID in the 1960s and 1970s. IID projects from the late

---

1. Some material is adapted from [LB03].

1980s forward are not emphasized, as by that time they were common.

Pre-1970

See "The Historical Accident of Waterfall Validity?" on p. 102.

Although IID in software is in the ascendancy as the "modern" approach to replace ad hoc or waterfall development, its practiced and published roots go back surprisingly far—at least as far back as the late 1950s, as a contemporary alternative to the nascent waterfall model, perhaps first described as the "stagewise model" for the USA air defense SAGE project by H. D. Benington in "Production of Large Computer Programs," *Proceedings of the ONR Symposium on Advanced Program Methods for Digital Computers*, June 1956.

Early roots for IID are found in the work of Walter Shewhart, the quality expert at Western Electric who proposed, in the 1930s, a series of PDSA cycles (the **Shewhart Cycle** or **Deming Wheel**) for quality improvement, an idea promoted by quality guru Edward Deming, starting in the 1940s. The application of iterative PDSA to software was explored by Zultner in "The Deming Approach to Quality Software Engineering," *Quality Progress*, 21(11) 1988.

A milestone 1950s project applying IID was the X-15 hypersonic jet (see W. H. Dana, "The X-15 Lessons Learned," NASA Dryden Research Facility, 1993):

> *A major contributor to the X-15's success over the long run was its emphasis on incremental development.*

Although not a software project, the X-15 is mentioned because some personnel (and hence, incremental experience) seeded NASA's 1961–63 Project Mercury, which did apply IID in software—and some of the latter project's personnel seeded the IBM Federal Systems Division (FSD), another early IID proponent.

Project Mercury was run with short half-day iterations. There was a technical review of all changes, and—interestingly—the Extreme Programming practice of test-first development was applied: Tests were planned and written in advance of each micro-increment, and then the code was written to pass the tests. Each mini-iteration required integration of all code and passing of tests.

The Project Mercury description came from the software engineering thought leader, Gerald M. Weinberg, who provided a window onto IID versus waterfall attitudes during this period, especially on the highly visible Project Mercury system [LB03]:

> *We were doing incremental development as early as 1957, in Los Angeles, under the direction of Bernie Dimsdale [at IBM's Service Bureau Corporation]. He was a colleague of John von Neumann, so perhaps he learned it there, or assumed it as totally natural. I do remember Herb Jacobs (primarily, though we all participated) developing a large simulation for Motorola, where the technique used was, as far as I can tell, indistinguishable from XP.*

> *When much of the same team was reassembled in Washington, DC, in 1958 to develop Project Mercury, we had our own machine and the new Share Operating System, whose symbolic modification and assembly allowed us to build the system incrementally, which we did, with great success. Project Mercury was the seed bed out of which grew the IBM Federal Systems Division. Thus, that division started with a history and tradition of incremental development.*

> *All of us, as far as I can remember, thought waterfalling of a huge project was rather stupid, or at least ignorant of the realities.*

Since the early 1960s, Weinberg has been a well-known consultant and author, is an inductee of the Computer Hall of Fame, and has written classics such as *Psychology of Computer Programming* and *Secrets of Consulting*.

1970s

Early practice of IID comes from the leadership of Mike Dyer, Bob McHenry, and Don O'Neill (and many others) during their tenure at the IBM FSD, which was responsible for building many aerospace and defense systems.

What is fascinating about the FSD story is the extent and success of IID use on large, life-critical DoD, space, and avionic systems during the 1970s.

The first major FSD documented application of IID (I could find) was in 1972. This was a major, high-visibility, life-critical system of over one million lines of code: the command and control system for the first USA Trident submarine. The project included Dyer, McHenry, and O'Neill as project manager. O'Neill conceived and planned the use of IID (later called **Integration Engineering** at FSD) on this project; it was a key success factor, and he was awarded an IBM Outstanding Contribution Award for it. Note the visible approval by IBM leadership for IID methods.

> To underline this point: IBM FSD created the IID method Integration Engineering, and it was a well-known practice on major FSD projects in the 1970s.

The Trident project could not be late: The system had to be delivered by a certain date; otherwise, FSD faced a $100,000 per day late penalty. The project was organized in four timeboxed iterations of about six months each. There was still a significant upfront specifications effort, and the iteration length was longer than normally recommended today. Although there was some feedback-driven evolution in the requirements, the IID approach was seen also as a way to manage the complexity and risks of development. See O'Neill, "Integration Engineering Perspective," *The Journal of Systems and Software*, No. 3, 1983.

Also in 1972, and outside of the IBM FSD, another major project that applied IID comes from an FSD competitor: TRW.

It applied incremental development on the $100 million TRW/Army Site Defense software project for ballistic missile defense. The project began in February 1972 and developed the system in five iterations. Iteration 1 did tracking of a single object, and by iteration 5, a couple of years later, the system was complete. The iterations were not strictly timeboxed, and there was significant up-front specifications work, but they were also refined in response to each iteration's feedback. See Williams, "Managing the Development of Reliable Software," *Proceedings, International Conference on Reliable Software*, ACM/IEEE, April 1975.

As with IBM FSD, TRW was another early adopter of IID practices. Indeed, Barry Boehm, the originator of the famous IID "spiral model" in the mid-1980s, served at TRW as Chief Scientist. Another key TRW employee relevant to this story was Winston Royce, author of the most frequently cited original paper on the waterfall. As will be explored later in "The Historical Accident of Waterfall Validity?" section on page 102, his message was misunderstood, and he was in fact a proponent of IID rather than the sequential waterfall, as it has come to be known.

Another early (mid-1970s), successful, and large application of IID at FSD was the USA Navy helicopter-ship system LAMPS. A four-year 200 person-year effort involving millions of lines of code, it was evolutionarily delivered in 45 timeboxed iterations (one month per iteration). This is the earliest project example I found where the length of iteration was in the range commonly recommended by today's IID methods. The project was quite successful. To quote,

Every one of those deliveries was on time and under budget.

It is described by the noted 1970s thought leader Harlan Mills in "Principles of Software Engineering," *IBM Systems Journal*, Vol 19(4), 1980.

Although unknown to most software professionals, another early and strikingly impressive example of an IID success is the heart of the NASA Space Shuttle software itself: the Primary Avionics Software System. This was built by FSD from 1977 to 1980, applying IID in a series of 17 iterations over 31 months, averaging around 8 weeks per iteration (see Madden and Rone, "Design, Development, Integration: Space Shuttle Flight Software System," *Communications of the ACM*, Sept. 1984). Their motivation for IID?

> *[The waterfall lifecycle was not suitable because] the requirements on the Shuttle program evolved during the software development process.*

(How unique). Ironically—in hindsight of the research evidence—the authors sound almost apologetic in having to forego the "ideal" waterfall for an IID approach,

> *Due to the size, complexity, and evolutionary [changing requirements] nature of the program, it was recognized early that the ideal software development lifecycle (the waterfall model) could not be strictly applied. ... However, an implementation approach (based on small incremental releases) was devised for STS-1 which met the objectives by applying the ideal cycle to small elements of the overall software package on an iterative basis.*

This Shuttle project exhibited classic IID practices: timeboxed iterations in the eight-week range, feedback-driven refinement of specifications, and so forth.

The IBM IID method Integration Engineering was so successful that it was incorporated into the FSD Software Engineering Practices (SEP) in 1977 and disseminated to the 2,500 FSD software engineers (see O'Neill, "The Management of Software Engineering," *IBM Systems Journal*, 19(4), 1980). The idea of IID stimulated substantial interest within IBM's commercial divisions, senior customer ranks, and among competitors, and presentations by SEP representatives on the value of IID, rather than the waterfall to visitors was not uncommon during this period.

Another early story and paper often cited on the subject of iterative development is "A Successful Software Development," by Wong, in *IEEE Transactions on Software Engineering*, No. 3, 1984. It describes an air defense system project that ran from 1977 to 1980 that combined significant up-front specifications followed by iterative development. The project was ostensibly meant to fit within DoD single-pass waterfall standards, with testing and integration in the last phase. However, Wong comments on the unrealism of this approach, and their need for and advantages using IID:

> *The [waterfall] model was adopted because software development was guided by DoD standards. ... In reality, software development is a complex, continuous, iterative, and repetitive process. The [waterfall model] does not reflect this complexity.*

1980s and Later

The earliest 1980s reference I could find to a large application successfully built via IID is the 1982 $100 million USD command and control project. See Tamanaha, "An integrated rapid prototyping methodology for command and control systems: Experience and insight," *ACM SIGSOFT Software Engineering Notes*, Dec. 1982.

From 1984 to 1988, Magnavox Electronic Systems built a large field artillery command and control system for the USA Army, ultimately a 1.3 million line Ada project. Under the methodology leadership of Don Firesmith, and with some consulting from

Grady Booch, it ran as a successful IID project composed of five iterations. The first iteration emphasized building the core architecture. The project had twice the productivity and three times the usual quality measures compared to other Magnavox projects [Firesmith87].

Dozens or hundreds more large IID projects in the 1980s can be discovered, but I'll close this brief early history of IID for large, risky projects with two related case studies started in the mid-1980s: the attempted next-generation USA and Canadian air traffic control (ATC) systems.

The attempted USA ATC project started in 1983 and ran as a classic and massive big-bang waterfall project: It was a herculean attempt to define the requirements before programming, a consequential lack of stakeholder feedback, analysis paralysis, complexity overload, and so on. The conclusion: In 1994 the government cancelled the project after having spent $2.6 billion USD, with nothing to show for it [GAO98]. The project was restarted in the late 1990s with an IID approach. To quote:

> *[in the new approach] FAA and the aviation community agreed to (1) use an incremental approach to modernizing the National Airspace System, referred to as the "build a little, test a little" approach; ... These practices differ from those of the past in which FAA tried to deploy large, complex projects all at once, known as the "big bang" approach. [GAO99]*

2167A, unsuccessful, has since been replaced. See p. 87

Similarly, in 1989, a new Canadian ATC project—CAATS—was started as a waterfall project, following guidance from the USA DoD waterfall-promoting standard 2167A. In 1992, after several hundred million dollars spent, requirements paralysis, and little progress deemed valuable, the Canadian government was considering cancelling the project. But, rather than abandon the effort, the project was restarted under the process leadership of Philippe Kruchten, an IID-experienced architect (and later, chief architect of the Rational Unified Process). Kruchten ran it as an iterative project, averaging six-months per iteration with a staff of several hundred, and CAATS re-surfaced as a successfully evolving system with early visible progress, ultimately with over one million lines of source code, mostly Ada. See Kruchten et al., "Modernizing ATC through Modern Software Methods," *1993 Proceedings of the Air Traffic Control Association*.

By the 1990s, IID use was relatively widespread, probably in the tens of thousands of projects worldwide, though varying adoption trends in different domains and cultures could be seen. Predictably, company and national cultures that emphasized hierarchical management and control, and detailed predictive planning, were the slowest adopters.

STANDARDS-BODY EVIDENCE

The transition of the USA DoD standards from waterfall to iterative and evolutionary is instructive. In 1980s a DoD standard for software development or procurement was released, DOD-STD-2167, based on a waterfall model and document-driven approach.[2]

As mentioned earlier, the DoD was experiencing failure in the acquisition of software based on a waterfall approach and the 2167 standard. For example, a 1995 report on failure rates in a sample of earlier DoD projects drew grave conclusions: Out of a total cost of $37 billion USD for the sample set, 75% of the projects failed or were never used, and only 2% were used without extensive modification [Jarzombek99].

---

2. It also had an influence on standards set by other governments. The story is explored in the "The Historical Accident of Waterfall Validity?" section on page 102.

Magnavox project p. 85 Thus, there was a motivation to improve the 2167 standard. In the latter 1980s, Firesmith, motivated from the stultifying influence of 2167 on the Magnavox project, helped lead the Ada community's promotion of IID to replace 2167 with a new IID-friendly 2167A standard. In collaboration with Lt. Colin Gylleat (who was deeply involved in producing 2167A), they were able to remove the legal requirements for functional decomposition and the waterfall development cycle. However, the original single-step waterfall *diagrams* remained in the updated 2167A from 2167, because (in the words of Firesmith):

> *Although the waterfall diagrams did not have any legal impact, I could not get them removed because the military logistics people would not agree with my assessment that they would continue to foster the waterfall mindset.*

His assessment would prove correct. Shortly thereafter, another push to replace the waterfall with evolutionary IID was made in a task force report [DSB87], chaired by Dr. Frederick Brooks. The report recommended to replace the waterfall, disproved on many large DoD projects, with iterative development:

> *DOD-STD-2167 likewise needs a radical overhaul to reflect modern best practice. Draft 2167A is a step, but it does not go nearly far enough. As drafted, it continues to reinforce exactly the document-driven, specify-then-build approach that lies at the heart of so many DoD software problems.*

And on incremental acquisition and development:

> *In the decade since the waterfall model was developed, our discipline has come to recognize that [development] requires iteration between the designers and users.*

Finally, in the section titled *Professional Humility and Evolutionary Development* (humility that it should be accepted that the waterfall goals of getting the specifications or design accurate without evolutionary implementation and feedback are rarely possible):

> *Experience with confidently specifying and painfully building mammoths has shown it to be simplest, safest, and even fastest to develop a complex software system by building a minimal version, putting it into actual use, and then adding functions [and other qualities] according to the priorities that emerge from actual use.*

> *Evolutionary development is best technically, and it saves time and money.*

The updated DOD-STD-2167A (Feb. 1988), which is often viewed by both DoD overseers and contractors as the epitome of a waterfall specification, was ironically actually an amendment promoted by Firesmith and Gylleat (and others) to allow lifecycle neutrality, to encourage IID alternatives to the waterfall:

> *This standard is not intended to specify or discourage the use of any particular software development method. The contractor is responsible for selecting software development methods (for example, rapid prototyping) that best support the achievement of contract requirements.*

Despite this intent, the new standard was interpreted—with justification—by many to still contain an implied preference for the waterfall model, due to its document-driven milestone approach.

Due to ongoing failure with waterfall projects, and to re-emphasize replacing the waterfall with IID for DoD projects, a *Report of the Defense Science Board Task Force on Acquiring Defense Software Commercially*, June 1994, was issued that stated:

> *DoD must manage programs using iterative development.*

> *Apply evolutionary development with rapid deployment of initial functional capability.*

As a consequence, 2167A was superseded by MIL-STD-498 in December 1994. In "Changes from DOD-STD-2167A to MIL-STD-498," *Crosstalk: The Journal of Defense Software Engineering*, April 1995, Maj. George Newberry summarizes the changes to encourage "evolutionary acquisition" and IID in the section *Removing the Waterfall Bias*:

> *MIL-STD-498 describes ... incremental builds. Each build implements a specified subset of the planned capabilities. The process steps are repeated for each build, and within each build, steps may be overlapping and iterative.*

The MIL-498 standard explains and promotes evolutionary requirements and design; for example:

> *If a system is developed in multiple builds, its requirements may not be fully defined until the final build. ... If a system is designed in multiple builds, its design may not be fully defined until the final build.*

In 2000 the DoD 5000.2 acquisition "instruction" was released, that again recommended evolutionary delivery and the use of IID:

> *There are two approaches, evolutionary and single step [waterfall] to full capability. An evolutionary approach is preferred. ... [In this] approach, the ultimate capability delivered to the user is divided into two or more blocks, with increasing increments of capability.*
>
> *... software development shall follow an iterative spiral development process in which continually expanding software versions are based on learning from earlier development.*

See also the scanned memo in Figure 6.6 that clearly communicates the DoD preference for evolutionary and "spiral" (iterative) development.

Thus, the DoD—perhaps the world's largest and most experienced procurement agency for software—started with the assumption that a waterfall model and up-front specifications was best (codified in 2167), and then—based on the experience of high rates of project failures—adopted iterative and evolutionary methods, demoting the waterfall.

The practice of IID is important to the DoD. For example, there is now an annual conference on the subject, *Evolutionary Acquisition & Spiral Development*, organized by the Institute for Defense and Government Advancement. See www.idga.org.

Unfortunately (for taxpayers worldwide) STD-2167 influenced the definition of standards in other countries, who did not keep up with the fact that the DoD later abandoned 2167 and the waterfall; many of these standard bodies still impose single-pass, document-driven processes.

The DoD is not the only standards group to make this shift. In 2002 the USA Food and Drug Administration (FDA) updated their prior waterfall model requirements [FDA97] for software development of FDA approved devices (e.g., medical devices) with a new standard that promotes iterative development [FDA02]. To quote,

> *Most software development models will be iterative. This is likely to result in several versions of both the software requirements specification and software design specification.*

Figure 6.6 scanned memo

THE UNDER SECRETARY OF DEFENSE

3010 DEFENSE PENTAGON
WASHINGTON, DC 20301-3010

APR 1 2 2002

ACQUISITION,
TECHNOLOGY
AND LOGISTICS

MEMORANDUM FOR SECRETARIES OF THE MILITARY DEPARTMENTS
CHAIRMAN OF THE JOINT CHIEFS OF STAFF
UNDER SECRETARIES OF DEFENSE
ASSISTANT SECRETARIES OF DEFENSE
INSPECTOR GENERAL, DEPARTMENT OF DEFENSE
GENERAL COUNSEL, DEPARTMENT OF DEFENSE
DIRECTORS OF THE DEFENSE AGENCIES

SUBJECT: Evolutionary Acquisition and Spiral Development

Since the publication of DoD Directive 5000.1 and DoD Instruction 5000.2, in which the Department established a preference for the use of evolutionary acquisition strategies relying on a spiral development process, there has been some confusion about what these terms mean and how spiral development impacts various processes such as contracting and requirements generation that interface with an evolutionary acquisition strategy. The purpose of this memorandum is to address those questions.

Evolutionary acquisition and spiral development are methods that will allow us to reduce our cycle time and speed the delivery of advanced capability to our warfighters. These approaches are designed to develop and field demonstrated technologies for both hardware and software in manageable pieces. Evolutionary acquisition and spiral development also allow insertion of new technologies and capabilities over time.

Although a number of European standards are still waterfall oriented, promising signs of change have emerged, such as the 2002 Bonn Germany *NATO Symposium on Evolutionary Software Development*.

EXPERT AND THOUGHT LEADER EVIDENCE

This section concentrates on some of the earliest and most well known software development thought leaders; many other experts reiterate their views. Where possible, the material is organized by date of publication.

Harlan Mills

The earliest iterative-promoting reference I could find from a prominent expert came in 1970 from Harlan Mills, who worked at the IBM FSD. Mills was perhaps the most well-known software engineering thought leader of the 1970s, winner of the DPMA and Warnier Prizes for lifetime contributions to information sciences, an inventor or contributor to structured programming, top-down design and programming, chief programmer teams, the Cleanroom Method, and incremental development.

In his well-known "Top-down Programming in Large Systems" he promotes iterative development. See *Debugging Techniques in Large Systems*, Prentice-Hall (reprinted in Mills' collected papers, *Software Productivity*, Dorset House, 1988). In addition to the paper's primary advice to develop starting from top-level control structures downwards, Mills gives the related lifecycle advice of building the system via "iterated expansions."

> *... it is possible to generate a sequence of intermediate systems of code and functional subspecifications so that at every step, each [intermediate] system can be verified to be correct, ...*

In 1976, after seeing the many successes with IID on IBM FSD projects, Mills reiterated and strengthened his IID message. In the widely read "Software Development," *IEEE Transactions on Software Engineering*, December 1976, he writes:

Software development should be done incrementally, in stages with continuous user participation and replanning, and with design-to-cost programming within each stage.

In the context of analyzing a failed three-year inventory control system project, he goes on to challenge the waterfall:

...there are dangers, too, particularly in the conduct of these [waterfall] stages in sequence, and not in iteration—i.e., that development is done in an open loop, rather than a closed loop with user feedback between iterations. The danger in the sequence [waterfall approach] is that the project moves from being grand to being grandiose, and exceeds our human intellectual capabilities for management and control.

Exasperated at the failures applying the waterfall, contrasted with IID at FSD, Mills asks:

...why do enterprises tolerate the frustrations and difficulties of such [waterfall] development?

And this complaint in 1976.

Further, Mills' Cleanroom Method included IID as part of the method.

Tom Gilb

In 1976 there was the (published) arrival of a long-standing and passionate voice promoting iterative and evolutionary methods: Tom Gilb. This was the first clear IID-promoting book reference I could find, in Gilb's *Software Metrics*, Studentlitteratur AB (Sweden). Some examples:

Evolution [or "Evo," the name of Gilb's iterative method] is a technique for producing the appearance of stability.

A complex system will be most successful if it is implemented in small steps and if each step has a clear measure of success- ful achievement as well as a "retreat" possibility to a previous successful step upon failure.

The advantage is that you cannot have large failures. You have the opportunity of receiving some feedback from the real world before throwing in all resources intended for a system, and you can correct possible design errors before they become costly live systems.

Gilb also wrote Evo articles in the 1978–79 issues of *Computer Weekly*. And in 1985, he published one of a growing number of arti- cles questioning the sequential lifecycle, in "Evolutionary Delivery versus the Waterfall Model" ACM *Sigsoft Software Requirements Engineering Notes*, July 1985.

Evo chapter: p. 211

Gilb has been developing and consulting since 1960, is the creator of one of the earliest iterative methods, Evo, and author of popular texts such as *Principles of Software Engineering Management*, Addison-Wesley, 1988, in which he expands on Evo in several chapters.

Frederick Brooks

In 1986 there was the release of a popular article in software engi- neering, one of whose main themes is the demotion of the waterfall and promotion of IID. It was "No Silver Bullet" by Frederick Brooks, published in *Proceedings of the IFIP Tenth World Comput- ing Conference* (and reprinted in *IEEE Computer*, April 1987). In this classic paper, Brooks criticizes the waterfall as undesirable, and extols the advantages of IID:

Nothing in the past decade has so radically changed my own practice, or its effectiveness [as iterative development].

He rejects waterfall advice and the promotion by requirements engineering advocates of detailed up-front specifications, and lays the blame for much software failure on it:

> *Much of present-day software acquisition procedures rests upon the assumption that one can specify a satisfactory system in advance, get bids for its construction, have it built, and install it. I think this assumption is fundamentally wrong, and that many software acquisition problems spring from that fallacy.*

Like Mills, Brooks was another famous software engineering thought leader. He was manager of the landmark IBM OS/360 operating system project, author of arguably the most widely read software engineering text, *The Mythical Man-Month* (Addison-Wesley, 1985), chair of the mid-1980s DoD study into software project failure (and what to change), and recipient of the highest awards in computer science and software engineering (the ACM Turing award, the IEEE John Von Neumann Medal, and the President's National Medal of Technology).

In the Silver Anniversary edition of *The Mythical Man-Month* Brooks tried to make it more plain by simply stating, *The waterfall model is wrong!*

Barry Boehm

Another well-known mid-1980s landmark in IID publications from an experienced expert comes with Barry Boehm's "A Spiral Model of Software Development and Enhancement," *Proceedings of an International Workshop on Software Process and Software Environments*, March 1985 (although more frequently cited in *ACM SIGSOFT Software Engineering Notes*, August 1986). Boehm's spiral model description promotes iterative and evolutionary development with a strong risk-driven emphasis. To quote:

A primary source of difficulty with the waterfall model has been its emphasis on fully-elaborated documents as completion criteria for early requirements and design phases. For some classes of software, such as compilers ..., this is the most effective way to proceed. But it does not work well for many classes of software, particularly interactive end-user applications.

Boehm, having ties to the DoD community, was successful in introducing the spiral model and its refinement, MBASE, on DoD projects, with a 90% rate of "highly satisfactory products" over several hundred projects. See, for example, "Balancing Discipline and Flexibility with the Spiral Model and MBASE," *Crosstalk: The Journal of Defense Software Engineering*, Dec. 2001.

Boehm has been involved in software development since the mid-1950s, has served as Chief Scientist for TRW (an experienced large systems contractor), Director of the USA DARPA Technology Office, and Chair of the Air Force Scientific Advisory Board. He is the creator of the well-known COCOMO estimation model, and has won the Warnier Prize, the NSIA Grace Murray Hopper Award, and the ACM Distinguished Research Award in Software Engineering.

James Martin

James Martin learned of iterative development and timeboxing from Scott Shultz at Dupont, where the practice was first given the name "timebox methodology" or "Rapid Iterative Production Prototyping" (RIPP). It was widely applied at Dupont in the early 1980s under Shultz's guidance.

Seeing its success, Martin started in the late 1980s to also promote development by timeboxed iterations for use both within and outside of the practice of rapid application development (RAD). See Martin, *Information Engineering: Design and Construction*,

Prentice-Hall, 1990. Based on its success with his customers, all subsequent method advice from James Martin promoted iterative development, rather than a sequential waterfall. He writes:

> *It is desirable [to use an iterative lifecycle] because the traditional lifecycle [the waterfall] is very slow. The traditional lifecycle often fails to meet the needs of end users. ... The traditional lifecycle prevents exploratory design and programming which is necessary to creative areas. ... Evolutionary development is needed in which systems continually grow.*

And:

> *While simple systems can be designed in one step, complex or subtle systems become understood only by attempting to build a [an evolutionary production-grade] prototype, learning from it, [and repeating]. The prototypes are improved a stage at a time until they converge to what the end users agree is a valuable system.*

The creators of DSDM, another popular iterative method, were RAD developers who were influenced by Martin's promotion of timeboxing and iterative development.

Martin has been involved in software development since the early 1960s, and was ranked by *Computerworld* among the top ten most influential people in the world of computing. He has served on the DoD Software Scientific Advisory Board, is an inductee of the Computer Hall of Fame, consulted to hundreds of organizations for decades, and is the author of over 100 texts on software development and technology.

Tom DeMarco

Tom DeMarco is a long-time practitioner and student of skillful software development practices, emphasizing people rather than lifecycle issues in his (and Tim Lister's) popular *PeopleWare* (Dorset House, 1987). In response to my question about his views on iterative development, he wrote (personal communication, email),

> *Craig, I have been a passive advocate of iterative methods since ever, but never wrote on the subject that I remember (my bag is the people side of management). However, my new book ["Waltzing With Bears: Managing Risk on Software Projects," Dorset House, 2003] with co-author Tim Lister has a whole part on iteration as a (read THE) risk mitigation technique.*

In their book, DeMarco writes:

> *The best bang-per-buck risk mitigation strategy we know is incremental delivery.*

DeMarco was winner of the 1986 Warnier Prize for "lifetime contribution to the field of computing" and the 1999 Stevens Award for "contribution to the methods of software development."

Ed Yourdon

In the early 1970s, with Larry Constantine and Tom DeMarco, Ed Yourdon founded Structured Analysis and Design, with a waterfall emphasis. But by the mid-1980s, Yourdon (and his colleagues) had shifted course and has since been a promoter of iterative development in many articles and books—for example, "The Future of Software: Best of Times, Worst of Times," *IEEE Software,* January 1998,

> *It's also easy to be optimistic when we look at the advances we've made in the "discipline" of our field. [New tools] have led many organizations to an iterative development approach that generally leads to more successful results than the waterfall development approach that was partly necessitated by the older generation of batch, mainframe tools.*

Yourdon has been in the field since 1964, is the author of dozens of books, was named one of the ten most influential people in the software field in *Crosstalk: The Journal of Defense Software Engineering*, and in 1997 was inducted into the Computer Hall of Fame.

A BUSINESS CASE FOR ITERATIVE DEVELOPMENT

As the evidence sections show, there is data to support the assertions that the waterfall is more failure-prone for software-intensive projects and that disciplined IID with evolutionary requirements and design is correlated with lower rates of failure and defects, and higher rates of productivity.

Thus, a business case can be made based on several factors, including:

❑ productivity

❑ quality (of both the product and the process)

❑ failure, delay, or cost-overruns

❑ fit of product to the true demand

This analysis draws special attention to *reduced failure rates*. Projects fail for many reasons, but evidence [e.g., Thomas01] has shown that waterfall practices rather than IID were associated with the most significant failure factors.

Figure 6.7 shows research on failure rates [Standish00] across 35,000 projects. On average, 23% of projects failed and were cancelled before completion in 2000.

Figure 6.7 success rates

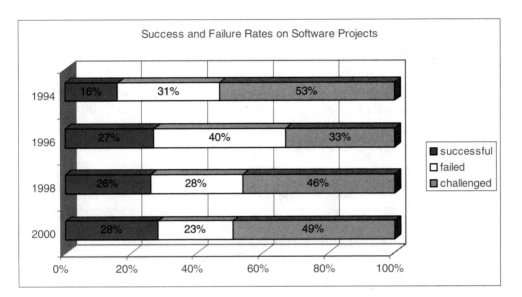

In addition, the average cost of these projects is:

Large Company	Medium	Small
$1.2M USD	$1.1M	$0.6M

Taking the average project cost for medium-sized companies, $1.1 million USD (let's round to $1 million), and the average year 2000 failure rate of 23%, if the organization attempts 20 projects in a year (a $20 million budget), it loses (conservatively rounding down) $4 million USD on four failed projects.

If—modestly—adopting IID leads to a slightly reduced failure rate of 17% (vs. 23%) then for every 20 projects attempted, one more succeeds—and roughly $1 million is saved.

In this case, even a substantial investment in education and consulting expertise to transition to IID pays off handsomely.[3] If a medium sized company with 10 projects per year and an annual $10 million project budget invested $100,000 in IID skills transfer, then—on average—in two years one more $1 million project will be successful. Assuming a two-year analysis and a 10% discount rate, this investment gives a (rounding) NPV of $700,000 with an IRR of 200%, not to mention reclaiming the lost opportunity cost of putting that $1 million project to work.

> In summary, although goals such as productivity and quality improvement are associated with IID, a primary, costly issue is reducing the expensive rate of failure of software projects—and IID is strongly correlated with the major factors to reduce failure and increase success. The opposite is true for waterfall practices.

THE HISTORICAL ACCIDENT OF WATERFALL VALIDITY?

The waterfall model was a response to ad hoc code-and-fix development in the 1960s. Note—as has been explored in the "Early Historical Project Evidence" section on page 79—disciplined IID did exist as a contemporary alterative. It was not inevitable that the waterfall be widely promoted (rather than IID) starting in the 1970s; it has a bit of an accidental quality to it, as I discovered in my historical research.

Misunderstanding started early, with the article and author most often cited for the waterfall: "Managing the Development of Large Software Systems" by Winston Royce, in *Proceedings of IEEE Westcon*, 1970.

---

3. Using experienced mentors to coach IID pilot projects is an adoption best practice.

In this article—sometimes (incorrectly) identified as the paragon of single-pass waterfall—Royce actually recommends an approach different than what devolved into the popular notion of waterfall, with its strict single-pass sequence of requirements analysis, design, and development phases. He recommends to "do it twice." To quote:

> *If the computer program in question is being developed for the first time, arrange matters so that the version finally delivered to the customer for operational deployment is actually the second version insofar as critical design / operations areas are concerned.*

He goes on to suggest that a 30-month project might have a 10-month throw-away "pilot model" and justifies its necessity when there are novel elements and unknown factors (hardly a unique case).

Winston's son Walker Royce described what his (deceased) father felt about the misinterpretation of the waterfall that was attributed to him, and the widespread promotion of a document-driven single-pass approach [LB03]:

> *He was always a proponent of iterative, incremental, evolutionary development. His paper described the waterfall as the simplest description, but that it would not work for all but the most straightforward projects. The rest of his paper describes [iterative practices] within the context of the 60s / 70s government contracting models (a serious set of constraints).*

It is ironic that the author of the seminal waterfall paper was a proponent of iterative and evolutionary development, that his paper was only describing a process for the most straightforward projects, and that Royce did not subscribe to the simplified single-pass waterfall, as it is often described.

Note also that the paper was not based on research into various successful lifecycle choices for large, novel projects. It did not cite any evidence, trends, or other projects. Indeed, the paper opens with this sentence:

I am going to describe my personal views about managing large software development.

Even by the time DOD-STD-2167 was adopted in the 1980s there was a growing body of experience and recommendations by thought leaders to avoid rather than embrace the (misunderstood) waterfall, but this knowledge did not find its way into the 2167 standard. Why? One part of the reason is that these standards were usually combined with and influenced by MIL-STD-1521B, another standard that required a series of document-driven reviews, such as a requirements review. I found another part of the answer in Boston.

In 1996 I visited the Boston area and had lunch with the principal author of 2167. He expressed regret for the creation of the rigid single-pass waterfall standard. He said he was influenced by common knowledge and practice of the time, plus other standards (e.g., 1521B). He was not familiar with the practice of timeboxed iterative development and evolutionary requirements at the time, and in hindsight, said he would have made a strong IID recommendation, rather than what was in 2167.

It is no small irony that 2167 was then used as input to other standards, both within the United States and internationally. For example, the British JSP-188, German V-Model (also the basis of the Austrian and Swiss standards), and the French GAM-T-17 were influenced by 2167, with an emphasis on single-pass waterfall phases, and early large, signed-off specifications before construction.

Although DoD reports started to publicly caution against 2167 and the waterfall in 1987, and 2167 was replaced with an IID-promoting standard in 1994, other governments and standards bodies that had drawn from 2167 did not likewise update their standards, apparently unaware of the changes afoot.

As I uncovered these stories, I was struck by the unintended influence a small number of individuals had on a world of standards and projects. And, how the misunderstanding and speculation that actually lay behind these standards led to a kind of accidental perception of validity for the waterfall, making of it a mirage as the "obvious tried-and-true" best practice for large, novel, complex projects, when in fact this was not the case.

Why Did Waterfall Promotion Continue?

H. L. Mencken quipped, "For every complex problem, there is a solution that is simple, neat, and wrong." In the history of science it is normal that lesser ideas first hold the dominant position, even in the absence of results. Western cosmology's Earth-centric universe dominated Europe for over a millennium until enough evidence and brave souls accumulated to depose the model. Software development is a young field, so it is no surprise the simple formula of "requirements, design, implementation" held sway during the first attempts to create a skillful development process. Other reasons for the early and ongoing adoption of the single-pass waterfall idea include:

❑ Few actually read Royce's original waterfall paper [Royce70]. Its iterative flavor was lost, and it devolved from the nuanced evolutionary description he gave, to a simple single-step lifecycle. This is seen in the many third-party diagrams supposedly depicting "Royce's waterfall," that do not correctly correspond to the original iterative picture Royce gave.

❏ Few realized that, as in the words of Royce's son, "[My father] was always a proponent of iterative, incremental, evolutionary development. His paper described the waterfall as the simplest description, but that it would not work for all but the most straightforward projects."

❏ The single-pass waterfall had simplicity of explanation and recall ("do the requirements, then design, and then implement"); IID is more complex to understand and describe. Note that even Royce's original two-iteration waterfall immediately devolved into a single step model by other adopters and writers.

❏ As discussed in the opening chapter, software projects have been inappropriately associated with a predictable manufacturing paradigm (such as mobile phones) that can be predictably specified and planned, rather than a new product development paradigm.

❏ Single-pass waterfall has been favored by some management because it gives the illusion of an orderly, predictable, accountable, and measurable process, with simple document-driven milestones (such as "requirements complete"). There is a special irony in choosing a simple-to-track process that yields higher levels of risk.

❏ Waterfall values and big up-front specification goals continued to be promoted by requirements engineering (and other groups) as appropriate or even ideal decades after large project experience, research, standards bodies, and the criticism of leading experts advised against it. Perhaps this was due to unfamiliarity with the evidence or with how disciplined iterative and evolutionary requirements could be made to work.

❑ The **Capability Maturity Model** (CMM) from the Software Engineering Institute (SEI) influenced some software process engineers in the late 1980s and 1990s towards gated, document-driven, waterfall practices [SEI03]. Although an IID-approach can be certified as CMM-mature, early CMM discussions had a tone of document and plan-driven, phase-oriented, and predictive planning. Many CMM certifiers and consultants had a background in waterfall values and practices and prescriptive process, without experience in iterative and adaptive methods. More recently, SEI CMM thought leaders have promoted IID and agile methods [Paulk01].

see www.sei.cmu.edu

CMM defines levels of process maturity. Level 1 is chaotic, heroic effort. Level 5 is a reflective, constantly improving system.

prescriptive process p. 32

❑ The Project Management Institute (PMI) educates and certifies managers, and influences management values via its Project Management Body of Knowledge (PMBOK). The PMI and PMBOK have valuable contributions, and acknowledge iterative and evolutionary methods. Yet, some early PMBOK content had a tone of "plan the work, work the plan," phases, and predictive planning more consistent with predictable manufacturing projects and the waterfall, than with evolutionary methods for high-change inventive projects.

see www.pmi.org

problems with "plan the work, work the plan" p. 62

WHAT'S NEXT?

Next are four related method chapters that explain the practices of Scrum, XP, UP, and Evo. After that, the book concludes with a practice tips chapter and a FAQ chapter.

RECOMMENDED READINGS

The many cited papers within this chapter are the place to go for more details, although in some cases I had to contact the original people to help fill in the story. Many older IEEE and ACM journal papers, and some older *IBM Systems Journals*, are now available on the Web.

SCRUM

*Ours is too great and too complex a nation for even such as I to
direct and lead every action.*
—Attila the Hun

OVERVIEW

❏ Classification of Scrum.

❏ Workproducts, roles, and practices.

❏ Common mistakes, adoption and process mixtures,
strengths and weaknesses.

Scrum appears simple, yet has practices that deeply influence the
work experience and that capture key adaptive and agile qualities.
Scrum's distinctive emphasis among the methods is its strong promotion of self-directed teams, daily team measurement, and avoidance of prescriptive process. Some key practices include:

prescriptive process
p. 32

❏ self-directed and self-organizing team

❏ no external addition of work to an iteration, once chosen

❏ daily stand-up meeting with special questions

❏ usually 30-calendar day iterations

❏ demo to external stakeholders at end of each iteration

❏ each iteration, client-driven adaptive planning

METHOD OVERVIEW

Classification

cycles and ceremony
p. 26

In terms of cycles and ceremony, Scrum classification is illustrated in Figure 7.1. Scrum is uniquely precise on the length of iterations: usually 30 calendar days, a more-or-less common length compared to other IID methods.[1]

Figure 7.1 Scrum on the cycles and ceremony scale

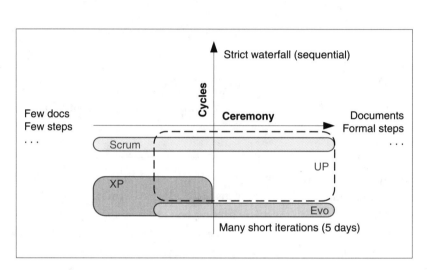

Scrum is flexible on the ceremony scale; discussion of what and how many workproducts is outside its scope, as is how much rigor is required. As a guiding principle, the Scrum founders would say, "as little ceremony as possible." Also on a Scrum project, the whole team—not a manager—will decide how much is appropriate.

High levels for a medical device are acceptable, as are low levels for a casual-information read-only Web site.

---

1. Shorter is legal, but 30-day iterations are encouraged.

In terms of scope on the Cockburn scale, Scrum covers the cells shown in Figure 7.2. Although one Scrum team should be seven or less, multiple teams may form a project. It has been used on both small projects and those involving hundreds of developers. Since Scrum practices include working in a common project room, it scales via a "scrum of scrums" where small teams work together and hold a daily stand-up meeting, and representatives from each those teams likewise meet daily. Scrum is complementary enough to other practices that it may be applied across all domains of software applications, from life-critical to more casual—and it has.

Cockburn scale p. 36

Figure 7.2 Scrum on the Cockburn scale

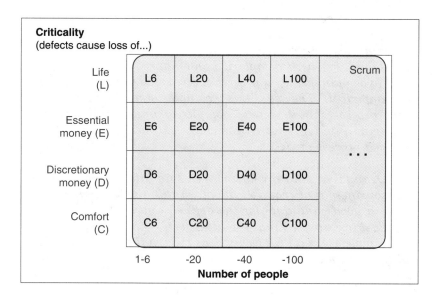

Introduction

Scrum [SB02] is an IID method that emphasizes a set of project management values and practices, rather than those in requirements, implementation, and so on. As such, it is easily combined with or complementary to other methods.

empirical and defined methods p. 32

A key Scrum theme is its emphasis on **empirical** rather than **defined** process. Ken Schwaber, one of the Scrum founders, tells a noteworthy story in this context [SB02]:

> *I wanted to understand why my customers' [waterfall and detailed-defined] processes didn't work for my [software] company, so I brought several methodologies to process theory experts at the DuPont Experimental Station in 1995. These experts, led by Babatunde Ogannaike, are the most highly respected theorists in industrial process control.[2]*

> *They inspected the systems development processes that I brought them. I have rarely provided a group with so much laughter. They were amazed and appalled that my industry [software], was trying to do its work using a completely inappropriate process control model. They said systems development had so much complexity and unpredictability that it had to be managed by a process control model they referred to as "empirical." They said this was nothing new, and all complex processes that weren't completely understood [or had changing inputs] required the empirical model [and not the defined process model].*

> *... [Ogannaike] said my business was an intellectually intensive business that required too much thinking and creativity to be a good candidate for the defined approach. ... He was particularly amused that the tasks were linked together with dependencies [in a PERT chart], as though they could predictably start and finish just like a well-defined industrial process.*

Shewhart and Deming p. 80

Ogannaike's words echo Deming and Shewhart's industrial process control emphasis on cyclic Plan-Do-Study-Act for complex, changing systems and environments.

---

2. Ogannaike has written one of the primary university textbooks on industrial process control; see [OR94].

LIFECYCLE

PRE-GAME		DEVELOPMENT	RELEASE
PLANNING	STAGING		
Purpose:	**Purpose**:	**Purpose**:	**Purpose**:
- establish the vision, set expectations, and secure funding	- identify more requirements and prioritize enough for first iteration	- implement a system ready for release in a series of 30-day iterations (Sprints)	- operational deployment
Activities:	**Activities**:	**Activities**:	**Activities**:
- write vision, budget, initial Product Backlog and estimate items	- planning	- Sprint planning meeting each iteration, defining the Sprint Backlog and estimates	- documentation
	- exploratory design and prototypes		- training
- exploratory design and prototypes		- daily Scrum meetings	- marketing & sales
		- Sprint Review	- . . .

The Scrum lifecycle is composed of four phases: Planning, Staging, Development, and Release. The following example illustrates a Scrum project and the lifecycle: Jeff Sutherland, one of the Scrum founders, serves at an organization that applies Scrum to build a hand-held medical system. Their evolutionary delivery release cycle is three months, composed of three Scrum Sprints (iterations). As this is a relatively mature and ongoing project, the vision-oriented Planning phase is bypassed (its goals having already been satisfied), and each release begins with Staging—addition and prioritization of items to work on in the first of the three Sprints. During the prior three-month release cycle, some subject matter experts were involved in enough requirements analysis to kick-start the release. In collaboration with the architect and some other team members, the new items are assigned tentative estimates, with no item larger than three person-days of effort. Staging is followed by three iterations of the Development phase. Quality assurance (QA) occurs in each, but the third Sprint has a special focus on QA, with less new development.

WORKPRODUCTS, ROLES, AND PRACTICES

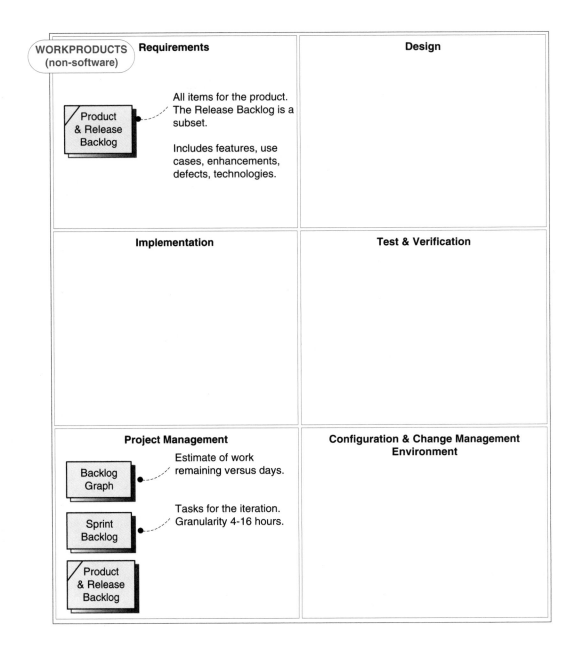

Roles

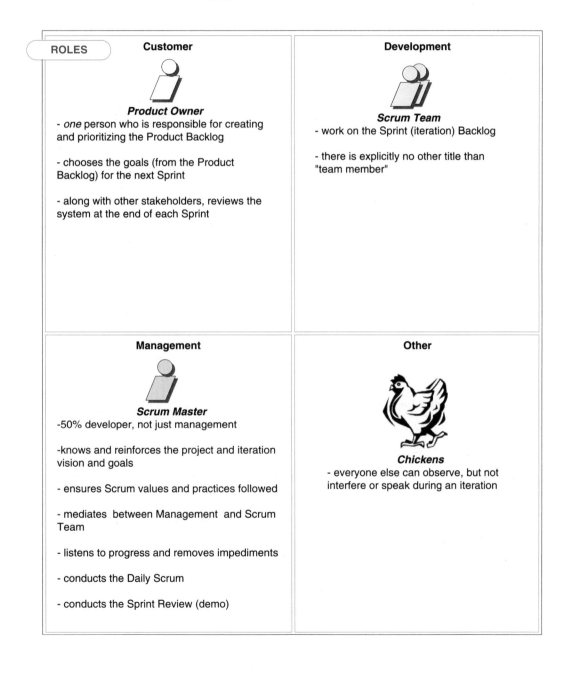

ROLES

Customer

Product Owner

- *one* person who is responsible for creating and prioritizing the Product Backlog

- chooses the goals (from the Product Backlog) for the next Sprint

- along with other stakeholders, reviews the system at the end of each Sprint

Development

Scrum Team

- work on the Sprint (iteration) Backlog

- there is explicitly no other title than "team member"

Management

Scrum Master

-50% developer, not just management

-knows and reinforces the project and iteration vision and goals

- ensures Scrum values and practices followed

- mediates between Management and Scrum Team

- listens to progress and removes impediments

- conducts the Daily Scrum

- conducts the Sprint Review (demo)

Other

Chickens

- everyone else can observe, but not interfere or speak during an iteration

Practices

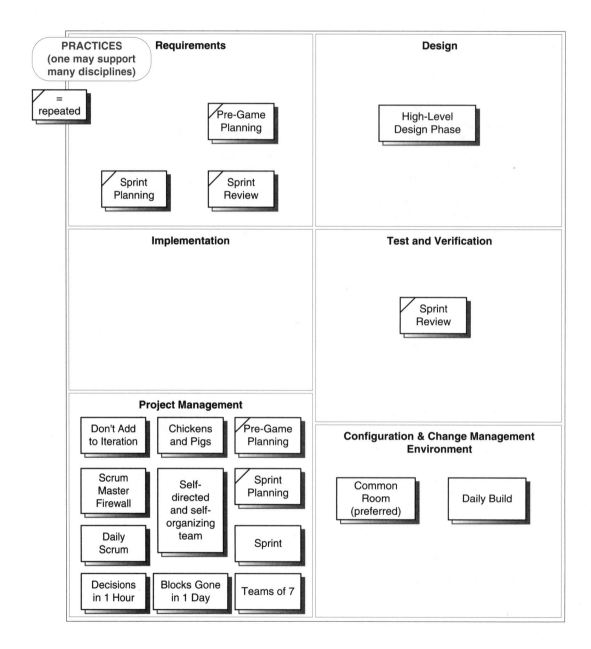

Core Practices

Practice	Description
Pre-game planning and staging	During Pre-game Planning, all stakeholders can contribute to creating a list of features, use cases, enhancements, defects, and so forth, recorded in the Product Backlog. One Product Owner is designated its owner, and requests are mediated through her. During this session, at least enough work for the first iteration is generated, and likely much more. Starting at these meeting and evolving over time, is identification of the Release Backlog, the subset of the Product Backlog that will make the next operational or product release.
Sprint planning	Before the start of each iteration—or Sprint—two consecutive meetings are held. In the first, stakeholders meet to refine and re-prioritize the Product Backlog and Release Backlog, and to choose goals for the next iteration, usually driven by highest business value and risk. In the second meeting, the Scrum Team and Product Owner meet to consider how to achieve the requests, and to create a Sprint Backlog of tasks (in the 4–16 hour range) to meet the goals. If estimated effort exceeds resources, another planning cycle occurs. As the iteration proceeds, the Sprint Backlog is updated, often daily during the early part of the iteration, as new tasks are discovered. As a history of many Sprint Backlogs grows, the team improves their creation of new ones.
Sprint	Work is usually organized in 30-calendar-day iterations; each is called a Sprint.

Practice	Description
Self-directed and self-organiz-ing teams	During an iteration, management and the Scrum Master do not guide the team in how to fulfill the iteration goals, solve its problems (other than to make decisions when requested, and remove reported blocks), nor plan the order of work. The team is empowered with the authority and resources to find their own way, and solve their own problems. This hands-off approach for 30 days, except to provide resources and remove blocks, is perhaps the most personally challenging aspect for management adopting Scrum.
Scrum meeting	Each workday at the same time and place, hold a meeting with the team members in a circle, at which the same special Scrum questions are answered by each team member. Details are described in the next section.
Don't add to itera-tion	During an iteration, management does not add work to the team or individuals. Uninterrupted focus is maintained. In the rare case something has to be added, something else should ideally be removed. But, before each new iteration, the Product Owner and Management have the right and responsibility to re-prioritize the Product Backlog, and indicate what to do in the next iteration, as long as the work request estimates don't exceed the resources.

Practice	Description
Scrum master firewall	The Scrum Master looks out to ensure the team is not interrupted by work requests from other external parties, and if they occur, removes them and deals with all political and external management issues. The Scrum Master also works to ensure Scrum is applied, removes reported blocks, provides resources, and makes decisions when requested. She also has to take initiative when she sees during the meeting that someone isn't completing work, if the team doesn't speak up.
Decision in one hour	Blocks reported at the Scrum Meeting that require decisions by the Scrum Master are ideally decided immediately, or within one hour. The value of "bad decisions are better than no decisions, and they can be reversed" is promoted.
Blocks gone in one day	Blocks reported at the Scrum Meeting are ideally removed before the next meeting.
Chickens and pigs	During the Scrum Meeting, only the Scrum Team can talk (the pigs). Anyone else can attend, but should remain silent (the chickens), even the CEO. An exception is management (e.g., CEO) feedback on survival points or explanation of the business relevance of the team's work. The Scrum needs to be a vehicle for communicating the product vision and organization goals. From this story: A pig and chicken discussed the name of their new restaurant. The chicken suggested *Ham n' Eggs*. "No thanks," said the pig, "I'd be committed, but you'd only be involved!"

Practice	Description
Teams of seven	Scrum can scale to large projects, but recommends one team have a maximum of seven members. Larger projects are multi-team.
Common room (preferred)	Ideally, the team work together in a common project room, rather than separate offices or cubes. Separate, private space is still available for other activities. However, teams composed of geographically spread members, participating by speakerphone in the Daily Scrum, have reported success.
Daily build	At least one daily integration and regression test across all checked-in code for the project. The XP practice of Continuous Integration is even better.
Sprint review	At the end of each iteration, there is a review meeting (maximum of four hours) hosted by the Scrum Master. The team, Product Owner, and other stakeholders attend. There is a demo of the product. Goals include informing stakeholders of the system functions, design, strengths, weaknesses, effort of the team, and future trouble spots. Feedback and brainstorming on future directions is encouraged, but no commitments are made during the meeting. Later at the next Sprint Planning meeting, stakeholders and the team make commitments. "Power Point" presentations are forbidden. Preparation emphasis is on showing the product.

The Scrum Meeting: Details

The Scrum Meeting—or scrum—is the heartbeat of Scrum and the project. Each workday at the same time and place, hold a meeting with the team members *standing* in a circle, at which time the same special questions are answered by each member:

1. What have you done since the last Scrum?

2. What will you do between now and the next Scrum?

3. What is getting in the way (blocks) of meeting the iteration goals?

I've added two more questions—since shortly after starting to apply Scrum in 1998—that have been useful:[3]

4. Any tasks to add to the Sprint Backlog? (missed tasks, not new requirements)

5. Have you learned or decided anything new, of relevance to some of the team members? (technical, requirements, ...)

The last question provides an efficient forum for a continuously improving and learning group—vital to agile development—and is often an interesting way to end the reports, increasing their perceived value.

Other points:

❏ The meeting is ideally held in a stand-up circle to encourage brevity.

❏ On average, 15 or 20 minutes for 7–10 people. Longer meetings are common near the start of an iteration.

❏ Non-team members (chickens) are outside the circle.

❏ It is held next to a whiteboard at which all the tasks and blocks are written when reported.

---

3. These additional questions have been reviewed and approved by Schwaber and Sutherland, the Scrum founders.

❑ The Scrum Master erases blocks only once they've been removed.

❑ There is a speaker-phone for offsite member participation—which is required.

❑ The Scrum Master ensures the rules are followed and prepares the location for an efficient meeting.

❑ Must start on time. Late fines collected by the Scrum Master and donated to charity are a popular rule.

❑ Chickens and Pigs rule enforced: Non-team members don't talk or ask questions. An exception is management feedback on survival points or explanation of the business relevance of the team's work. The Scrum needs to be a vehicle for communicating the product vision and organization goals.

❑ No other discussion is allowed beyond the three (or five) questions. The Scrum Master has authority to refocus the discussion.

❑ If other issues need discussion, secondary meetings immediately after the Scrum Meeting occur, usually with subsets of the team. For example, during the Scrum meeting, I may say to Jill, during her answer report, "We need to talk about that. Let's meet after the Scrum."

The Value of the Scrum Meeting

Value: Since there is a self-directing and organizing team, with no manager directing workers or solving problems (unless asked) during an iteration, the Scrum Meeting creates the daily mechanism to quickly inform the team about the state of the project and people. Then, people can take action. External people can observe the daily Scrums to get an accurate, timely, and information-rich measure of progress and issues. It supports openness and allows resolution of dependencies and conflicts in real time to maximize throughput.

Value: When a person reports on what they are doing for the next day, they are expressing a kind of social promise to the team. This increases responsibility and follow-through.

Value: Scrum is based on the insight that software development is creative and unpredictable new product development, and therefore empirical rather than defined methods are needed. The Scrum Meeting provides the frequent measuring and adaptive response mechanism that empirical methods require.

Value: Project risks include not accounting for all tasks, poor estimates, and not quickly resolving blocks. The Scrum Meeting provides a daily forum to update tasks, and surface and remove impediments.

Value: It is important to have people (and teams) that are continuously improving and learning. The Scrum Meeting supports this, especially with the addition of Question 5. Unspoken (or *tacit*) information and knowledge becomes spoken and shared.

Value: Shared language, values, and practices help a development team. This is created and reinforced in the daily Scrum.

Workproducts

In addition to the workproducts illustrated on p. 114, Scrum allows any other workproducts of value to the project. For example, it can be combined with some UP practices, and one can create a Vision or Risk List, using UP terminology.

Product Backlog—A sample, partial Product Backlog is shown in Figure 7.3. Note that all conceivable items go in the backlog and are prioritized by the Product Owner. The estimates (in person-hours of effort) start as rough guidelines, refined once the team commits to an item.

Figure 7.3 sample Product
Backlog

	A	B	C	D	E	F
1	**Product Backlog**					
2						
3	**Requirement**	**Num**	**Category**	**Status**	**Pri**	**Estimate**
4	log credit payments to AR	17	feature	underway	5	2
5	process sale-simple cash scenario	232	use case	underway	5	60
6	slow credit payment approval	12	issue	not started	4	10
7	sales commission calculation	43	defect	complete	4	2
8	lay-away plan payments	321	enhance	not started	3	20
9	PDA sale capture	53	technology	not started	1	100
10	process sale-credit pmt scenario	235	use case	underway	5	30

Sprint Backlog—A sample Sprint Backlog is shown in Figure 7.4. Note the daily estimate of work remaining for each task; these columns also show the date (e.g., 6 of Jan) and total hours remaining on each day (e.g., Jan 6, 362 hours). It is updated daily by the responsible members or by a daily tracker who visits each member. New estimates are allowed to increase above the original estimate. The simplest (and thus preferred) tool is a spreadsheet; Sutherland uses a customized version of the open-source GNU GNATS tracking tool, with a Web interface.

Figure 7.4 sample Sprint
Backlog

	A	B	C	D	E	F	G	H	I
1	**Sprint Backlog**								
2	**Task Description**	**Origi nator**	**Respon sible**	**Status**	**Hours of work remaining**				
3					**6**	**7**	**8**	**9**	**10**
4					362	322	317	317	306
5	Meet to discuss the goals and	JM	JM/SR	Completed	20	10	0	0	0
6	Move Calculations out of	TL	AW	Not Started	8	8	8	8	8
7	Get GEK Data		TN	Completed	12	0	0	0	0
8	Analyse GEK Data - Title		GP	In Progress	24	20	30	25	20
9	Analyse GEK Data - Parcel		TK	Completed	12	12	12	12	12
10	Define & build Database		BR/DS	In Progress	80	80	75	60	52

Sprint Backlog Graph—A Sprint Backlog Graph is shown in Figure 7.5. It is a visual summary of estimated task hours remaining in the Sprint Backlog. In Scrum, this is considered the most critical project data to track. Recommended: Post an updated version of this each day on the wall by the Scrum meeting.

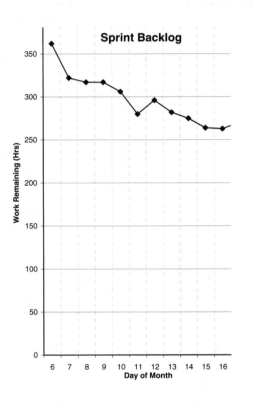

Figure 7.5 sample Backlog Graph

Other Practices and Values

❑ **Workers daily update the Sprint Backlog**—Once tasks are underway, individuals are responsible for daily updates estimating the time remaining for their tasks.

❑ **No PERT charts allowed**—A PERT chart is built on the assumption that the tasks of a project can be identified, ordered, and reliably estimated, that there is minimal change and noise in the system, and in general that a defined process can be applied. This is inconsistent with the recognition in iterative and agile methods that software is semi-chaotic new product development with high degrees of change and noise, and defined processes can't apply.

❑ **Scrum Master reinforces vision**—She needs to daily share and clarify the overall project vision, and goals of the Sprint, perhaps at the start of the Scrum meeting.

❑ **Replace ineffective Scrum Master**—The manager/Scrum Master is the servant of the developers, not vice versa. If Scrum Master is not removing blocks promptly, acting as a firewall, and providing resources, the Scrum founders encourage replacing the Scrum Master.

VALUES

The Scrum values are described in [SB02]:

❑ **Commitment**—The Scrum Team commits to a defined goal for an iteration, and is given the authority and autonomy to decide themselves how best to meet it. Management and the Scrum Master commits to not introduce new work during an iteration, avoid directing the team, and work to provide the resources and quickly remove blocks that the team reports in their daily Scrum meeting. The Product Owner commits to define and prioritize the Product Backlog, guide choice of the next iteration's goals, and review and provide feedback on the result of each iteration.

❑ **Focus**—The Scrum Team has to be able to focus on the stated goals of the iteration, without distraction. Thus, management and the Scrum Master focus on providing the team with resources, removing blocks, and avoiding interrupting the team with additional work requests.

❑ **Openness**—The openly accessible Product Backlog makes visible the work and priorities. The Daily Scrums make visible the overall and individual status and commitments. Work trend and velocity are made visible with the Backlog Graph.

❑ **Respect**—Or, team responsibility rather than scapegoating. The individual members on a team are respected for their different strengths and weaknesses, and not singled out for iteration failures. The whole team rather than a manager, through self-organization and direction, adopts the attitude of solving "individual" problems through group exploration of solutions, and is given the authority and resources to react to challenges, such as hiring a specialist consultant to compensate for missing expertise.

❑ **Courage**—Management has the courage to plan and guide adaptively and to trust individuals and the team by avoiding telling them how to get the iteration done. The team has the courage to take responsibility for self-direction and self-management.

COMMON MISTAKES AND MISUNDERSTANDINGS

or, How to Fail with Scrum

Error: Not a self-directed team; managers or Scrum Master direct or organize the team—The urge may be strong during an iteration to tell or suggest to team members how to work, or solve a problem. Many managers are used to an emphasis on directing and planning, rather than their role in Scrum: To quickly remove blocks, provide resources, act as a firewall to the rest of the organization, and otherwise stay out of the way. This is especially true for the Scrum Master during the Scrum Meeting, when there is a natural tendency for the team to look to a leader for direction and solutions.

Error: No daily update of the Sprint Backlog by members or daily tracker—Self-explanatory.

Error: New work added to iteration or individual—In a sea of constant change, some stability is required. Not changing the requirements for an iteration, once begun, is Scrum's point of control.

Error: Product Owner isn't involved or doesn't decide—Scrum is customer driven; the Product Owner needs to decide what the Product Backlog priorities are and choose the requirements for the next iteration.

Error: No Sprint Review—Feedback and adaptation drive Scrum; the demo and review are needed to inform the customers, so they can steer the next iteration.

Error: Many masters—Scrum requires one voice on the Product Backlog requirements, priorities, and work for the next iteration: the Product Owner.

Error: Documentation is bad—Scrum isn't anti-documentation; discussion of project workproducts is simply outside the scope of its definition. As with all agile methods, non-code workproducts are expected to add real value, rather than be created for the sake of following a process formula.

Error: Design or diagramming is bad—Scrum is pragmatic rather than doctrinaire on the team's approach to design: If they find value in some pre-programming design or diagramming work during an iteration, it's done.

Error: Full team (including customers and management) not briefed in Scrum and its values—Self-explanatory.

Error: Scrum Meeting too long or unfocused—Keep it below 20 minutes, and focused on the Scrum questions.

Error: Iteration doesn't end in an integrated and tested partial product—An iteration doesn't just finish on the end date. The goal is that all the software has been integrated, tested, and baselined.

Error: Each iteration ends in a production release—Although a Scrum iteration *may* end in a production release, it is not a requirement. It may require many iterations before readiness.

Error: Predictive planning; PERT chart planning—As with all IID methods, it is a misunderstanding to create a plan laying out exactly how many iterations there will be for a long project and what will occur in each, or to create a PERT chart identifying many tasks, their order and estimated duration.

You Know You Didn't Understand Scrum When...

Some of the key misunderstandings expressed as a checklist:

- ❏ You think a manager or Scrum Master should tell the team what to do, or how to solve its problems.

- ❏ Customers are not involved in each iteration, not prioritizing requirements, not attending each demo, and are not choosing the highest business value set for the next iteration.

- ❏ New requirements or extra-project tasks are added to team members during an iteration.

- ❏ You create a plan laying out how many iterations there will be for the project, and what will occur in each, and think you can enforce it.

- ❏ You create a PERT chart or a plan of dependent, ordered tasks, with estimated durations.

SAMPLE PROJECTS

The following projects had significant Scrum influence:

Large—IDX Web-enabled benefits suite

- One year, 330 people across multiple related projects, an E300 project on the Cockburn scale, [SB02]
- A suite of 15 related applications were developed within one year of adopting Scrum, after three years of struggle to deliver one application.
- Prime developer: IDX.

Medium—Caremark

- Four months, 20 people, an E20 project, [SB02]
- After two years of struggle, 160 staff at its height, and no delivery, Scrum was introduced with a reduced team size of 20 developers (10 new hires). In four months, a successful production release was created.
- Prime developer: Caremark and consultants.

Small—Individual Personal NewsPage

- One month, eight people, a C20 project [SB02]
- After nine months without delivery, Scrum was adopted, and a usable production release emerged after one 30-day iteration. After five months of releases, most of the original goals were achieved.
- Prime developer: Individual Inc.

PROCESS MIXTURES

Scrum + Evo

Some Evo practices are compatible with Scrum. Scrum does not discuss specific specification methods, and thus Evo's Planguage is applicable. Evo's measurement emphasis is compatible; indeed, Sutherland, one of the Scrum creators, takes a strong interest in measurement when applying Scrum.

Evo p. 211
Planguage p. 231

Scrum's 30-day iteration length is not consistent with Evo—too long.

Scrum + UP

The Scrum practices are either equal to or specializations of UP practices, or are consistent additions. If some workproducts are required on a Scrum project, using the UP versions is reasonable. The Product Backlog is an acceptable portion of the UP Project Plan, and the Sprint Backlog is an acceptable version of the UP Iteration Plan.

UP p. 173

One area of different emphasis is the presence in the UP of optional but predefined activities; the UP describes a set of possible activities related to requirements analysis, testing, and so forth. And, the UP indicates some dependent ordering of these optional activities; for example, that a project vision is created before a detailed requirement is described. Scrum's rejection of defined process and predictable steps is inconsistent with this structure, if the UP activities are viewed as a required formula. But, if the activities are treated as optional advice, performable in any order, and without attempt to schedule their order and duration on a project, it is within Scrum.

See "UP as a Heavy, Defined Process versus an Agile UP Approach" on p. 192.

Scrum + XP

XP p. 137

Most Scrum practices are compatible with XP or refinements, such as the Scrum Meeting. Indeed, Kent Beck borrowed the XP stand-up meeting idea from Scrum.

The Scrum practice of a demo to external stakeholders at the end of each iteration enhances XP's feedback and communication goals. The Scrum Backlog and progress tracking approaches are minor variations of XP practices, and so simple that they are well within the XP spirit of "do the simplest thing that could possibly work."

Scrum's 30-day timeboxed iteration length is not completely consistent with XP, which prefers shorter—even one-week—iterations.

see www.xbreed.net

Mike Beedle, one of the original Scrum contributors, has developed **XBreed**—a combination of Scrum and XP practices applied (at least originally) to the creation of reusable components in the context of a concurrent multi-project development.

ADOPTION STRATEGIES

As always, coaching by an experienced method expert on the first project is recommended.

1. In contrast to the recommended gentle, pilot-project adoption strategy of UP (for example), the Scrum creators encourage organizations to first adopt it on their single most difficult and critical project. This brave advice underscores the Scrum creators' view that it is strong medicine with a high success rate. They feel the crucible of a critical project best spurs real change to the new values and practices of Scrum.

2. After the first project is underway, but not before the second iteration (so that all the practices have been practiced), extra-project management and potential customers may be invited to observe Scrum Meetings, Sprint Planning, and Sprint Reviews.

3. Second-generation Scrum projects can start before the completion of the first, although the first should be given some time to "ripen," such as three completed iterations. The Product Owner, Scrum Master, and some team members of the new projects will benefit from attending some of the first project's meetings (daily, planning, review) shortly before embarking on their new project. Coaching is useful—during the first iteration—for the new Product Owner and Scrum Master by those on the first project.

4. Jeff Sutherland, one of the Scrum creators and a VP Engineering or CTO at several organizations, recommends ultimately expanding Scrum practices to the highest levels of the development organization. Every level is team based. Projects hold daily Scrums, including a daily Scrum of Scrums among Scrum Masters of subsystem teams. Project representatives in a product line family meet weekly for a Scrum, and upper management holds monthly Scrums.

FACT VERSUS FANTASY

First, a standard disclaimer:

Process is only a second-order effect. The unique people, their feelings and qualities, are more influential.

Scrum practitioners do not report significant variation from the ideals of Scrum compared to its concrete use, presumably due to the relatively small and unambiguous set of practices. The most commonly reported reality checks are the encroachment of non-iteration work on to team members, and attempts by management to direct or organize the team, or solve—unasked—its problems.

Scrum iterations have also failed when the Scrum Master does not regularly reinforce the project vision and Sprint goals, and the team drifts.

STRENGTHS VERSUS "OTHER"

Strengths

❑ Simple practices and management workproducts.

❑ Individual and team problem solving and self-management.

❑ Evolutionary and incremental requirements and development, and adaptive behavior.

❑ Customer participation and steering.

❑ Focus.

❑ Openness and visibility.

❑ Easily combined with other methods.

❑ Team communication, learning, and value-building.

❑ Team building via the daily Scrum, even if not in common project room.

Other[4]

❑ Minimal guidance within disciplines other than project management (e.g., programming). That is, Scrum's emphasis is the lifecycle and project management aspects of develop-

---

4. Could be viewed as a weakness, strength, or deliberate desirable exclusion, depending on point of view.

ment, rather than—for example—software or requirements engineering techniques.

- For example, the Product Owner has the domain knowledge and requirements vision. But, they will describe a function in only brief terms in the Product Backlog. How to transfer and expand this domain knowledge or requirement? Scrum does not address such issues related to workproducts, requirements analysis, and so forth.

❑ Many projects will need some documents. Scrum does not define what these may be, and thus each project may create ones with similar intent, but varying names and content. In other words, no common, standard workproducts that are shareable with common names across projects. This impedes reuse of workproducts and impedes a common workproduct vocabulary in larger organizations.

HISTORY

The roots of Scrum are found in a well-known article summarizing common best practices in 10 innovative Japanese companies, "The New New Product Development Game," *Harvard Business Review*, Jan 1986, by Takeuchi and Nonaka. It introduced the terms *Sashimi* (slices) for IID, and *Scrum* for the adaptive and self-directed team practices. The name was taken from the game of rugby, for the adaptive team behavior moving a ball up the field.

Jeff Sutherland is one of the Scrum creators and was VP at Easel Corporation in 1994 when he introduced some of its practices; he had read the article. He was also influenced by a report on a hyper-productive project at Borland Corporation that effectively used structured daily meetings [Coplien94]. In 1995 Ken Schwaber worked with Sutherland at Easel on the formalization of Scrum. Their results were described in a workshop paper [Schwaber95]. In 1996 Sutherland joined Individual Inc., and asked Ken Schwaber to assist in the adoption of Scrum ideas. Schwaber refined and extended Scrum, in collaboration with Sutherland, into the versions ultimately described in [BDSSS98] and [SB02].

What's Next?

The next chapter covers XP, another popular agile method. That's followed by chapters on UP and Evo. Finally, there are chapters on more practice tips and a FAQ.

Recommended Readings

The bible of Scrum is *Agile Software Development with Scrum*, primarily by Schwaber, with contributions from Beedle and Sutherland.

Several books and articles influenced the Scrum creators, and are worth mention as recommended readings because of their widespread or seminal influence:

❑ "The New New Product Development Game," *Harvard Business Review*, Jan 1986, by Takeuchi and Nonaka. Discusses common best practices of innovative Japanese companies.

❑ *Wicked Problems, Righteous Solutions*, by DeGrace. Discusses why the waterfall is unsuitable for most software projects, and explores various iterative feedback-based practices for development.

❑ *Hidden Order: How Adaptation Builds Complexity*, 1995, and *Emergence: From Chaos to Order*, 1998, by Holland. Both discuss the dynamics and value of adaptive, self-organizing groups to solve problems.

EXTREME PROGRAMMING

It's easy to have a complicated idea.
It's very very hard to have a simple idea.
—Carver Mead

OVERVIEW

❑ Classification of XP.

❑ Workproducts, roles, and practices.

❑ Common mistakes, adoption and process mixtures, strengths and weaknesses.

Extreme Programming (**XP**) is a well-known agile method; it emphasizes collaboration, quick and early software creation, and skillful development practices. It is founded on four values: communication, simplicity, feedback, and courage. In addition to IID, it recommends 12 core practices:

1. Planning Game	*7. pair programming*
2. small, frequent releases	*8. team code ownership*
3. system metaphors	*9. continuous integration*
4. simple design	*10. sustainable pace*
5. testing	*11. whole team together*
6. frequent refactoring	*12. coding standards*

METHOD OVERVIEW

Classification

cycles and ceremony p. 26

In terms of cycles and ceremony, XP classification is illustrated in Figure 8.1. For average projects, the recommended length of a timeboxed iteration is between one and three weeks—somewhat shorter than for UP or Scrum.

Figure 8.1 XP on the cycle and ceremony scale.

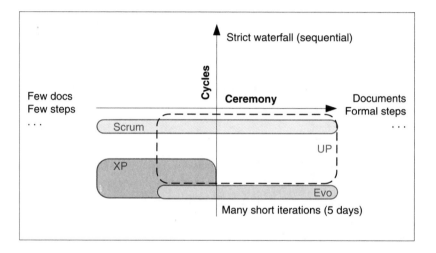

XP is low on the ceremony scale; it has only a small set of a pre-defined, informal workproducts, such as paper index cards for summarizing feature requests, called **story cards**.

A refreshing quality of the original XP description was the statement of known applicability: It had been proven on projects involving roughly 10 developers or fewer, and not proven for safety-critical systems. Nevertheless, it has been more recently applied with larger teams. Consequently, in terms of the Cockburn scale, XP perhaps covers the cells shown in Figure 8.2.

Cockburn scale p. 36

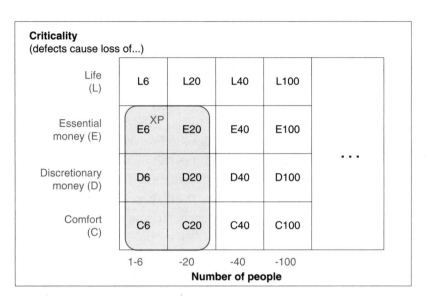

Figure 8.2 XP on the Cockburn scale

Introduction

XP[1] [Beck00], created by Kent Beck, is an IID method that stresses customer satisfaction through rapid creation of high-value software, skillful and sustainable software development techniques, and flexible response to change. It is aimed at relatively small team projects, usually with delivery dates under one year. Iterations are short—usually one to three weeks.

As the word *programming* suggests, it provides explicit methods for programmers, so they can more confidently respond to changing requirements, even late in the project, and still produce quality code. These include test-driven development, refactoring, pair programming, and continuous integration, among others. In contrast to most methods, some XP practices truly are adopted by

---

1. Some writers capitalize the full name as "eXtreme Programming" but Beck does not.

developers—they sense its practical programmer-relevant techniques.

XP is very communication- and team-oriented; customers, developers, and managers form a team working in a common project room to quickly deliver software with high business value.

XP is distinctive in not *requiring* detailed workproducts except for program code and tests. However, it doesn't disallow other detailed workproducts. Although all evolutionary methods avoid detailed up-front specifications and plans that span the entire release cycle, most of these methods encourage writing down details for at least the next iteration. In contrast, XP emphasizes *oral communication* for requirements and design. For example, a feature is summarized "Find lowest fare" on a handwritten paper index **story card**. Then, when work starts on the feature, the programmers learn details by talking with the customers working full-time in the project room. This may sound disorganized or naive, but Beck is experienced and well aware of the implications of sloppy requirements. Instead, XP is posing this interesting question:

> *Is there a sane and disciplined way to quickly succeed—on typical small projects—by focusing on code and tests, while avoiding most other documentation overhead?*

XP's premise isn't hacker code-and-fix programming; rather, its premise is that there is a new, structured, and sustainable way to succeed with a focus on rapid code production and oral communication, while avoiding most other overhead. To reiterate, XP is not hacking. Quite the contrary, an XP project involves constant practice of highly disciplined—yet agile—software development practices and values.

XP consultant Don Wells explains the influence of the XP values [Wells01]:

XP improves a software project in four essential ways; communication, simplicity, feedback, and courage. XP programmers communicate with their customers and fellow programmers. They keep their design simple and clean. They get feedback by testing their software starting on day one. They deliver the system to the customers as early as possible and implement changes as suggested. With this foundation XP programmers are able to courageously respond to changing requirements and technology.

There is a considerable set of practices in XP: 12 core practices and many ancillary ones. Speaking of these, Wells writes [Wells01]:

It is a lot like a jig saw puzzle. There are many small pieces. Individually the pieces make no sense, but when combined together a complete picture can be seen.

Many of these practices work *in synergy*, and thus *it is risky to customize XP by removing some elements.* For example, XP aims to produce software quickly by—in part—avoiding detailed requirements documentation. But, this is compensated by the practice of onsite customers sitting in the project room to fill in the details.

The word *extreme* in XP comes from Beck's conviction that it is hard to have too much of a good thing in software development. That is, take known good practices and "turn the dial up to 10," or to extreme levels. For example:

❑ Testing is good, so write unit tests for (almost) all code, and acceptance tests for all features.

❑ Code reviews are good—even better close to creation date—so do code reviews in real time and all the time via pair programming.

❑ Frequent integration of code across all team members is good, so do it 24/7 with an automated, continuous integration process on a dedicated build machine.

❑ Short iterations and early feedback are good, so make iterations one or two weeks long, if possible.

❑ More customer involvement is good, so bring customers into the project full-time, sitting in the common project room.

❑ Communication is good, so have everyone sit together, pair program, include onsite customers, and involve the customer frequently in planning, steering, and evaluation.

LIFECYCLE

EXPLORATION	PLANNING	ITERATIONS TO FIRST RELEASE	PRODUCTIONIZING	MAINTENANCE
Purpose: - Enough well-estimated story cards for first release. - Feasibility ensured.	**Purpose:** - Agree on date and stories for first release.	**Purpose:** - Implement a tested system ready for release.	**Purpose:** - Operational deployment	**Purpose:** - Enhance, fix. - Build major releases
Activities: - prototypes - exploratory proof of technology programming - story card writing and estimating	**Activities:** - Release Planning Game - story card writing and estimating	**Activities:** - testing and programming - Iteration Planning Game - task writing and estimating	**Activities:** - documentation - training - marketing - . . .	**Activities:** - May include these phases again, for incremental releases.

Some comments on the XP lifecycle phases defined by Beck:

1. Like many projects, XP can start with exploration. Some story cards (features) may be written, with rough estimates.

2. In the Release Planning Game, the customers and developers complete the story cards and rough estimates, and then decide what to do for the next release.

3. For the next iteration, in the Iteration Planning Game, customers pick stories to implement. They choose stories—and

thus steer the project—based on current status, and their latest priorities for the release. Developers then break the stories into many short, estimated tasks. Finally, a review of the total estimated task-level effort may lead to readjustment of the chosen stories, as XP does not allow overworking the developers with more than they can do based on "family-friendly" work days, such as an eight-hour day. Overtime is seriously discouraged in XP; it is viewed as a sign of a dysfunctional project, increasingly unhappy people, and dropping productivity and quality.

4. Developers implement the stories within the agreed time-boxed period, continually collaborating with customers (in the common project room) on tests and requirement details.

5. If not finished for release, return to step 3 for the next iteration.

WORKPRODUCTS, ROLES, AND PRACTICES

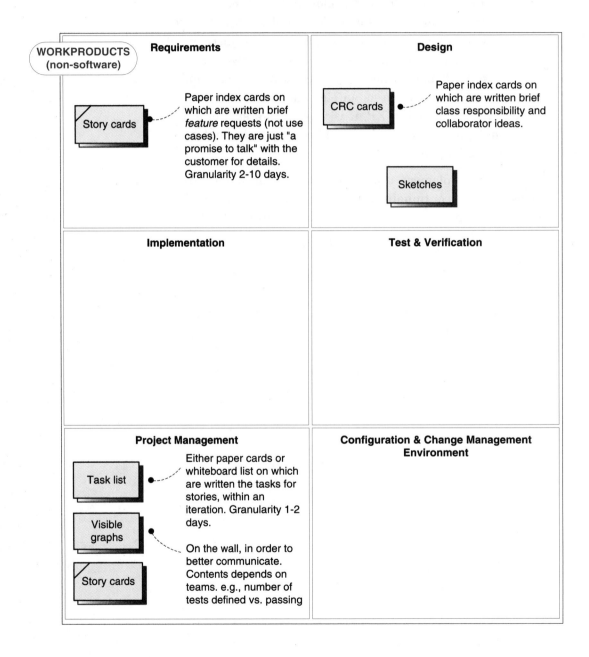

Roles

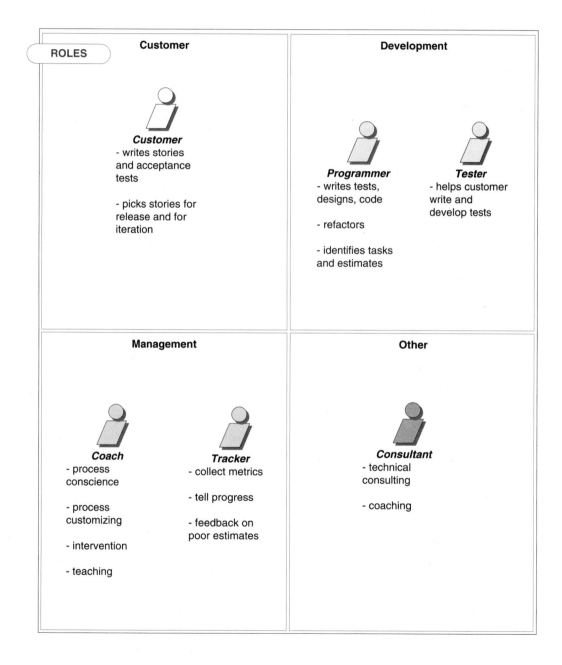

ROLES

Customer

Customer
- writes stories and acceptance tests

- picks stories for release and for iteration

Development

Programmer
- writes tests, designs, code

- refactors

- identifies tasks and estimates

Tester
- helps customer write and develop tests

Management

Coach
- process conscience

- process customizing

- intervention

- teaching

Tracker
- collect metrics

- tell progress

- feedback on poor estimates

Other

Consultant
- technical consulting

- coaching

Practices

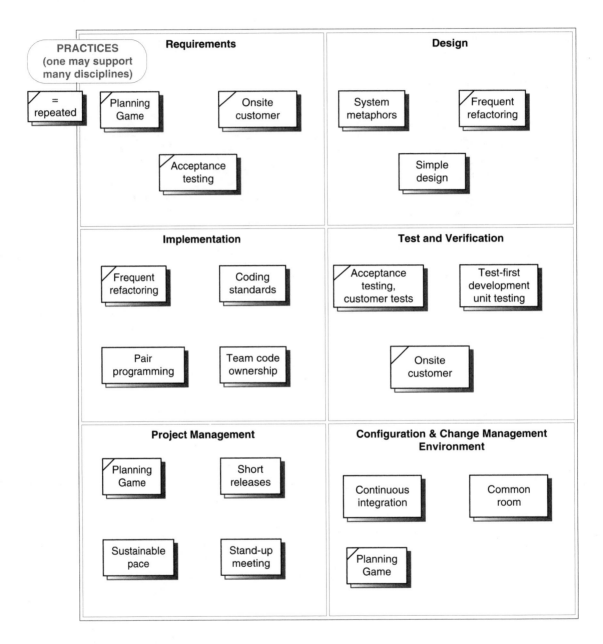

Core Practices

Practice	Description
Whole team, or Onsite customers	The whole team—programmers and customers—work together in a common project room. One or more customers sit more-or-less full time with the team; they are expected to be subject matter experts and empowered to make decisions regarding requirements and their priority. The customer contribution includes detailed explanation—to the programmers—of the features briefly summarized on story cards, Planning Game participation, clarification, and writing acceptance tests in collaboration with a programmer. The purpose is in response to the consistent project failure research indicating that more customer involvement is paramount to successful projects. The first release of XP spoke of only one onsite customer; this has been recently revised to emphasize a group of customers.
Small, frequent releases	Evolutionary delivery. Not applicable to all projects. Not to be confused with organizing one release cycle into many short iterations.
Testing: Acceptance testing & Customer tests	Testing practices in XP are very important. All features must have **automated acceptance (functional) tests**. All tests (acceptance and unit) must run with a binary pass/fail result, so that no human inspection of individual test results is required. The acceptance tests are written with collaboration of the customer—they define a testable statement of what acceptance means. This is called **Customer Tests** in XP.

Practice	Description
Testing: Test-driven development and unit testing	Unit tests are written for most code, and the practice of **test-driven development** (and **test-first development**) is followed. This includes the practice that the unit test is written by the programmer *before* the code to be tested. It is a cycle of test $\rightarrow$ code, rather than code $\rightarrow$ test. Usually, the open-source XUnit testing framework family (such as JUnit) is applied (see www.junit.org). All acceptance and unit tests are automatically run repeatedly in a 24/7 continuous integration build and test cycle. See p. 292 for a detailed example.
Release planning game	The **Release Planning Game** goal is to define the scope of the next operational release, with maximum value (to the customer) software. Typically a half-day one-day session, customer(s) write **story cards** to describe features, and developers estimate them. There may also exist story cards from prior exploration phase work. The customer then chooses what's in the next release by either 1) setting a date and adding cards until the estimate total matches the time available, or 2) choosing the cards and calculating the release date based on their estimates.
Iteration planning game	The **Iteration Planning Game** goal is to choose the stories to implement, and plan and allocate tasks for the iteration. It happens shortly before each new iteration (1–3 weeks in length). Customer(s) choose the story cards for the iteration. For each, programmers create a **task list** (on cards or whiteboard) that fulfill the stories. This is followed by a volunteering step in which the programmers choose a set of tasks. They then estimate their task lengths. If tasks are not estimated in the half-day to two-day range, they are refactored.

Practice	Description
Simple design	Avoid speculative design for possible future changes. Avoid creating generalized components that are not immediately required. The design should avoid duplicate code, have a relatively minimal set of classes and methods, and be easily comprehensible.
Pair programming	All production code is created by two programmers at one computer; they rotate using the input devices periodically. Pairs may change frequently, for different tasks. The observer is doing a real-time code review, and perhaps thinking more broadly than the typist, considering tests and so forth. Certainly, team productivity is not simply a function of the number of hands typing—it is more nuanced. The XP claim is that the combination of cross learning, the peer pressure of more disciplined practice observance and more hours actually programming than procrastinating, defect reduction due to real-time code review, and the stamina and insight to carry on when one programmer is stuck, all add up to an overall team improvement.
Frequent refactoring	Refactoring in the XP context is the continual effort to simplify the fine-grained code and larger design elements, while still ensuring all tests pass. That is, cleaning the code and design, without changing functionality. There is supposed to be "lots" of refactoring in XP. This practice is also known as **continuous design improvement**. The goal is minimal, simple, comprehensible code. It is achieved by small change steps, verifying tests after each, and ideally the use of refactoring tools, now available in some IDEs.

Practice	Description
Team code ownership	Any pair of programmers can improve any code, and the XP value system is that the entire team is collectively responsible for all the code. The value of "it's her code, and her problem" is not endorsed; rather, if a problem or chance to improve is spotted, it's the spotter's responsibility. A related goal is faster development by removing the bottleneck associated with change requests in an individual code ownership model. The obvious danger of modifying code one did not originally write is ameliorated in XP by some of the other practices: The guaranteed-present unit and acceptance tests running within an automated continuous integration build process inform you if you broke the code, your pairing partner brings another set of eyes to the change, and common adherence to coding standards ensures all the code looks the same.
Continuous integration	All checked-in code is continuously re-integrated and tested on a separate build machine, in an automated 24/7 process loop of compiling, running all unit tests and all or most acceptance tests. There are several open-source tools for this, built on the ubiquitous Ant technology, including CruiseControl and Anthill.
Sustainable pace	Frequent overtime is rightly considered a symptom of deeper problems, and doesn't lead to happy, creative developers, healthy families, or quality, maintainable code. XP doesn't support it—rather, it promotes "no overtime."
Coding standards	With collective code ownership, frequent refactoring, and regular swapping of pair programming partners, everyone needs to follow the same coding style.

Practice	Description
System metaphors	To aid design communication, capture the overall system or each subsystem with memorable metaphors to describe the key architectural themes. For example, the C3 payroll system was described in terms of an assembly line of checks with posting rule "machines" operating on them, extracting money from different "bins." Many have reported this the least necessary practice.

Workproducts

Story Cards—Figure 8.3 shows a simple story card: A handwritten note on a paper index card. During the Planning Game, many of these are written. This spartan example was chosen to emphasize the minimalist approach to recorded requirements that XP encourages.[2]

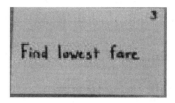

Figure 8.3 sample story card

The story cards record **user stories**: features, fixes, or nonfunctional requirements that the user wants. There can even be a story card to create documentation. Stories are usually in the one-day to three-week range of estimated duration. Contrary to some misunderstanding, XP stories are *not* use cases or scenarios. They usually represent features. Note that XP prefers a feature-driven

---

2. In fact, when XP expert Ron Jeffries reviewed this chapter, he felt even the number "3" on this real-example card was excessive.

approach to describing requirements rather than the use-case-driven approach that UP promotes.

In XP, oral communication is preferred, and the story card purpose is *not* to detail the user story, but to jot a summary, make references to other documents, and in general, to view the card as "a promise to talk" (in Alistair Cockburn's words) with the customer who wrote it, by the developers implementing it. Since *whole team together* is an XP practice, the card donor should be readily available. XP coaches vary on their advice regarding granularity for estimation. Some say stories can be in the two-day to two-week range of effort, others recommend stories be estimated in units of one, two, or three weeks, but not in finer person-day units.

Task List—During an Iteration Planning Game, the team convenes around a whiteboard, and generates a list of tasks for all the stories chosen for the iteration. Another popular alternative is to generate individual task cards. Once a task is chosen by a volunteer, they enter an effort estimate (in *ideal engineering hours*)—tasks should be in the 1–2 day range.

Visible Graphs—The idea is to easily communicate—to the team—something they find useful to measure. Measure at least one thing. XP doesn't mandate what that should be, though known examples include acceptance tests defined and passing, story progress, and task progress.

Other Practices and Values

- ❑ **Onsite customer proxies**—Many groups wishing to apply XP cannot find full-time "ultimate" customers to work in the project room. For example, consider a new internal system for (very busy) commodity traders. And this problem is common for commercial products for an external market. The common solution is to designate **customer proxies** that do join the team in the project room, have good (though not as ideal as true customer) knowledge of the domain and requirements, and that represent the ultimate customers. If proxies are used, it is important that the true customers at least participate in end-of-iteration demos, and preferably, in the Planning Games.

- ❑ **Customer on call**—When the onsite customer is not present, arrange matters so that the customer representative is committed to fast access, such as via a mobile phone.

- ❑ **Embrace change**—The overarching attitude that XP promotes is to embrace rather than fight change, in the requirements, design, and code, and be able to move quickly in response to change.

- ❑ **Only by volunteering (accepted responsibility)**—Tasks are not assigned to people. Rather, during the Iteration Planning Game, people choose or volunteer for tasks. This leads to a higher degree of commitment and satisfaction in the self-accepted responsibility, as has been explored in [DL99].

- ❑ **Very light modeling**—XP encourages programming very early and does take to "extreme" the avoidance of up-front design work. Any more than 10 or 20 minutes of design thinking (e.g., at the whiteboard with sketches or notes) before programming is considered excessive. Contrast this with Scrum or the UP, for example, where a half-day of design thought near the start of an iteration is acceptable.

- ❑ **Minimal or "just enough" documentation**—With the goal of getting to code fast, XP discourages writing *unnecessary* requirements, design, or management documents. The use of small paper index cards is preferred for jotting brief descriptions, as are verbal communication and elaboration. Note that the practice of "avoiding documentation" is compensated by the presence of an onsite customer. XP is not anti-documentation, but notes it has a cost, perhaps better spent on programming.

- ❑ **Metrics**—XP recommends daily measurement of progress and quality. It doesn't mandate the exact metrics, but to "use the simplest ones that could work." Examples include numbers of completed tasks and stories, and number and success rate of running tests.

- **Visible wall graphs**—The collected metrics are daily updated on wall graphs for all to easily see.

- **Tracking and Daily Tracker**—The regular collection of task and story progress metrics is the responsibility of a tracker. This is done with a walk-about to all the programmers, rather than email; commenting on this—and very telling of the XP attitude—Ron Jeffries (one of the XP founders) said, "XP is about people, not computers." Test metrics can be automatically collected by software.

- **Incremental infrastructure**—XP recommends (as do the other iterative processes) that the back-end infrastructure (for example, a persistence layer) not be the main focus of implementation in the early iterations, but rather, only enough is implemented to satisfy the user-functional requirements of each iteration.

- **Common project room**—XP projects are run in a common project room rather than separate offices. Pair programming tables are in the center of the room, and the walls are clear for whiteboard and poster work. Of course, people may have a private space for private time, but production software development is a team sport in XP.

- **Daily stand-up meeting**—As in Scrum, there is a daily short stand-up (to keep it short) meeting of status.

- **Ideal engineering hours (IEH)**—Task estimates—and possibly story estimates—are done in terms of IEH, or uninterrupted, dedicated, focused time to complete a task.

- **Story estimates**—To estimate larger stories, some XP practitioners recommend using only coarse values of one, two, or three week durations rather than IEH or day-level estimates.

VALUES

Beck's XP description is noteworthy in the process world for being perhaps the first to explicitly state the values that underly the attitude and practices on a healthy XP project. To quote Beck on the relationship of values and practices:

The [practices] are what you do. The values are how you decide if you are doing it right.

They are:

❏ **Communication**—XP accepts the widely appreciated observation that problems in communication underly most project difficulties. Communication between programmers is promoted through pair programming, the daily stand-up meeting, and the Planning Game. Communication is promoted through customer involvement in writing acceptance tests and the Planning Game.

❏ **Simplicity**—or, "Do the simplest thing that could possibly work." This applies not only to the design of software, but to other things such as requirements and project management "tools." For example, XP encourages the use of simple paper index cards to write a brief description of feature and task requests, if more formal artifacts can be avoided. In terms of software design, XP avoids speculative design for possible change ("future proofing") or the creation of more generalized components that aren't immediately justified by current requirements.

❏ **Feedback**—This value drives quality and adaptation. Feedback in the short term is driven by the XP practice of test-first development with unit tests. It also comes from the practice of continuous integration; a broken build tells the story. When a customer writes a story card (a feature description), programmers immediately estimate it, so the customers know the effort. The practice of daily tracker provides feedback to the team and customer on progress for the iteration. On a longer scale, the customer written acceptance tests provide feedback. Short iterations give the customer the chance to see (and perhaps operate) an incrementally evolved partial system, and clarify or redirect the requirements. And the practice of frequent operational releases generates feedback from production users.

❏ **Courage**—The courage to develop fast, and make changes fast emerges from the support of the other values and practices, and modern technologies. For example, without a massive set of unit tests, acceptance tests, and continuous integration, making deep "architectural" changes in the code base is tricky business—difficult to tell what will break. But the presence of these, combined with a simple design, very clean code refined from frequent refactoring, and modern automated refactoring tools provided by many IDEs enables more rapid and radical change.

COMMON MISTAKES AND MISUNDERSTANDINGS

or, How to Fail with Extreme Programming

Error: No onsite customer; rather, use specifications written for the next iteration—It is normal and acceptable to create written specifications for the iteration (for example, two use cases) if the adopted method is Scrum, UP, Evo, etc. An iterative or agile project that takes this approach can work well, but is better characterized as being based on another method (e.g., the UP) that allows written evolutionary requirements. It is a cornerstone of XP to avoid detailed specifications, use oral communication of the requirements, and onsite customers.

Error: Applying a subset of uncompensated practices; customizing before trying—Many XP practices work as a synergistic whole, and it is a mistake to remove one that compensates or supports another. For example, collective code ownership isn't feasible without testing, continuous integration, and coding standards. Minimal requirements documentation isn't possible without an onsite customer. Frequent refactoring doesn't work without the tests. That is why Beck, while not wishing to be rigid, in general recommends adoption of all or most of the core practices. To quote Beck, "Do all of XP before trying to customize it."

Error: XP is just iterative development + minimal documentation + unit testing—Although there is some flexibility in what practices must be present to define an XP project, it is more than this—common to several IID methods. One could run a Scrum, UP, DSDM, or other evolutionary methods primarily with just these practices. XP is characterized by a larger set of practices, including pair programming, onsite customers, customer-written acceptance tests, and more.

Error: Not writing the unit tests first—Test-first development has a more subtle dimension than first glance, and is an important XP practice. Writing the tests *first* influences how one conceives, clarifies, and simplifies the design. Test-first has an interesting psychological quality of satisfaction: I write the test, and then I make it succeed. There is a feeling of accomplishment that sustains the practice.

Error: Customer doesn't decide—XP is customer driven; they need to decide what the acceptance criteria are (via tests), and what stories go in a release and iteration.

Error: No customer-owned tests—Ron Jeffries has said, "The failure to have customer-owned acceptance tests [in each iteration] is one of the most common mistakes in XP."

Error: Minimal refactoring—The XP avoidance of design thought before programming is meant to be compensated by a relatively large refactoring effort, such as 25% of total effort applied to refactoring. Beck's point is that one can't avoid both design thought before programming and refactoring; it's either/or.

Error: Must have only one onsite customer—The original XP books talked of *one* onsite customer in the project room. Beck and the XP leaders have since refined this to emphasize that the customer team needs to be considered as a whole, with requirements coming from perhaps many customers participating in the Planning Games. Thus, they have replaced the practice "onsite customer" with "whole team together."

Error: Many fine-grained task cards—Most task cards should be in the one or two-day range of effort. Most in the "few hours" range creates unnecessary information management.

Error: Pairing with one partner too long—XP pairing changes frequently, often in two days or less. Variation also helps spread the learning.

Error: Customer or manager is tracker—Programmers will feel awkward reporting slow progress.

Error: Not integrating the QA team—Many organizations have a separate Quality Assurance team, used to having a completed system "thrown over the wall" to them. One or more dedicated QA people need to be brought onto the project full-time—the whole team practice—usually to write the acceptance tests in collaboration with the customer.

Error: Post-development design documentation is wrong—XP isn't anti-documentation, but prefers programming if that's sufficient to succeed. XP can support the creation of design documentation to reflect the existing code base, once the program is complete. As always, the simplest approach that can work is the goal, such as video recording an explanation.

Error: Diagramming is bad—Although XP advice is minimal modeling or diagramming, such as 15 minutes before programming, a very little is acceptable.

Error: Only young pair programmers—Some XP projects have suffered in the pair programming practice when most of the developers were quite young, without the patience or maturity to handle working closely with others.

Error: Pairing newbies—One of the two partners should have pair programmed before.

Error: One partner going too fast—When pair programming, the quicker or more experienced partner needs to be sensitive to the speed or comprehension differential of their partner, and slow down their activities and explanations.

Error: Observer can't easily see the monitor—Self-explanatory, but a surprisingly frequent problem.

Error: Not willing to learn; not willing to explain—For successful pair programming, an attitude of openness to learning and of explaining yourself is required.

Error: Full team (including customers) not briefed in XP and its motivations—Self-explanatory.

Error: Dissenter on team—XP is about communication and collaboration, and a culture of development; lone programmers who don't wish to accept it can impair the team culture and project progress.

Error: Stand-up meeting too long or unfocused—Keep it below 20 minutes, and on status of tasks, not a discussion of design and requirements.

Error: Lumping into one big "bug fix" story—As defects accumulate, don't group them into one task or story card; keep them with their original related cards.

Error: No dedicated acceptance tester—One is needed to work with the customer on transforming their acceptance criteria into runnable tests. An exception is very small projects—the tester may fulfill that role part-time.

Error: Onsite customer and Big Boss aren't aligned—XP talks of the Big Boss, or the person ultimately owning or responsible for the project goals and milestones. These two stakeholders need to be in agreement.

Error: Customer writing acceptance tests isn't the reviewer of their execution—A classic problem of serving different masters.

Error: Iterations too long—XP iterations should be 1–3 weeks.

Error: Iterations aren't timeboxed—It is a misunderstanding to let the iteration length expand when it appears the goals can't be met within the original time frame. Rather, the preferred strategy is usually to remove or simplify goals for the iteration. And, analyze why the estimates were off.

Error: Iteration doesn't end in an integrated and tested baseline—An iteration doesn't just successfully end on the end date. The goal is that all the software has been integrated, tested, and baselined.

Error: Each iteration ends in a production release—The baselined software produced at the end of an iteration is an *internal* release rather than shippable code. It represents a subset of the final production release, which may only be ready after a dozen or more short iterations. It is true that in iterative development one goal is that each iteration release is stable enough to potentiality release to production, if necessary. However, this is not the normal intent of an iteration release.

Error: Predictive planning—It is a misunderstanding to create, *at the start of the project*, a believable plan laying out exactly how many iterations there will be for a long project, their lengths, and what will occur in each. This is contrasted with the agile approach: adaptive planning. The XP team and customer plans the next iteration, and then planning adapts iteration by iteration, based on current feedback.

You Know You Didn't Understand XP When...

Some of the key misunderstandings expressed as a checklist:

- ❑ You think you should customize the choice of practices without having first applied them all.
- ❑ You think "doing XP" means to avoid the waterfall model and develop iteratively, or just to avoid documentation, or just to write some unit tests.
- ❑ Customers are not involved in the Planning Game, creating acceptance tests, or reviewing the iteration results.
- ❑ You create a plan laying out how many iterations there will be for the project, their lengths, and what will occur in each.

SAMPLE PROJECTS

The following projects had significant XP influence:

Large—Atlas leasing system

- – Three years, 60+ people, Java technologies, an E100 project, [Schuh01]

- *Fully adopted practices*: simple design, testing, frequent refactoring, collective code ownership, continuous integration
- Pair programming was attempted, but did not stick. There was no onsite customer.
- Prime developer: ThoughtWorks.

Medium—Orca security incident-response

- One year, 25 people, a D40 project, [Morales02]
- *Fully adopted practices*: most practices, with the exception of small, frequent releases as this was a commercial product.
- Prime developer: Symantec.

Small—C3 payroll

- One year, 10+ people, an E20 project [C3Team98]
- *Fully adopted practices*: This was the original project that defined XP, coached by Kent Beck and Ron Jeffries. All practices were adopted.
- Prime developer: Chrysler.

PROCESS MIXTURES

XP + Evo

Evo p. 211

Evo specifications p. 231

XP values and spirit regarding specifications is not compatible with Evo. XP's value of avoiding written or precise requirements, and preferring oral communication between developers and requirement donors is very different than Evo's emphasis that when a specification is required, it be done so with clarity and measurable qualities.

On the other hand, many XP development practices may be consistently applied with Evo, such as test-driven development, pair programming, and so forth.

XP's client-driven adaptive planning is also consistent with Evo. The XP stand-up meeting, common project room, and whole team together supports Evo's feedback goals.

adaptive planning
p. 253

XP's 1–3 week iteration length is relatively consistent with Evo, which prefers 1–2 week iterations.

XP + Scrum

Most Scrum practices are compatible with XP. The Scrum meeting is a refinement of the XP stand-up meeting (in fact, Beck got the idea from Scrum), using special questions. Both recommend a common project room. The Scrum practice of a demo to external stakeholders at the end of each iteration enhances XP's feedback and communication goals. The Scrum Backlog and progress tracking approaches are minor variations of XP practices.

Scrum p. 109
Scrum meeting p. 120

Scrum's 30-day iteration length is not consistent with XP—too long.

A Scrum practice is to have only one customer representative, the Product Owner, who is ultimately responsible for the requirements and priorities. But in recent updates to XP, there is an emphasis on collaborating with a *group* of customers—avoiding just a single person. It is nice to have a single customer voice, and it is useful to know and resolve multiple people's goals. XP and Scrum tackle this tension differently, shifting whether development or business is responsible for resolving the conflict.

Mike Beedle, one of the early Scrum practitioners, has explored combinations of XP and Scrum under the name "XBreed."

see www.xbreed.net

XP + UP

UP p. 173

UP practices p. 186

Most XP practices are either equal to or specializations of UP practices, and many XP practices can be applied in the context of an overarching UP project. For example, test-first development is a specialization of the UP *continuously verify quality* best practice. The UP does not require or promote unnecessary document creation—all artifacts are optional—and so it is a misunderstanding to assume the methods are fundamentally incompatible. Although speaking of some XP within UP can have conceptual integrity, the opposite is not true, as there are some differences in style and emphasis.

One area of difference is in the accepted degree of up-front modeling (diagramming, etc.). For example, within a UP project and a two-week iteration, it is considered acceptable to spend a half-day near the start to consider design ideas "at the whiteboard" before programming. In XP, no more than 10 or 20 minutes before programming is considered suitable.

Another difference is in the goal of the early iterations. In the UP the goal is to identify and drive down the high risks: technical, political, satisfying the customer, and so forth. Although this may happen in the XP, it is not an explicit guiding principle.

A third difference is in requirements specifications. The UP allows and supports the creation of relatively detailed specifications (evolutionarily, over a series of iterations), assuming that an onsite customer is not going to be present. These will usually take the form of use cases and an associated nonfunctional specifications document, created in a series of timeboxed requirements workshops. The idea in the UP is, during the early programming iterations, to have a parallel track of requirements analysis where the majority of requirements are being written, while the development team is also programming something critical. The programming work is meant, in part, to help clarify the requirements work.

XP stories are normally features, rather than use cases. Thus, XP promotes a feature-driven approach to requirements. On the other hand, the UP promotes a use-case-driven approach, although the UP accepts and allows features rather than use cases.

ADOPTION STRATEGIES

As always, coaching by an experienced method expert on the first project is recommended.

Similar to Scrum, but in contrast to the recommended gentle, pilot-project adoption strategy of UP (for example), XP recommends adoption like this:

1. Pick the worst project or problem.

2. Apply XP until solved.

3. Repeat.

If all the XP practices can't be swallowed at once, Beck recommends starting with:

❏ whole team together in a common project room

❏ test-first development

❏ acceptance tests written/owned by customers

❏ Planning Game

❏ pair programming

That said, there are dangers in only adopting a few of the practices, especially if one does not understand how they support each other. Avoidance of up-front design (even on a per-iteration basis) is compensated by frequent refactoring. Frequent refactoring is supported by continuous integration, and test-first development. And so forth.

Introducing customers to this new engaged approach is a challenge. The key is to help them see the early, tangible business value that they want, and emphasize that they will be steering the team to meet their needs in short cycles. An XP goal is to so delight the customer with this new-found control and responsiveness, that after a few iterations they will love the process.

On the common problem of customers wanting more and more in an iteration, one technique is to exploit the physical nature of story cards: Once the cards have been estimated and chosen for an iteration—and therefore consuming all available development resources—they are laid out on a table. Clearly, with the "no overtime" rule of XP, adding a new card means an existing one must be physically removed. This visual and tangible impact teaches a clear lesson.

If you can't get a customer into the room, what to do? First, look for another related representative, such as a product manager. If no luck, establish the closest possible communications. Visit them frequently, use a mobile phone, spend time at their job, have them use an instant messenger service to simulate the feel of close communication, have them attend the Planning Games, and show lots of demos.

Programmers will adopt most of the practices without concern, except pair programming. XP recommends not inviting programmers opposed to the idea to an XP project. Do not put only young programmers together; the maturity and patience of some older developers is necessary to make pairing work. Ensure the pairs mix regularly, the typing developer rotates frequently, and that people are learning from each other; i.e., sharing with their partners what they know, and what they are thinking. If pairs aren't frequently talking together, something isn't working.

For XP, the physical environment must change: open common room with development stations near the center, and the walls exposed for visible graphs, sketching, and so forth. And, the stations need to support pair programming. Ensure the non-typing partner can easily see the monitor.

Since pair programming implies lots of talk, a culture of quiet talking needs to be encouraged.

FACT VERSUS FANTASY

Reading the XP method practices can create the impression that they are a silver bullet, but of course, they are not. As always,

Process is only a second-order effect. The unique people, their feelings and qualities, are more influential.

One fantasy regarding XP adoption is found in groups that believe by just adopting iterative and evolutionary development and avoiding up-front specifications, they are "doing XP." Likewise with unit testing, working in a common project room, and so forth. Although data is still sketchy, it seems that many of the projects claiming to be doing XP are simply applying some iterative and evolutionary practices common to many IID methods (such as short iterations), and the group mistakenly believes these are unique XP ideas.

Probably the most common XP fantasy is getting onsite customers. It seems to be rare as hen's teeth to achieve this. Also, there is no shortage of so-called "XP" projects one investigates that could not arrange pair programming, which Beck considers one of the basics of an XP project.

Resistance to pair programming is perhaps the most common issue among developers. Some just don't want to do it.

It is also rare to find a common project room, or enough white-boards.

Test-first development, early acceptance tests defined with customers, constant refactoring, and continuous integration are all widely confirmed as sustainable, excellent practices.

STRENGTHS VERSUS "OTHER"

Strengths

❑ Practical, high-impact development techniques, many of which are easily and sustainably adopted by developers (e.g., continuous integration, test-driven development).

❑ Emphasizes customer participation and steering.

❑ Evolutionary and incremental requirements and development, and adaptive behavior.

❑ Programmers estimate the tasks they have chosen, and the schedule follows this, not vice versa (i.e., scheduling is rational).

❑ Emphasizes communication between all stakeholders.

❑ Emphasizes quality through many practices. Test-first development, continuous integration, and team code ownership are examples.

❑ Clarifies what is an acceptable system by requiring the customer to define the acceptance tests.

❑ Daily measurement, and developers are involved in measuring and defining what to measure.

❑ Every iteration, developers get practice (during the Planning Game) identifying tasks and estimating them, leading to improvement in these vital skills.

❏ Frequent, detailed reviews and inspections, as all significant work is done in pairs. Inspection is strongly correlated with reduced defect levels.

Other[3]

❏ Requires the presence of onsite customers (or proxies). This is often not possible, and their absence makes difficult or impossible the practice of "oral requirements" and using short story cards. XP has no standard solution for written requirements. That takes us back to other methods, such as the UP, which have a mechanism for iteratively recording detailed requirements.

❏ Relies on oral history for knowing the design and requirements details. This has limitations related to quickly helping new members, or scaling to larger projects.

❏ The XP practices are interdependent and mutually supporting. It isn't really a pick-and-choose process; most need to be done. Yet, people avoid some in the urge to avoid "unnecessary" steps, and thus failure ensues. Then, XP is unfairly criticized.

❏ No standard way to describe or document the software design as a learning aid.

❏ Some developers do not want to do pair programming.

❏ Many projects will need a set of documents other than code. XP does not define what these may be, and thus each project may create ones with similar intent, but varying names and content. In other words, no common, standard workproducts that are shareable with common names across projects. This impedes reuse of workproducts and impedes a common workproduct vocabulary in larger organizations.

---

3. Could be viewed as a weakness, strength, or deliberate desirable exclusion, depending on point of view.

❑ Lack of architecture-oriented emphasis in the early iterations. Lack of architectural design methods. XP advocates claim simple design and refactoring lead to the same goal.

HISTORY

In the mid-1980s, Kent Beck and Ward Cunningham worked together in a research group at Tektronix. They founded the idea of CRC cards and (the seminal contribution of) design patterns, while building many Smalltalk systems. The roots of XP come from this collaboration. Eventually, Beck branched into private consulting, slowly (re-)discovering the various XP practices, such as the value of working in a common room. Cunningham went on to create the popular and unique Web concept of Wiki Webs.

In the mid-1990s, Beck was retained by Chrysler to help with a new Smalltalk-based payroll system, the C3 project. One aim of the project was the education of the staff in object-technology skills; a successful payroll system was desirable, but not the only goal. Beck introduced the majority of practices that became XP, and brought in Ron Jeffries to daily lead and coach the team. Martin Fowler was also invited for some consulting. Primarily led by the vision of Beck, the XP practices coalesced on this project.

Beck says that at its heart, XP is expressing what he learned with and from Cunningham.

There has been some mis-information that the C3 project "failed." In fact, management felt that the team received good object-technology education, and the C3 payroll system did successfully go into production for several thousand employees, but was eventually phased out and the team reassigned, as management—with direction from the new Daimler owners—developed different ideas for handling payroll at the new-found DaimlerChrysler company.

WHAT'S NEXT?

The next chapter presents the practices of the UP, an iterative method with a somewhat different emphasis than XP. Following that, Evo is introduced—one of the first evolutionary methods.

RECOMMENDED READINGS

There are many XP books but only a few essentials. *Extreme Programming Explained* by Kent Beck is required reading. A good practical companion by three members of the original C3 team is *Extreme Programming Installed*.

Supporting or related texts that are recommended include:

- ❏ *Test-Driven Development: By Example*, by Kent Beck. Teaches the essentials of this key XP practice.

- ❏ *Refactoring: Improving the Design of Existing Code*, by Martin Fowler. The bible on refactoring skills.

- ❏ *Peopleware*, by Tom DeMarco and Tim Lister. Discusses some of the people-side issues that inspired Beck in XP.

- ❏ *The Deming Management Method*, by W. Edwards Deming and Mary Walton. Discusses the critical role of personal pride in workmanship. This also influenced Beck and XP.

- ❏ *Toyota Production System: Beyond Large-Scale Production*, by Taiichi Ohno. This book—by the creator of the Toyota method—on "lean manufacturing" is something of the physical-goods equivalent to XP for software. Although Beck did not read this work until after creating XP, he has since highly praised it for capturing many of his goals and values in XP.

- ❏ "Episodes: A Pattern Language for Competitive Development" in *Pattern Languages of Program Design 2*. Article by Ward Cunningham, edited by John Vlissides. Cunningham presents some of the key ideas that became XP.

UNIFIED PROCESS

*The true measure of a man is how he treats
someone who can do him absolutely no good.*
—Samuel Johnson

OVERVIEW

❏ Classification of UP.

❏ Workproducts, roles, and practices.

❏ Common mistakes, adoption and process mixtures, strengths and weaknesses.

The **Unified Process (UP)** is a popular iterative process framework, particularly its refinement in the **Rational Unified Process** or **RUP**. Some of the UP key practices and guidelines illustrate its spirit:

UP versus RUP p. 207

❏ Develop in short timeboxed iterations.

*practice details
p. 188*

❏ Develop the high-risk and high-value elements (for example, the core architecture) in early iterations, preferring re-use of existing components.

❏ Ensure that you deliver value to your customer.

❏ Accommodate change early in the project.

❏ Work together as one team.

The UP organizes iterations within four phases. The **elaboration phase** iterations emphasize programming the risky, core architecture, **construction phase** iterations build the remainder.

METHOD OVERVIEW

Classification

cycles and ceremony
p. 26

In terms of cycles and ceremony, UP classification is illustrated in Figure 9.1. For average projects, the recommended length of a timeboxed iteration is between two and six weeks—somewhat longer than XP, for example.

Figure 9.1 UP on the cycles and ceremony scale.

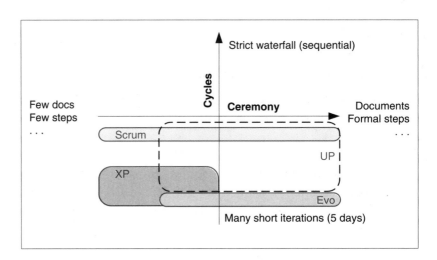

Perhaps the most noteworthy quality of the UP, in comparison with other popular IID methods, is its ability to scale up and down on the ceremony spectrum, with *optional* support for higher degrees of formality and documentation. Contrary to some misunderstanding, the UP encourages a relatively light footprint in terms of ceremony, although in general it recommends more documentation and modeling than in XP. It offers a set of around 50 optional workproducts for many contingencies.

Cockburn scale p. 36

In terms of the Cockburn classification, the UP covers all cells. See Figure 9.2.

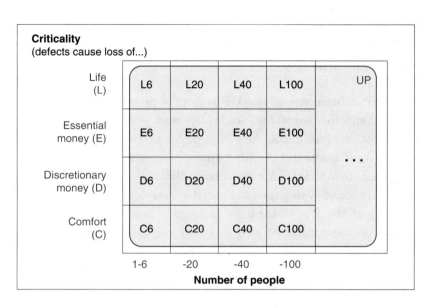

Figure 9.2 UP covers all cells on the Cockburn scale

The UP can be applied to small three-person projects with no more than loss of comfort, and up to hundreds of developers working on life-critical systems. For example, the core UP practices were applied on the Canadian Air Traffic Control System project, involving many hundreds of developers.

Introduction

The UP [JBR99] is an **iterative process framework**—a general process description that can and should be refined into a more detailed process description for an organization or project, such as the RUP [Kruchten00].[1] A UP specialization may itself be a more detailed process *framework* (as is the RUP) or a concrete process description for one particular project.

---

1. IBM bought Rational in 2003, maintaining the "RUP" branding.

See "UP as a Heavy, Defined Process versus an Agile UP Approach" on p. 192.

The UP is more of a defined process, and more broad and ambitious than the other iterative processes described in this text. However, all activities and workproducts, and their ordering, are optional and arbitrary.

The RUP refinement of the UP is both a process framework (for creating specific processes), and a licensed product. As a product, it is a set of around 100 core Web pages of process description—with several thousand detailed supporting pages—and with templates for its artifacts. A customizing "RUP Builder" tool can configure the set of Web pages to describe your organization's specific tailoring of the RUP. Many organizations purchase and install a version on their intranet as a learning aid, quality assurance aid, and template resource. See Figure 9.3. It is not required to own the RUP product to adopt and apply the UP's general ideas or practices.

The UP defines a set of approximately 50 optional (non-software) **artifacts** (workproducts), such as the **Vision**. A particular project may create zero or more, and "less is better" is a guiding rule, although a couple of workproducts are usually recommended, including a **Vision** and **Risk List**. Note that workproducts in the UP are *information abstractions* rather than necessarily computer documents; for example, the Risk List could be realized with a poster on the wall of the project room. Nevertheless, the RUP product includes document templates (for example, in HTML) for those wishing to use them.

The workproducts are organized within **disciplines**—such as the Requirements discipline—that define major areas of concern and activity on a software project. See Table 9.1 for a sample.

Figure 9.3 sample Web page from the RUP product

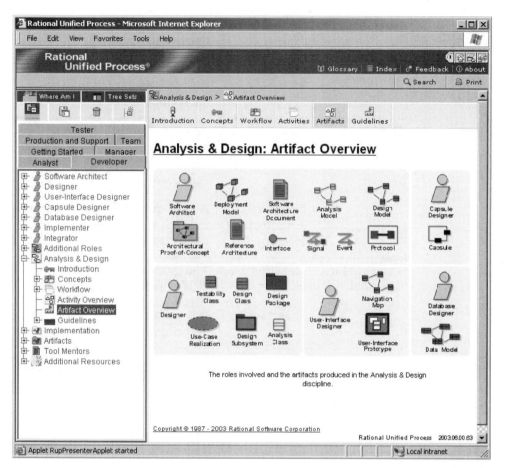

Table 9.1 sample UP
disciplines and
workproducts

Discipline	Workproduct	Comment
Requirements	Vision	Summary of stakeholders' key needs and features.
	Use-Case Model	The set of use cases describing the intended functions and environment.
Design	Design Model	An object model describing the hardware and software realization of the use cases in terms of collaborating objects.
	Software Architecture Document	A system overview or learning aid that includes several architectural views.
Project Management	Iteration Plan	The goals and tasks for the current or next iteration.
	Risk List	A list of prioritized risks with associated mitigation plans.

Figure 9.4 sample UP
disciplines and iterations

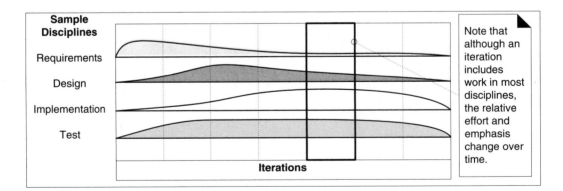

In terms of disciplines and iterations, the UP envisions a project approximating Figure 9.4. In each iteration, activity occurs in most disciplines, though the relative efforts vary over time.

The UP requires that it be **tailored** for each project; that is, choosing the set of practices and UP workproducts to create, from the large but optional set available. This unique tailoring is called the **Development Case** of the project; a simple example is shown in Table 9.2. In general, "less is better" is the guideline, and a Development Case is encouraged to contain the minimal set of workproducts needed to address the risks and goals of the project.

Table 9.2 Sample partial UP Development Case

Discipline	Techniques	Artifact Iteration→	Incep. I1	Elab. E1..En	Const. C1..Cn	Trans. T1..Tn
Requirements	one-day timeboxed requirements workshops, prototypes, paper-based UI mock-ups.	Vision	s[a]	r		
		Supplementary Specification	s	r		
Design	Pair designing doing whiteboard sketches captured with camera, test-first design, reverse engineering.	Design Model		s	r	
		SW Architecture Document		s		
Project Mgmt	All Scrum management practices	Risk List	s	r	r	r
Implementation	Pair programming, test-first development, continuous integration	code, graphics, etc.	s	r	r	r
...	...					

a. s = start. r = refine.

LIFECYCLE

INCEPTION	ELABORATION (iterations ...)	CONSTRUCTION (iterations ...)	TRANSITION (iterations ...)
Purpose: - High-level objectives, business case, vision, and scope defined and agreed	**Purpose**: - Core, architectually significant parts of system coded and tested	**Purpose**: - System completed and ready for deployment	**Purpose**: - System verified as ready for deployment
- "10%" of the signficant requirements defined in detail	- Significant risks identified and mitigated	- Efficient and predictable development, building on the stable architecture coded in elaboration	- Deployed system
- Key risks identified	- "80%" of major reqs *evolved* & defined in detail		
- Elaboration effort estimated	- Enough stability and information to estimate duration and effort		
Possible Activities: - requirements workshop	**Possible Activities:** - testing, programming, designing in short iterations	**Possible Activities:** - testing, programming, designing in short iterations	**Possible Activities:** - beta or release candidate testing and feedback
- start Vision and Risk List	- requirements workshops, refining the vision	- stakeholder evaluation and steering; ideally only minor req changes	- final programming and documentation
- start Use-case Model and Supplementary Specs	- refining the environment (process and technical)	- create all documents	- educating, marketing, ...
- prototyping		- alpha testing	- deployment
Requirements phase	Design phase	Programming phase	Test phase

1. **Inception** is ideally short, such as a few days. Iterations are possible, but rare. Activities could include a short requirements workshop, 10% of the requirements captured in detail (the most architecturally influential ones), a "top ten" high-level requirements list, and a first draft of the vision and business case for the project. If this phase is long, it is usually a sign of excessive up-front specifications or planning.

2. In **elaboration**, the core, architecturally significant elements are programmed and tested in a series of short time-boxed iterations, and by its end a semi-reliable plan and estimate is possible. This phase includes *programming* work, not only requirements or design modeling. In addition to development, with feedback from the growing system, there may be a series of short requirements workshops (one per iteration) to refine most of the requirements. This is a step of discovery and creativity; when complete, the core of the system and most requirements have stabilized through an iterative, evolutionary process.

3. In **construction**, the remainder of the system is built—in short iterations—on top of the solid foundation laid in elaboration. Requirements may still change, but ideally the big surprises were provoked and discovered earlier in elaboration. Other activities include alpha testing, performance tuning, and document creation (for example, user aids).

4. In **transition**, the system is ultimately deployed. First, a release candidate is exposed for review and feedback. This may occur in several iterations. Finally, there is deployment, that may include distribution over various channels, education, parallel run with an older system, data conversion, and so on.

The UP identifies **milestone objectives** in a project that define the boundaries of these phases. These come from the work of the Barry Boehm, in [Boehm96].[2] Boehm called the end of inception the Life Cycle Objectives (LCO) milestone. The end of elaboration was called the Life Cycle Architecture (LCA) milestone.

Each phase may contain multiple iterations. The milestone goals of each phase are described in Table 9.3, and an example of phases and iterations is shown in Figure 9.5.

---

2. Boehm and the UP creators have a long history of collaboration.

Table 9.3 UP phases

Phase	Milestone Goals	Comments
Inception	Agreement on scope, vision, and priorities. Some risks identified. A plan to start elaboration exists.	*Establish a common vision.* Typically a very short phase, such as a few days or weeks. A first requirements workshop might be held.
Elaboration	The vision, requirements, and architecture are stabilized. The core executable architecture is implemented; major risks are mitigated. The majority of requirements are defined. Estimates and coarse-grained plan are defined.	*Build and test the risky core.* This phase contains significant production programming and testing, combined with evolutionary requirements and design work. Usually composed of several iterations. In addition to programming, perhaps a series of requirements workshops; one per iteration. Semi-reliable plans and estimates at *end* of elaboration.
Construction	System is believed ready to be deployed. Stakeholders are ready for deployment.	*Build and test the rest.* Typically the largest set of iterations. As in elaboration, major testing occurs in each iteration.
Transition	System is deployed. Users are satisfied.	*Deploy.* Beta testing, release candidate evaluation, training.

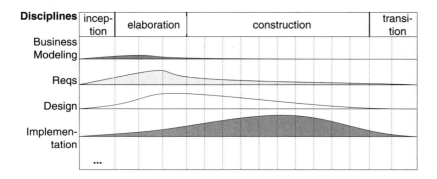

Figure 9.5 shows an *example* of iterations across the phases: three iterations in elaboration and 10 in construction. As usual, iterations are not necessarily the same length. Often, early elaboration iterations are longer (e.g., three weeks) due to the demands of creative and unpredictable discovery. Later construction iterations could be one or two weeks long. The resources or staffing also varies. Ideally, the elaboration phase is staffed by a small, cohesive, co-located team who shape the core. During construction, larger teams and more parallel development may occur. See Figure 9.6.

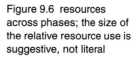

Figure 9.6 resources across phases; the size of the relative resource use is suggestive, not literal

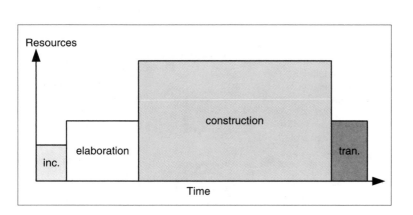

WORKPRODUCTS, ROLES, AND PRACTICES

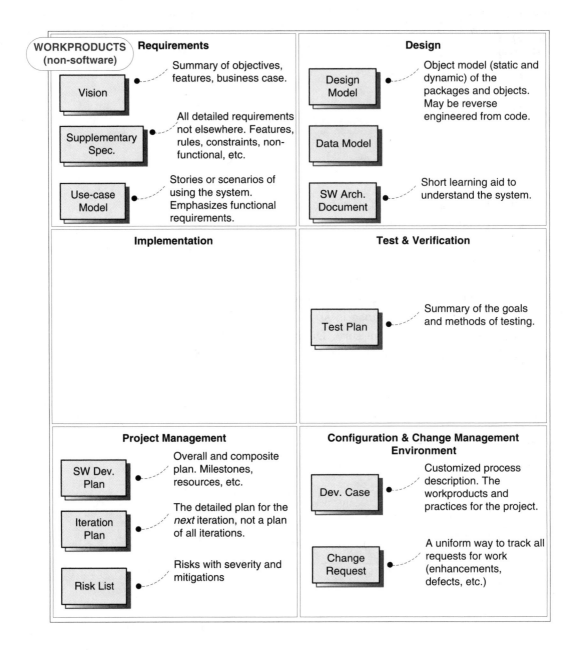

WORKPRODUCTS (non-software)

Requirements

Vision — Summary of objectives, features, business case.

Supplementary Spec. — All detailed requirements not elsewhere. Features, rules, constraints, non-functional, etc.

Use-case Model — Stories or scenarios of using the system. Emphasizes functional requirements.

Design

Design Model — Object model (static and dynamic) of the packages and objects. May be reverse engineered from code.

Data Model

SW Arch. Document — Short learning aid to understand the system.

Implementation

Test & Verification

Test Plan — Summary of the goals and methods of testing.

Project Management

SW Dev. Plan — Overall and composite plan. Milestones, resources, etc.

Iteration Plan — The detailed plan for the *next* iteration, not a plan of all iterations.

Risk List — Risks with severity and mitigations

Configuration & Change Management Environment

Dev. Case — Customized process description. The workproducts and practices for the project.

Change Request — A uniform way to track all requests for work (enhancements, defects, etc.)

Roles

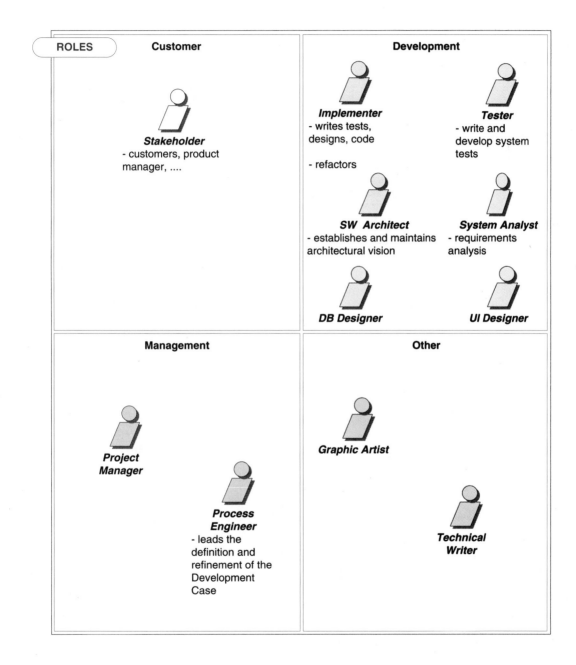

Practices

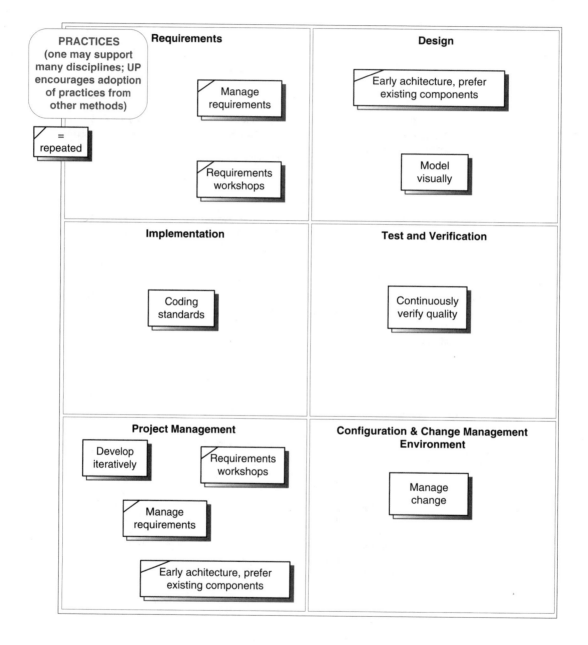

Core Practices

To be called a UP project, it arguably should illustrate at least the following:

❏ Follow the UP guidelines and best practices.

❏ Create at least a couple of UP artifacts, such as the Vision and Risk List.

    – Conform to the UP workproduct names rather than use other or prior names, to establish a common vocabulary.

❏ Organize the iterations and milestone goals according the goals of inception, elaboration, construction, and transition.

UP Guidelines

Although the original UP creators had in mind a preference for a relatively light approach to process, this was not well communicated in their early learning aids. In their more recent material, this has improved. For example, [KK03] presents the "spirit of the RUP" guidelines for success—core attitudes to hold on a UP/RUP project:

❏ Attack risks early and continuously, or they will attack you.

❏ Deliver value to your customer—early and often.

❏ Stay focused on developing executable software in early iterations, not specifications or other documents.

❏ Accommodate change early in the project. Provoke and managing change via early development, multiple requirements workshops, change management tools, and so on.

❏ Baseline an executable architecture early.

❏ Prefer component-oriented architectures and the reuse of existing components.

❏ Work together as one team (e.g., cross-functional teams)

❑ Quality is a way of life, not an afterthought.

The Six Best Practices

The UP is not really limited to only six best practices, but these are an important minimal set to focus on. UP adopters should understand these practices, and most or all should be applied on UP projects:

1. The most important of the UP practices is to develop using *timeboxed iterations*, recommended between two and six weeks. In other words, do not apply a waterfall lifecycle or attempt to do thorough requirements analysis first. Rather—as with all iterative lifecycle processes—start programming early, when only a portion of the most significant requirements are understood in detail. Refine the requirements and design based on feedback and adaptation from the programming effort instead of attempting large, up-front requirements analysis or speculative "Power Point architectures."

2. Emphasize programming the high-risk and high-value elements, and a *cohesive architecture* in early iterations, and strive to re-use *existing components*—large and small—to reduce new code and defects. For large projects, ideally the requirements analysis and core architecture is developed by a co-located small team; later, the early team members divide into subproject leaders coaching subteams doing parallel development.

3. *Continuously verify quality*. Test early, often, and realistically by integrating and testing all the software each iteration—unit, system, and load testing. This best practice includes techniques such as test-driven development and continuous integration, both promoted in XP. Plus, it extends beyond code to include early verification of usability, the quality of non-code artifacts (such as requirements), and of

the process itself via regular team meetings to reflect on the value or lack thereof in different activities.

4. Before starting programming in an iteration, do at least a little *visual modeling*, such as sketching at the whiteboard for an hour, to explore and communicate creative design ideas while ignoring low-level code details. Oftentimes, sketches will be loosely based on the industry-standard Unified Modeling Language (UML). Practices promoted by Agile Modeling, such as creating multiple visual models in parallel, using digital cameras to capture sketches, and so on, are applicable to this best practice. Sometimes, CASE tools for visual modeling can add value, to regularly reverse engineer the growing code base into UML diagrams that offer a big-picture view of the software.

5. *Manage requirements* through skillful means to *find*, *organize*, and *track* them. *Find* and refine requirements iteratively and incrementally rather than via major up-front analysis—for example, through a series (once per iteration) of short timeboxed one-day requirements workshops in the early phases of the project. Where suitable, *find* functional requirements by writing use cases to record functional requirements, rather than older-style function lists. Using a tool, *organize* requirements with attributes, such as risk, priority, and status (e.g., new, assigned), and with traceability to other dependent requirements, so that they can be analyzed; using a tool for this task is especially valuable on large projects where it is difficult for any one person to envision and reason about all the requirements. And using a tool, *track* the status of requirements so that we know what's finished, underway, and so forth.

6. *Manage change* through disciplined configuration management and version control, a change request protocol, and baselined releases at the end of each iteration.

Workproducts

The workproduct diagram (p. 184) shows a subset of common UP workproducts (artifacts). There are approximately 50 in total. The details are outside the scope of this introduction; see [Larman01] for many examples, or the RUP product.

Important overarching points regarding the UP workproducts:

- ❑ **Unfair criticism?**—Some have criticized the UP as having too many workproducts in comparison with some other IID methods. Yet, when you examine the full UP list, it contains workproducts such as *Release Notes*, *Bill of Materials*, *Training Materials*, and so forth. These are workproducts that a team makes for many products, regardless of method. It is just that the UP has identified them, whereas XP and Scrum, for example, have not. And, all are optional.

- ❑ **Common vocabulary**—For larger organizations, especially those with hundreds of developers or multiple offices, it is useful to have a common vocabulary of workproducts (*Vision*, *Software Architecture Document*, etc.). It helps communication between people and offices. It helps during scavenging for reusable artifacts from prior projects.

- ❑ **Information abstractions**—The UP artifacts are information abstractions rather than concrete computer documents, although the RUP product provides sample document templates. The *Risk List* can be a poster on the wall; the *Software Architecture Document* can be a video; the *Design Model* can be UML-ish whiteboard sketches captured on a digital camera.

Other Practices and Values

Absorbing practices—The UP is a broad and general IID process definition. It defines or endorses many detailed practices, both "local" to the UP or adopted from other methods, such as XP testing or Scrum meetings. Note that many practices, such as XP's *test-driven development*, are specializations or variations of the UP practices, such as *continuously verify quality*. If the RUP product is used, the "RUP Builder" can configure the process definition to include documentation on absorbed practices.

Use-case driven—The UP does not require the application of use cases to capture functional requirements; feature lists and feature-driven development are possible. However, when use cases are suitable for the problem domain, their use is encouraged in the UP. In that case, the UP recommends organizing iterations by scenarios of use cases, tackling the most architecturally significant, risky, and highest business value scenarios early. Then, one designs and implements to fulfill use case scenarios. Further, the UP recommends basing system-level acceptance tests on these scenarios. Thus, use cases drive the iterative development and acceptance testing.

iteration planning with use cases and scenarios p. 269

VALUES

In contrast to XP and Scrum, the UP does not make explicit a set of underlying values, although some can be inferred. And whereas the XP values emphasize human and communication qualities, the UP values emphasize a project-oriented rather than people-oriented focus. These include:

❑ It is important to apply the UP guidelines and best practices. Some UP values logically follow from this, such as iterative is better than waterfall, having a cohesive architecture is good, change control must be formalized, and so forth.

❑ Be risk- and value-driven. That is, in early iterations, identify and drive down the high risks and build elements deemed of highest value to the stakeholders.

❑ It is important to define a clear vision (in the UP Vision workproduct) for the project that summarizes the stakeholders' real needs.

❑ It is critical that the UP process be tailored to the unique needs of each project while still observing the best practices. Plus, be tailored to the minimal set of workproducts and activities that add value.

❑ It is useful to have a well-defined process that provides guidance on activities, on what artifacts to create, and on the tasks of individuals and the team.

UP as a Heavy, Defined Process versus an Agile UP Approach

for a discussion of defined vs. empirical methods, see p. 111

It is this last value that is a point of contention in the UP compared to the classic agile methods. Some in the agile process community have dismissed off-handedly the idea that a defined process such as the UP is useful, and that it is too "heavyweight," but the issue is more nuanced.

First, the UP creators did not intend the process to be applied or adopted in a rigid or heavyweight manner; they are experienced and practical software developers who also appreciate simplicity and agility. They view the UP as a suite of options to pick from, within the constraints of adopting its spirit and best practices.

Another perspective on this issue is offered by Cockburn, who describes three levels of behavior and listening as people mature in learning a subject [Cockburn02]: 1) following, 2) detaching, and 3) fluent. He relates this to literature and guidance for software methods by noting that Level-3 advice such as terse "work in a common project room and deliver usable software every four weeks" may be suitable for the *fluent* master, but not for the novice *following* developer. The detailed defined process aspects of the UP are aimed especially at a Level-1 audience, and in that context are of some value for learning, and as quality assurance checklists.

Level-2 and Level-3 developers may ignore the prescriptive and defined aspects of the UP, such as what tasks to do in what order, and instead focus more simply on choosing a set of UP workproducts to create, applying the best practices, and realizing these according to the creative judgment of the team in a more empirical process spirit.

A second issue in the value of defined processes is repeatability and avoiding re-invention. There *are* at least a few predictable, repeatable, useful steps in deploying a system to production, such as writing release notes. The UP makes explicit this advice (which is especially useful for the Level-1 audience), whereas the agile methods do not.

A third point in the value of defined processes is having a common vocabulary for artifacts, such as the UP Vision and Design Model. The UP provides such a vocabulary, which removes the need for each project to recreate one, and promotes communication across projects and organizations.

The issue of defined versus empirical processes for software projects boils down to a matter of balance and moderation. Certainly, rigid command-control sequencing of fine-grained, pre-defined activities is not skillful on most software projects, but on the other hand, some aspects of defined processes add value and can be applied in an agile and empirical spirit, as some activities are predictable—for example, many related to deployment.

Given a set of iteration goals, a self-directed team doing daily Scrum meetings can be characterized as applying the UP if it creates a few UP workproducts and follows its best practices, but is driven by the dynamic and creative judgment of the team, rather than by following a UP recipe of ordered activities.

In summary, the UP—although a semi-defined process—can be and is applied by some in an agile style.

COMMON MISTAKES AND MISUNDERSTANDINGS

or, How to Fail with the Unified Process

There are internal IT organizations, books, Web pages, articles, consulting organizations, and speakers that demonstrate these misunderstandings. Be cautious in receiving UP advice or hiring consultants, and apply the tests in the "Signs the UP "Expert" Is Not an Iterative Expert" section on page 198.

Superimposing Waterfall Ideas

The most common of the significant UP misunderstandings, and a quick sign that the UP "expert" actually is not, is to describe the four phases akin to the waterfall phases (requirements, design, implementation, test):

THIS IS INCORRECT; it is a sign of misinformation by those not truly understanding the UP

1. **Inception**—requirements analysis, detailed specifications.

2. **Elaboration**—more detailed requirements analysis, modeling, and design work.

3. **Construction**—programming the design.

4. **Transition**—testing.

This *incorrect* description of the UP phases illustrates the most common misunderstanding: superimposition of waterfall phases onto the UP. A corollary of misapplying the waterfall phases includes other common waterfall mistakes in UP adoption:

❑ Attempting to do most requirements analysis or design before programming.

❑ Deferring major testing or QA till near the end of the project.

Other Common Misunderstandings

Error: Iterations too long—It is usually a misunderstanding to define iterations of several months long. The UP recommends an iteration length between two and six weeks, excluding massive projects involving hundreds of people and many subteams. Skilled iterative project leaders strive towards shorter timeboxed iterations in the two to four-week range, all other things being equal. One project may be composed of dozens of short iterations.

Error: Iterations aren't timeboxed—It is a misunderstanding to let the iteration length expand when it appears the goals can't be met within the original timeframe. Rather, the usual expert strategy is to remove or simplify goals for the iteration.

Error: Iteration doesn't end in an integrated and tested baseline—An iteration is not properly complete unless all the software, across all or most subteams, has been integrated, tested, and baselined. It is a misunderstanding to think an iteration simply ends arbitrarily on the end date; the goal is to pull everything together.

Error: Each iteration ends in a production release—It is a misunderstanding to think each iteration must end in a production release. Although this is possible (especially during maintenance) it is less common than requiring many iterations before a production release.

Error: Elaboration phase goal is to create a throwaway prototype—Prototypes are perfectly acceptable in the UP (usually during inception), but the goal of elaboration is not a throwaway prototype but rather a production subset of the final system. Some have misunderstood this (and some UP books have misadvised on this point) because the original UP and RUP literature itself used the unfortunate choice of phrase "architectural prototype" in a few places to describe the output of elaboration. This confusing term was meant to imply "architectural subset of the final production system" but many interpreted "prototype" to invariably mean throwaway code.

Error: Development Case too complex; too many workproducts—It is a misunderstanding to define a Development Case with dozens of UP workproducts, when fewer will suffice. The guideline is "less is better." This is not advice to avoid demonstrably useful documentation, or the forethought that accompanies its creation; the UP recommends creating workproducts that really add value, and abandon make-work or low-value document or model creation.

Error: Predictive planning—It is a misunderstanding to create, *near the start of the project*, a believable plan laying out exactly how many iterations there will be for a long project, their lengths, and what will occur in each.

Error: The team should do lots of modeling and UML diagrams, and use a CASE tool—The UP contains several optional models, with many opportunities to apply the UML for diagramming speculative designs before programming. However, these are optional, and if a team can successfully and easily develop software with little or no prior diagramming, they may. Modeling and UML diagramming in the UP are aids to help with complexity and creativity, no more. And it is certainly not necessary to use a CASE or UML drawing tool while modeling on a UP project. The Agile Modeling approach that recommends the simplest possible tool—perhaps whiteboard hand sketches and digital cameras—is perfectly suitable.

Error: Need many tools—It is a misunderstanding to think many software tools need to be applied on an UP project. Rather, it can be run as low-tech, high-touch as paper cards, wall posters, and whiteboards, combined with a sprinkling of CVS, Anthill (for continuous integration), and Bugzilla (for issue and defect tracking).

Error: Software Architecture Document (SAD) "finished" before end of elaboration—The UP SAD is a learning aid that summarizes the big ideas and motivation in the architecture. It is a misunderstanding to create the final SAD before the end of elaboration, as that would imply major up-front design, and speculative definition of the architecture without programming. In the UP, the architecture evolves iteration by iteration through an interplay of some educated guesses combined with programming and testing. The architecture is not stabilized until the end of elaboration, after significant programming to build and prove it. Thus, the SAD, which summarizes the architecture, cannot be finished until elaboration is over.

Error: Not conforming to the official UP workproduct names or phase names—One purpose of the UP is to establish a common vocabulary, both within an organization and globally across UP-conforming teams, for workproducts and major lifecycle phases. For an organization that is adopting the UP to replace a prior process, it is a misunderstanding to rename the UP workproduct to the older familiar names, rather than surrender to the new terms.

You Know You Didn't Understand the UP When...

Some of the key misunderstandings expressed as a checklist:

- ❑ You think a sequence of requirements → design → implementation express the way to run a UP project.

- ❑ You think inception is like requirements analysis, elaboration is like design and detailed requirements analysis, construction is like programming after the design, and transition is a testing phase.

❑ You want to do most requirements analysis or design before programming.

❑ You defer the major testing until near the end of the project.

❑ You define iterations months long rather than weeks long.

❑ You create the SAD before the end of elaboration.

Signs the UP "Expert" Is Not an Iterative Expert

UP consultants, authors, and speakers from both major well-known consulting organizations and small shops may exhibit a misunderstanding of the UP and iterative development. Here are some of the key ones illustrated in the behavior of a UP "expert":

❑ Describes the UP phases similar to waterfall phases; recommends doing most requirements or design before programming; encourages creation of more and more detailed specifications and plans, before starting development work.

❑ Suggests iterations more than six weeks long. Does not strive towards short iterations.

❑ Recommends an inception phase that is weeks (or worse, months) long, involving major planning and analysis; is not encouraging a rapid transition to early programming in an elaboration phase.

❑ Is not stressing the importance of early programming starting in the first elaboration iteration, well before all requirements, plans, and design are known.

❑ Recommends creating many UP artifacts, rather than seeking ways to reduce the number. Some UP consultants do this out of ignorance; others out of a justification for their presence and guidance in the creation of these and handling a more complex process.

❑ Builds only a throwaway prototype in the elaboration phase.

❏ Defers unit, load, usability, or acceptance testing until near the end of the project.

❏ Insists that the team follow the UP activities "by the book."

❏ Insists on the team using UML CASE tools to draw many diagrams, whereas hand sketches on whiteboards, or simply bypassing drawing and just programming, would suffice.

❏ Creates the "final" SAD before the end of elaboration and before significant programming has occurred.

❏ Near the start, defines a "believable" plan laying out how many iterations there will be for the project, their lengths, and what will occur in each (i.e., predictive planning).

❏ If hired as an UP auditor to verify the team is skillfully applying the UP, encourages more or more thorough work-product creation or more detailed planning, rather than early programming, evolutionary requirements, and adaptive planning.

SAMPLE PROJECTS

The following projects applied many of the values and practices that characterize a UP project:

Large—Canadian Automated Air Traffic Control System

- Ten years, 400 people, Ada and C++, an L400 life-critical project, [PKT93].

- This was a large test bed for the practices that were later refined as the RUP. The chief architect was Dr. Kruchten (who drove the adoption of these practices), also the lead architect of the RUP. It was first attempted as a waterfall project, failed, and then was restarted under the new process direction of Kruchten as an iterative project. As a successful iterative ATC project, it is an instructional contrast to the failed attempt (after 11 years and $2.6 billion USD) to replace the USA ATC, which was unsuccessfully run as a waterfall project [GAO98].

– Prime developer: Raytheon Systems Canada. Originally, Hughes Canada Systems Division.

Medium—Ogre Nextgen Economic Modeling System

– Two years, 15 people, Java technologies, an E20 project.

– A Java technology decision support system used by oil/gas asset holders (e.g., potential oil fields). Development involved 19 iterations that on average were four weeks. Included the Scrum practice of a demonstration to external stakeholders at the end of each iteration.

– Prime developer: Valtech USA.

Small—QUICKcheck point-of-sale

– One year, six people, Java technologies, [Evans01].

– A self-checkout POS system for grocery stores.

– Prime developer: Kyrus.

PROCESS MIXTURES

UP + Evo

The UP is especially for software development, and usually for projects involving multiple iterations before production delivery. Consequently, the UP could be applied to Evo backroom development work. However, Evo's very frequent evolutionary delivery and project management style is not exactly in the same spirit as the UP, although both share an interest in early identification and mitigation of risks. The UP has its own set of workproducts and approach to requirements capture: the Use-Case Model (and thus, use cases), and Supplementary Specification for description of functions, features, and nonfunctional requirements. Evo Planguage elements, such as the Performance Requirement Specification, may be used within the UP Supplementary Specification. Evo's measurement emphasis is compatible or acceptable with the UP. The upper bound of UP's 2–6 week iteration length is not consistent with Evo—too long.

Evo p. 211

backroom p. 217

Planguage p. 231

UP + Scrum

The Scrum practices are consistent with UP practices. The Scrum Product Backlog is an acceptable portion of the UP Project Plan, and the Sprint Backlog is an acceptable version of the UP Iteration Plan. One area of potential conflict is the presence in the UP of optional but predefined activities; the UP indicates some dependent ordering of these optional activities—for example, that a project vision is created before a detailed requirement is described. Scrum's rejection of defined process and predictable steps is inconsistent with this structure if the UP activities are viewed as a required formula. But, if the activities are treated as optional advice, performable in any order, and without attempt to schedule their order and duration on a project, and without

Scrum p. 109

Product and Sprint Backlog p. 123

See "UP as a Heavy, Defined Process versus an Agile UP Approach" on p. 192.

assignment of tasks to individuals by a manager, it is not in conflict with Scrum.

UP + XP

XP p. 137

test-driven development p. 292

Most XP practices are consistent with UP practices, and many XP practices can be applied in the context of an overarching UP project. For example, test-driven development is a specialization of the UP *continuously verify quality* best practice. Since all UP workproducts are optional it is a misunderstanding to assume the methods are fundamentally incompatible, given XP's promotion of minimal modeling and documentation.

However, although speaking of some XP practices within a UP project can have conceptual integrity, the opposite is not true, as there are some differences in style and emphasis. One area of difference is in the accepted degree of up-front modeling (diagramming, etc.). For example, within a UP project and a two-week iteration, it is considered acceptable to spend a halfday near the start to sketch and explore design ideas "at the whiteboard" (visual modeling) before programming. In XP, no more than 10 or 20 minutes before programming is considered suitable.

Another difference is in the goal of the early iterations. In the UP the goal is to identify and drive down the high risks: technical, political, satisfying the customer, and so forth. Although this may happen in the XP, it is not an explicit guiding principle.

A third difference is in requirements specification. The UP allows and supports the creation of relatively detailed specifications (incrementally, over a series of iterations), assuming that an onsite customer is not going to be present. These will usually take the form of the Use-Case Model and Supplementary Specification.

ADOPTION STRATEGIES

As always, coaching by an experienced method expert on the first project is recommended. UP adoption is meant to be iterative, incremental, and adaptive. "Big bang" process adoption, where many people are trained near the same time, and/or many UP projects start at once, should be avoided.

First, executive management will benefit from education in some UP concepts (for example, through a short seminar). An executive sponsor should be identified, and discussion of a suitable pilot project initiated.

Then, a pilot project starts. The project should be large enough to be meaningful and interesting, yet not bet-the-bank risky. For example, a 10-person, six-month project.

A UP coach should be responsible for leading the definition of the Development Case, and its refinement during the elaboration phase. Ideally, the coach should be a hands-on developer during the pilot, so that *eating their own dogfood* is strongly experienced, and the process is realistically refined.

See "Signs the UP "Expert" Is Not an Iterative Expert" on p. 198.

To contrast that, a *worst practice* is if a "Methods and Practices" group within the organization defines how the organization or a project should adopt the UP. "Armchair process engineers" are not helpful, should be avoided, and often superimpose waterfall values on to the UP, or promote excessive workproduct creation. Take advice on what to do or adopt in the UP from hands-on developers and managers doing early UP projects, in collaboration with a UP coach participating and developing as well. If corporate process engineers are involved in UP adoption recommendations, they should discover and refine recommendations by serving as hands-on developers during pilot projects, rather than by speculation.

A related worst practice is to attempt to fit the UP into the organization's existing concepts and workproduct vocabulary. For example, taking the organization's current lifecycle phases, and believing the UP phases fit within them, or are equal to them. They won't be, and it usually leads to waterfall superimposition. It is a similar mistake to rename the UP artifacts (Vision, etc.) to the old names used by the organization. In short, UP adoption is best done by incremental surrender to a new set of ideas and terms, not by dressing up an old horse in new clothes.

There are many possible practices in the UP. Thus, it is useful in the early iterations—assuming a prior culture of low software engineering maturity—to start simple and add some practices as the iterations proceed.

After project completion, assuming it was successful and positive, "in-selling" of the UP practices by the project members or customers themselves to others in the organization is better than promotion by outside consultants or management. For example, a lunchtime session where team members share their experiences, pros and cons, with a wider audience.

Assuming there will be a second generation of UP projects, some of the members from the first generation project will ideally move into process engineering roles, and help coach these new projects. The Development Case from the prior projects should be carried forward as a starting point. Therefore, the adoption spreads incrementally.

Another useful activity is a project retrospective that looks at the refined Development Case and ensures it accurately reflects what worked well, and what didn't.

FACT VERSUS FANTASY

As implied earlier, perhaps the most common fantasy regarding UP adoption is that it is widely being applied in the iterative and adaptive manner its creators intended. Rather, a non-trivial percentage of organizations and consulting companies are incorrectly applying it in a predictive and waterfall spirit, with up-front specifications and planning.

Another fantasy is when the organization purchases many copies of the RUP product for their development staff, and continue with the mistaken belief that the presence of the installed product implies true iterative and evolutionary development is underway.

Another common and related fantasy is when the organization decides to adopt the RUP, thinking it is simply a more detailed, well-defined, and well-documented version of what they already expect in development (e.g., the waterfall), and they do not themselves have to make deep changes in their expectations and behavior. For example, in the RUP, reliable estimates for the entire project are not to be expected until the *end* of elaboration.

Instead, this happens:

> *Memo: Congratulations! We've adopted the UP. Please ensure the requirements are finished for our upcoming UP projects so we can estimate them before moving on to the programming phase.*

STRENGTHS VERSUS "OTHER"

Strengths

❑ Focus on risk- and value-driven priorities.

❑ Emphasizes building a cohesive architecture early, preferring existing components.

❑ Evolutionary and incremental requirements and development, and adaptive behavior.

❑ Well-defined workproducts, offering a common vocabulary.

❑ The guidelines and best practices are a good foundation.

❑ Offers guidance on many disciplines, from requirements to configuration management.

❑ Easily combined with techniques from other methods.

❑ Easily customized; encourages minimal "light" versions.

❑ RUP product has easily accessible useful advice, and standard project templates.

❑ Proven to scale to large or small projects.

❑ Encourages use cases where appropriate.

❑ Widely adopted; hence, learning and consulting resources.

❑ Created with many customers, refined on many projects; not a speculative process.

Other[3]

❑ Many details.

❑ UP phases are often incorrectly applied in a waterfall style.

❑ Minimal attention to the social dynamics and communication aspects of successful and sustainable development practices. Contrast to Scrum and XP.

❑ The RUP product can give the (unintended) impression of promoting a very defined and predictable development pro-

---

3. Could be viewed as a weakness, strength, or deliberate desirable exclusion depending on point of view.

cess, as though software was mass manufacturing rather than new product development.

HISTORY

Some of the roots of the UP/RUP exist in the work of Barry Boehm and his spiral model. Its risk-driven and iterative approach influenced key UP/RUP contributors at Rational Corporation, including Philippe Kruchten, Grady Booch, Mike Devlin, Rich Reitman, and Walker Royce. Indeed, Royce collaborated with Boehm on research, writing, and projects. Boehm's well-known "anchor point" milestones [Boehm96] became the milestones that defined the boundaries between inception, elaboration, and construction. More directly, the Rational team created the UP/RUP based on the Objectory process they acquired from the RUP founder Ivar Jacobson, and taking input from the "Rational Approach" they had developed through the 1980s and 1990s, in collaboration with customers. So, some key architecture was inherited from Objectory. The core initial development was around 1995–98. The chief architect of the UP/RUP was Philippe Kruchten, an experienced architect or process leader on major applications such as the new Canadian air traffic control system, and a well-known architecture thought leader, e.g., [Kruchten95]. Although Rational had *Rational* Unified Process and a commercial product in mind from the start, they also wanted to communicate and promote the idea of a process more public domain and open—a generalized *Unified Process*. This was consistent with their open Unified Modeling Language initiative. Hence, Ivar Jacobson wrote the first book to present this view, *The Unified Software Development Process* (1999). As indicated, the UP included key ideas from Jacobson's Objectory process, and in collaboration with the RUP team he described their evolving process vision.

WHAT'S NEXT?

The next chapter presents Evo, a very early iterative and evolutionary method. After that are two final chapters on practice tips and a FAQ.

RECOMMENDED READINGS

❏ An excellent introduction is *The Rational Unified Process Made Easy* by Per Kroll and Philippe Kruchten.

❏ Another very readable introduction to the RUP is *The Rational Unified Process—An Introduction* by Philippe Kruchten, its lead architect.

❏ *Applying UML and Patterns: An Introduction to OOA/D and the Unified Process* [Larman01] takes a case-study approach to introducing the UP and OOA/D. The concepts and workproducts are introduced incrementally over a series of casestudy iterations.

❏ As a caution, there are a number of so-called UP and RUP texts that give incorrect descriptions.

Worthwhile readings that influenced some UP creators:

❏ "A Spiral Model of Software Development and Enhancement" by Barry Boehm, *ACM SIGSOFT Software Engineering Notes*, August 1986 (the reprint in *IEEE Computer*, May 1988 is often cited). A widely cited paper that describes the spiral model of iterative and risk-driven development.

❏ Tom Gilb's iterative Evo method, described in *Principles of Software Engineering Management*, 1988.

❏ Grady Booch's *Object Solutions—Managing the OO Project*, 1995.

❑ "Anchoring the Software Process" by Barry Boehm, *IEEE Software*, July 1996. Describes the milestones from which the inception, elaboration, and construction phases were inspired.

❑ The PMBOK (www.pmi.org). Some of the Project Management discipline was influenced by the PMBOK.

EVO

There is only one move that really counts: the next one.
—Chess master Jose Capablanca

OVERVIEW

❑ Classification of Evo.

❑ Workproducts, roles, and practices.

❑ Demonstrate Planguage for Evo specifications.

❑ Common mistakes, adoption and process mixtures, strengths and weaknesses.

Evo (short for **Evolutionary Project Management**) is perhaps the oldest IID method with a significant agile and adaptive quality, first taking shape in the 1960s and then published in 1976. Evo emphasizes:

❑ short iterations, with evolutionary delivery each iteration

❑ evolutionary requirements and design

❑ adaptive client-driven or value-driven planning

❑ quantifiable measurements of value and progress

❑ defining all quality requirements with numeric measures

❑ optional use of a language, Planguage, for specifications

METHOD OVERVIEW

Classification

In terms of cycle and ceremony, Evo classification is illustrated in Figure 10.1. For average projects, a common length of a timeboxed iteration is one or two weeks.

Figure 10.1 Evo on the cycles and ceremony scale.

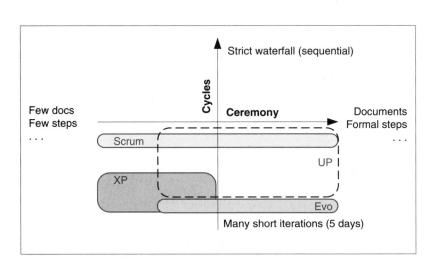

Evo recommends some initial work to define a "critical top ten" list of measurable project objectives, and when specifications are written, Evo encourages unambiguous precision. It also encourages brevity, promoting one page summaries. Evo avoids big up-front specifications, although evolving specs—that could be part of a small or large set—are acceptable if shown to be valuable.

When describing high-level requirements, a structured language call **Planguage**[1] is possible; it encourages clarity, precision, and measurement. If used, it raises Evo on the ceremony scale.

---

1. Rhymes with "language."

Similar to Scrum, it has only a small set of predefined workproducts, such as an **impact estimation table**. Others may be adopted from different methods as needed.

impact estimation table p. 235

In terms of the Cockburn scale, Evo covers the cells shown in Figure 10.2. Since the 1970s, it has been applied on a wide range of projects of many sizes.

Figure 10.2 Evo on the Cockburn scale

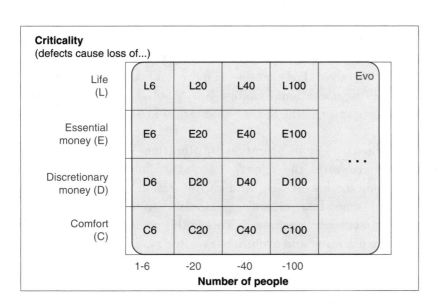

Introduction

Evo [Gilb76, Gilb88] was created by Tom Gilb, a pioneer of iterative and evolutionary development.

I'm including this chapter on Evo—less well known than Scrum, XP, and UP—not only because of its inherent interest, but to balance the historical oversight of this pioneering iterative method and to show that some agile method principles have long been part of Evo, such as a adaptive, client-driven planning of iterations.

Agile Principles p. 28

Gilb has been an advocate for an iterative, light, and adaptive approach to systems development since the 1960s; he first wrote about this in 1976, and his 1988 *Principles of Software Engineering Management* is a milestone early book presenting an evolutionary and iterative process.[2]

Evo's evolutionary emphasis is consistent with the Shewhart/ Deming cycle of Plan-Do-Study-Act (PDSA), and makes reference to PDSA as an underlying conceptual model.

Evo is not just for software. It is applicable in a larger systems engineering context—new software is just one solution to fulfill project objectives. For example, if more education (on the existing software) or operational change has a better value-to-cost ratio than new software, the former approaches are preferred.

It emphasizes—short iteration by iteration—making maximum progress towards the client's current highest-priority requirements, for the lowest cost. And each iteration, delivering into the hands of some stakeholders some useful results, so that early benefit and feedback is achieved. This is the practice of client-driven adaptive planning and evolutionary delivery.

Agile Manifesto p. 28

Evo is pragmatic, has some qualities similar to newer agile methods, is customer focused and results oriented—in the spirit of the Agile Manifesto and Principles. Anything necessary can change (based on the PDSA model) to reach the requirements (function or performance) within the project constraints.

these bold terms are official Evo terms

One of Evo's distinguishing ideas is its emphasis on clearly defining, quantifying, estimating, and measuring the **performance requirements** that need improvement over time.

---

2. Gilb also wrote the first book on software metrics, coining the term in [Gilb76], and continues to refine Evo, e.g., [Gilb03].

Performance includes **quality requirements** such as reliability, **workload capacity requirements** such as throughput, and **resource savings requirements** such as money. The impact of Evo steps on budgeted resource consumption is monitored both in design activity and iteration project management activity.

example requirements
p. 233

Evo requires evaluating proposed solutions for their impact on the state of these requirements, and then actually measuring the impact of those introduced.

> This structured approach and emphasis on improving the *performance* characteristics, rather than just on delivering functionality, is a key part of Evo's unique flavor.

Thus, note that in Evo there is explicit recognition that the requirements delivered may be either functions *or* performance objectives (quality, workload capacity, or resource saving).

Evo expects that each iteration there is a re-evaluation of solutions which yield the highest value to cost ratio, guided by feedback and estimates. As such, Evo requires active stakeholder participation to steer the project each iteration—client-driven adaptive planning. These practices are part of **evolutionary project management**.

adaptive planning
p. 253

Measurable progress is a key principle of Evo, which takes seriously Drucker's maxim: *If you can't measure it, you can't manage it*. Quantifiable measures for performance requirements, and their regular measurement, is required. Unproven improvements, and vague quality goals such as "usable" are discouraged.

In Evo, the value system is that management doesn't schedule the details of the entire project, but they must be able to measure, control, and steer a dynamically evolving project. In other words, adaptive planning.

Planguage p. 231

Evo encourages *precision* and (where relevant) *quantification* in specifications. It does so by encouraging (but not requiring) the use of a compact, structured specification language called Planguage to record requirements—iteratively and incrementally.

It is a misunderstanding to interpret Evo's promotion of high-quality, low-volume critical specifications as an attempt at large up-front analysis. Evo promotes avoiding unnecessary analysis and detail—until it is needed.

inspection p. 230

Inspection—especially of these specifications—is encouraged in Evo as an economical method to improve quality. Indeed, research verifies this [Russell91], and Gilb has been an active promoter of inspections for decades, including co-authoring the text *Software Inspections*.

Evo also encourages a risk-driven approach, as does the Unified Process. As Gilb has aptly said,

> *If you do not actively attack the risks in your project, they will actively attack you.*

LIFECYCLE

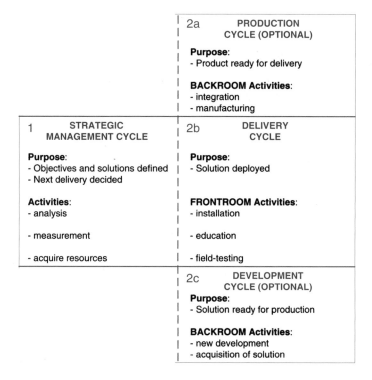

	2a **PRODUCTION CYCLE (OPTIONAL)**	
	Purpose: - Product ready for delivery	
	BACKROOM Activities: - integration - manufacturing	
1 **STRATEGIC MANAGEMENT CYCLE**	**2b** **DELIVERY CYCLE**	
Purpose: - Objectives and solutions defined - Next delivery decided	**Purpose**: - Solution deployed	
Activities: - analysis - measurement - acquire resources	**FRONTROOM Activities**: - installation - education - field-testing	
	2c **DEVELOPMENT CYCLE (OPTIONAL)**	
	Purpose: - Solution ready for production	
	BACKROOM Activities: - new development - acquisition of solution	

1. In the **Strategic Management** cycle, stakeholders decide which solutions ready for delivery (perhaps from the backroom activities) will actually be delivered, usually based on highest value-to-cost and risk. This activity also includes approving changes to objectives and solutions, analyzing feedback measurements, and obtaining resources.

2. These cycles may be concurrent. Ideally, each week something is delivered to stakeholders for use and feedback. In parallel, timeboxed development and production cycles work on incrementally building solutions ready for delivery, although it may be weeks (or longer) before they are eligible

for delivery. The analogy Evo offers is a business with the following organization:

- **Backroom**—products are prepared, and when ready, are "placed on a delivery shelf" available for delivery.

- **Frontroom**—some eligible products are taken off the shelf and delivered to stakeholders (see Figure 10.3).

Figure 10.3 backroom and frontroom delivery

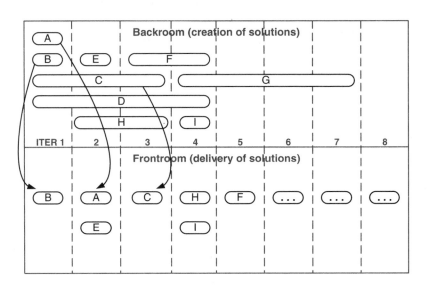

Projects carry on, driven by the goal of maximizing stakeholder value at lowest cost, until there are no more profitable requirements to fulfill.

Niels Malotaux, another Evo consultant, describes the lifecycle of Evo projects from his experience working with clients [Malotaux03]:

1. A project kick-off "Evo Day" that includes the project manager, architect, and all other development team members. Activities include presenting an overview of Evo ideas and practices, explaining the product vision and architectural

ideas, identifying and estimating tasks for the first two-week iteration, and prioritization. Finally, people choose and commit to a set of individual tasks for the next week.

2. Execution of the two-week iteration.[3]

3. On the last day of the iteration:

   - First, the project manager visits each developer and discusses the task results and completion. If things were not completed, there is reflection on the causes.

   - Second, the project manager discusses the project status with stakeholders (e.g., the product manager). Requirements are revisited and re-prioritized. Those chosen for the next iteration are analyzed and specified in greater detail, with measurements and so forth.

   - Third, the project manager and development team generate a new set of tasks. Again, developers choose and commit to the highest-priority tasks for the next week. In a team meeting, experiences of the last iteration may be discussed for process improvement ideas, and the product vision and evolving architecture may again be summarized or refined, to promote a common team goal.

---

3. Malotaux has found that two-week delivery iterations are more sustainable than one-week delivery iterations.

WORKPRODUCTS, ROLES, AND PRACTICES

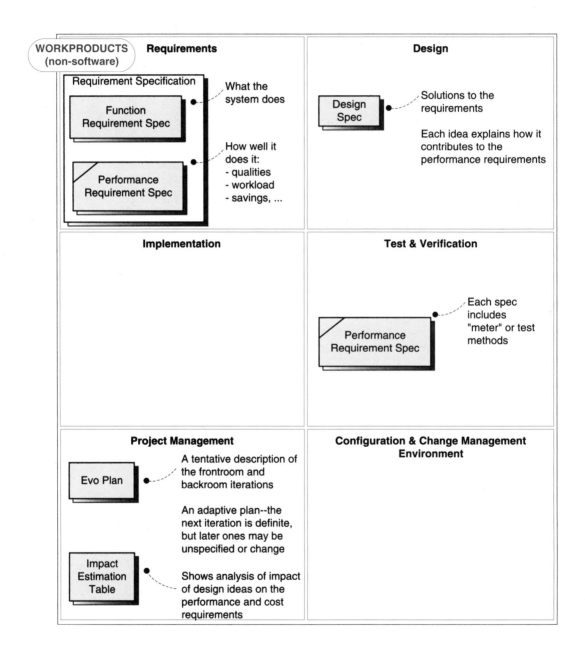

Roles

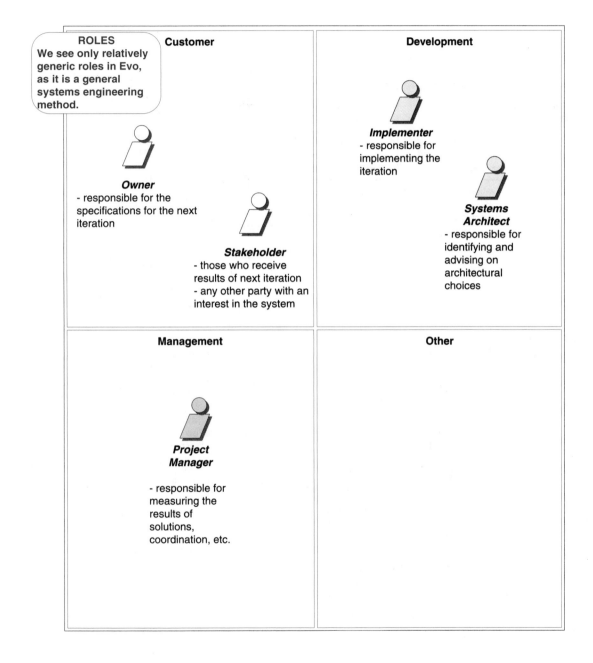

Practices

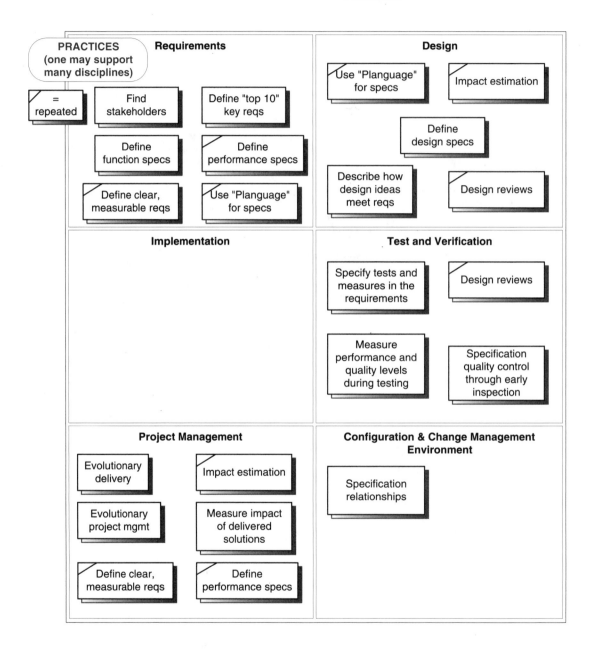

Core Practices

Evo applies to systems engineering in general—not only software development—although software projects are a common domain of application.

As with the other IID methods covered, Evo promotes evolutionary requirements analysis. Yet, when requirements and design ideas are written, Evo requires analysis with respect to a measurable evaluation of the value and impact of requirements and designs. Evo is infused with the practice and value of *measurable, measuring*, and *adaptive response* to the results.

Requirements Practices

Practice	Description
Find stakeholders	Both internal and external, friendly and foe, and across the lifecycle of the system.
Define "top 10" key reqs	Evo, as with other IID methods, encourages an early definition (in Planguage) of "critical top ten" *high-level* requirements. They need not all be decomposed into fine details, although those facing early implementation may be. Each iteration, they are reviewed and refined.
Define function specs	Evo functions describe what the system does. Evo does not promote major up-front detailed functional requirements analysis, but it does require at least clear definitions for the next iteration, *optionally* described in the **Function Requirement Specification**, using Planguage. *example p. 232*

Practice	Description
Define performance specs	Evo promotes describing system performance—how well the system works, its benefits, and how it affects the environment. Written and refined incrementally. Performance attributes are attached to functions. Specifically, Evo performance attributes fall into three categories: 1) quality—how well it performs (usability, reliability, …), 2) workload capacity, and 3) resource savings. The Performance Requirement Specification captures this information using Planguage. *example p. 233*
Define clear, and (where possible) measurable, specs	When specifications are written, do so in a manner and language which exposes and minimizes misunderstanding or ambiguity. The Evo Requirement Specification examples illustrate this. Evo promotes a balance between too little and too much detail in requirements. It wants clarity and detail for the key specifications you have chosen to implement in the next short iteration. Other more speculative or unassigned requirements can wait. Evo's performance specifications should have measurable impact, which should be identified. *examples p. 231*
Use Planguage for specs	Planguage is Evo's structured language for specifications in both requirements and design. It is optional, but encouraged. Evo includes **Planguage templates** for its requirements and design specifications. *notation p. 231, examples p. 231*

Practice	Description
Evolution-ary project manage-ment	Key ideas include: – evolutionary delivery to stakeholders for real use and feedback – small steps (ideally bi-weekly, or between 2–5% of total project financial cost and time) – steps with highest quality-to-cost ratios given highest priority for delivery – the existing system is preferred as the initial system base – feedback modifies future plans and requirements; adaptive planning and evolving specifications – total systems approach; do anything that helps – early results-orientation *discussion p. 227*
Evolution-ary deliv-ery	Evolutionary delivery emphasizes delivering a partial solution into production early, in order to obtain early business value, and feedback to guide and evolve future deliverables. A common delivery frequency in Evo is weekly, or more specifically, every 2–5% of duration and budget. In Evo, the solution chosen for delivery in the next iteration is based on highest value-to-cost ratio and early risk reduction. Each iteration's solution can be of a different type. For example, within a project to replace an older mainframe payroll application, early deliverables could be quick-fix operational changes in the existing system, or adding a Web-based front end to the old system, while work on the new system is underway in the backroom. *discussion p. 227*

Practice	Description
Measure impact of delivered solutions	Evo embraces Shewhart and Deming's core principle of improvement: PDSA. Plus, Drucker's maxim that you can't manage what you can't measure. The *study* step requires measuring, each iteration, the effect of the solution on the objectives. This data is used to help drive evolutionary project management (*act* in response to *study*), iteration by iteration. *Evo plan table p. 229*

Design Practices

Practice	Description
Define design specs	Design ideas are also recorded in Planguage, in the **Design Specification**, and are incrementally evolved, as with requirements specs. *example p. 234*
Impact estima-tion	A method to numerically analyze and compare the effectiveness of design ideas to meet cost and performance requirements—the qualities, workload capacity, and resource savings. The results are expressed in an **Impact Estimation Table**. *example p. 235*
Describe how design ideas meet reqs	The design specifications in Evo should explain why and to what degree they fulfill the requirements. This information is used in impact estimation, and discourages "resume-driven design" in which over-engineered or unfocused designs arise that are not really pertinent to business goals and value. *example p. 234*

Test and
Verification
Practices

Practice	Description
Specify tests and measures in the reqs	The *study* step in Plan-Do-Study-Act step requires measurements or **meters**, in Evo terms. Although new meters can always be adopted, Evo recommends that during performance analysis, the meters for that performance attribute be defined, within the Performance Requirement Specification. *example p. 233*
Specification quality control through early inspection	When goals or specifications are written, research shows that defects and misunderstanding are likely. Research also shows that early inspection is a powerful, cheap tool to reduce those defects. Note that **specification defects** have a precise meaning in Evo: failure to observe a formal, written, required specification rule. Gilb is an expert in the effective use of inspection—which is *not* the same as informal review. The Evo quality control practice includes *sampling*, and application of the **Defect Detection Process**, and **Defect Prevention Process**. *details p. 230*

Configuration &
Change
Management

Practice	Description
Specification relationships	The Planguage specification templates contain relationship sections to support requirements traceability. *example p. 234*

Evolutionary Project Management

As with Scrum, XP and UP, Evo's project management philosophy is adaptive rather than predictive planning. And, as with the other

adaptive planning p. 253

methods, there is still attention to the long-term vision, objectives, and a robust architecture. Some controlling principles:

- ❏ **Financial Control**—An iteration should be between 2–5% of the total initial financial budget before delivering some measurable results. This excludes larger capital costs that must be incurred in an iteration, such as buying a server, as these are "backroom" expenses.

- ❏ **Deadline Control**—A delivery (or frontroom) iteration should be between 2–5% of total project time, with a lower-bound of one or two weeks. This leads to the official Evo rule of thumb of one-week iterations for a one-year project. The Evo consultant Niels Malotaux has found two-week delivery iterations are more sustainable than one week.

- ❏ **Value Control**—Choose design ideas for the next iteration that deliver the best stakeholder value for costs.

With these control guidelines, the next iteration is chosen in response to the latest measurements and evolving understanding of the requirements. A misstep that doesn't deliver expected value consumes no more than (say) 2% of resources.

Future iterations may be tentatively assigned to specific design ideas, and ordered with respect to dependencies, but Evo encourages only very light investment in this kind of predictive planning, as it is central to Evo to adapt the plan at each step.

impact estimation table p. 235

Unless there is a specific stakeholder request for the next iteration, Evo recommends the use of impact estimation table analysis to choose design ideas for the next step.

For tracking and adapting, Evo also recommends the use of an impact table to record the results of delivered solutions, and to indicate the steps of the Evo plan. See Table 10.1 for a simplified example after the first iteration.

Target Requirements	Iteration 1 (plan, actual)	Iteration 2	Cumulative to date
Responsive Browsing	5%, 2%[a]	10%, __	2%
System Reliability	10%, 5%	20%, __	5%
Capital Costs	0%, 0%	5%, __	0%
Development Costs	2%, 2%	2%, __	2%

Table 10.1 simplified Evo plan and results table

the capitalization in Evo implies these are terms defined in Planguage elsewhere

a. the percentage of the final target

Regarding evolutionary delivery: A common Evo project management question is, "If I'm making a new plane (for example), how can I deliver it for use by stakeholders in weekly increments?" Although evolutionary delivery of software is often possible—such as bi-weekly refinement to a Web site, or new updates which can be downloaded—this of course will not apply to new products with long development lead times. In this case, Evo's approach is to work on their development in the *backroom*. It could be months before something from the backroom is available for delivery. Meanwhile, Evo still requires that *something* of measurable value be delivered to stakeholders each *frontroom* iteration (e.g., every two weeks). For example, early documentation samples, improvements to the existing system or operational environment, and so forth.

backroom / frontroom
p. 218

The last point underlines Evo's total systems approach: Do anything that helps. It is not limited to new software or hardware constuction. Gilb believes there is an expensive and risky tendency to avoid looking at the existing system (when there is one) for the desired improvements—sometimes due to technologists' delight in new technologies—and thus he promotes in Evo a preference for considering the existing system as the base for improvement.

Specification Quality Control (SQC) Through Early Inspection

When specifications are created (iteratively), Evo recommends the use of classic systems engineering process control through sampling and inspection. Evo promotes defect removal in specs, done with agility, through its Defect Detection Process and Defect Prevention Process.

Evo's SQC draws from IBM's research and practice [e.g., MJHS90], and Gilb's experience; he is co-author of *Software Inspection* (which emphasizes specification inspection).

A key idea in SQC is that specifications are not informally inspected for any kind of fault; rather, there is only a search for defects—meaning a violation of a written rule from a rule set or checklist that the "checker" is working against. Here's a simplified defect rule set[4]:

- ❏ **Clear**—They must be unambiguously clear to the intended readers.

- ❏ **Scale**—Performance and cost requirements must specify a scale of measure to define the concept.

Other key practices in SQC include:

- ❏ Two to five checkers for an inspection.

- ❏ Specification pages are *sampled* for inspection; the entire document is not checked. If the sampled defect level is above a threshold, the specification is not released for use.

- ❏ The checkers do not volunteer solution or correction advice to the author. They only note issues. It is up to the author to determine solutions or take the initiative to ask the checkers for suggestions.

---

4. Adapted from [Gilb03].

Defect *prevention* in Evo is a process improvement activity that comes from collecting inspection data, reflecting on the results, and experimenting with changes in source workproduct creation.

Planguage

Planguage is Evo's compact specification language. Figure 10.4 shows common notation for one partial specification.

examples: See "Workproducts" on p. 231.

Figure 10.4 Planguage

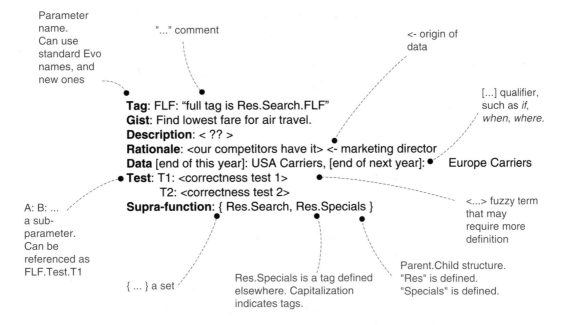

Parameter name. Can use standard Evo names, and new ones

"..." comment

<- origin of data

[...] qualifier, such as *if, when, where.*

Tag: FLF: "full tag is Res.Search.FLF"
Gist: Find lowest fare for air travel.
Description: < ?? >
Rationale: <our competitors have it> <- marketing director
Data [end of this year]: USA Carriers, [end of next year]: ● Europe Carriers
● **Test**: T1: <correctness test 1>
　　　T2: <correctness test 2>
Supra-function: { Res.Search, Res.Specials }

A: B: ...
a sub-parameter. Can be referenced as FLF.Test.T1

{ ... } a set

Res.Specials is a tag defined elsewhere. Capitalization indicates tags.

<...> fuzzy term that may require more definition

Parent.Child structure. "Res" is defined. "Specials" is defined.

Workproducts

Full description of Evo's workproducts and how they can be expressed in Planguage is beyond the scope of this introduction. Nevertheless, the following examples provide a sample of Evo's flavor. More detailed examples are given than for the

Scrum, XP, and UP chapters, as Evo examples are less well-known and less widely available.

Planguage specifications are incrementally developed over the iterations, and only to the extent that doing so adds value.

Function Requirement Specification

Individual functions are recorded in an Evo Function Specification, using Planguage. These could be a high-level top-ten list of functions, or detailed and decomposed functions. The following example illustrates standard parameters (e.g., "Gist") from the Evo Planguage template. Some statements are purposefully undefined, both for brevity and to emphasize the normal process of partial and evolving specifications in Evo. All capitalized tag elements (e.g., Call Center) refer to other specifications previously defined, probably hyperlinked and clickable. Observe that opinions or "facts" in a specification are sourced to a party; Evo expects claims to have some substantiation, or at least explicit acknowledgment that they are wild guesses.

Planguage
p. 231

Tag: <u>FLF</u>:
Type: Function Specification
======= Basic Information =================
"version, status, owner, stakeholders are elided"
Gist: Find lowest fare for air travel.
Description: <input: dates, airports, carriers. output: flights sorted by cost>

Relationships: Evo supports requirements traceability in this section.

============= Relationships ===============
Supra-functions: Res.Search
Sub-functions: none
Is Impacted By: { Call Center, Web Front End }
Linked To: Supports: Res.Booking

Measurement: Goals in Evo should be testable and measurable.

============= Measurement ===============
Test: T1: <correctness test 1>
============= Priority and Risk Management ==

Rationale: <Our competitors have it> <- Marketing Director
Assumptions:
A1 [before end of next year]: Competitor X doesn't upgrade
A2: < ?? >
Dependencies: Res.DB
Risks: R2, R6
Priority: Must be in first public release <- Marketing Director
============= Specific Budgets =============
Financial Budget: < ?? >

Performance Requirement Specification

Individual performance requirements (quality, workload capacity,
resource saving) are recorded in the Planguage form shown in this
example.

Tag: Responsive Browsing:

Type: Workload Capacity Requirement: Response:
Budget: < ?? >
============= Basic Information ========
"version, status, owner, stakeholders are elided"
Ambition: <Many> Res.Users with <acceptable> response time.

============= Measurement ===========
Scale: Average HTTP response time in seconds
Meter: Automated HTTP server monitor
============= Targets ===============

*Measurement:
Illustrating the
quantifiable emphasis
in Evo.*

Goal
[First Release]: response under 3 seconds for up to 1,000 requests
per second <- Marketing,
[Second Release]: response under 2 seconds for up to 1,000
requests per second <- Marketing
============= Constraints ==============
Fail [First Release]: response over 6 seconds <- Marketing
============= Benchmarks ===============

Past [Old System, last year]: response under 5 seconds for up to 1,000 requests per second <- ABC Research Report

Record [CompetitorY, this year]: response under 1 second for up to 3,000 requests per second <- ABC Research Report

============= Relationships ===============

Is Impacted By: Res.DB.Response <- DBA

Impacts: Usability

============= Priority and Risk Management ==

Value <this level will retain 95% of first-time users> <-Marketing "assumptions, dependencies, etc."

Relationships: Illustrates the performance requirement relates to other performance requirements (or perhaps, directly to functions).

Design Specification

Design ideas are expressed in the Planguage template form demonstrated in this next example.

Tag: Server Cluster:

Type: Design Idea

============ Basic Information ==============

"version, status, owner, stakeholders are elided"

Gist: Cluster of 10 application servers with an IP sprayer.

Description: < ?? >

============= Design Relationships ===========

Design Constraints: { Use Moon Spark 5000s, Use Java Technologies, Use Open Source }

Sub-Designs: < replication, fail over >

============== Impacts Relationships ==========

Impacts [Functions]: { Res.Search, Res.Transaction, Res.Browse }

Impacts [Intended]: { [Good] Responsive Browsing, [Good] System Reliability, <more> }

Impacts [Cost]: { Operations Budget, [if not open source] Development Budget }

Impacts [Other Designs]: { Deployment Model, Data Model }

Value: < meeting responsiveness and reliability goals will maintain customer retention at 95% <- Marketing Director >

Impacts: design ideas must be connected to functions and / or performance requirements

== Impact Estimation of Design on Selected Requirements ==

Tag: Responsive Browsing

Type: Performance Requirement Cross Reference

Scale: Average HTTP response time in seconds

Scale Impact: under 3 seconds for up to 1,000 requests per second

Scale Uncertainty: ± 1 second <- Jill Jones

Percentage Impact: [if Use Moon Spark 5000s] 100%[5]

Percentage Uncertainty: ± 33%

Evidence: CompetitorX has this configuration and response

Source: Jill Jones (Chief Architect)

Credibility: 0.5 as Jill worked for CompetitorX on similar project

Tag: System Reliability

"repeat analysis using the above set of parameters"

============== Priority and Risk Management ====

"assumptions, dependencies, risks, priority, issues are elided"

Impact Estimation: a design idea should contribute to performance objectives. Its impact on each is analyzed.

Note that claims are sourced, and uncertainty and credibility estimated.

Impact Estimation Table

This tool is used in Evo to analyze the impact of alternative (or complementary) design ideas on performance requirements. Barring "obvious" priorities for the next iteration as indicated by stakeholders, this table is used to rationally choose the set of design ideas to implement next, based on the best benefit-to-cost ratio. Note that the horizontal and vertical summing of impact percentages do not always accurately predict a result; they may or may not provide a sense of aggregate impact. For example, can one sum the *Responsive Browsing* impact of both a server cluster and high-performance hardware? Perhaps...

---

5. From some baseline (such as "Past") in the requirement.

Table 10.2 simplified
impact estimation table

Design Ideas -> Requirements	Server Cluster	High-performance hardware	Sum of Impact[a]
Responsive Browsing Baseline: 5 sec. Goal: 3 sec.			
Scale and % impact[b]	3 ± 1 sec. 100% ± 50	4 ± 1 sec. 50% ± 50	150% ± 100
Evidence and Credibility	CompetitorX has this configuration and response <- Jill Jones 0.2	Moon Microsystems has customers achieving this <- Moon Sys Eng. 0.1	
System Reliability Baseline: 3000 hours MTBF. Goal: 3500			
Scale and % impact	3200 ± 200. 40% ± 40	3100 ± 200. 20% ± 40	60% ± 80
Evidence and Credibility	CompetitorX has this config and "suspected" reliability <- Jill Jones 0.2	Moon Microsystems has customers achieving this <- Moon Sys Eng. 0.1	
Sum of Impact[c]	140%	70%	
Capital/Dev Cost Baseline: $0 USD. Budget: $200K			
Amount and %	$20K ± 10K. 10% ± 5	$100K ± 10K. 50% ± 5	60% ± 10
Evidence and Credibility	Bob's friend guesses this cost on another project <- Bob Bones 0.1	Moon firm quote <- Moon Sales Rep. 1.0	
Benefit-to-Cost Ratio[c]	14 (140% / 10%)	1.4 (70% / 50%)	
Impact Credibility Adjust Cost Credibility Adjust	0.84 (14 * .3 *.2)[d] 0.08 (0.84 * .1)	0.01 (1.4 * .1* .1) 0.01 (0.01 * 1.0)	

a. Sum of impacts on a requirement may or may not be cumulative.
b. The % impacts are with respect to the baseline.
c. The sum of impacts of one design idea may or may not be cumulative. The total may or may not work as an estimate for comparison.
d. Multiplying probabilities is a heuristic to reduce total to a reasonable magnitude.

There is a lighter alternative (for prioritization) to these tables that Evo also offers: the use of simple benefit-cost estimates: Each design idea is given a 0-9 ranking for both benefit and cost. Ideally, this is in a group "delphi" ranking session. The best benefit-to-cost ratio ideas are implemented next.

Other Practices and Values

Evo has many detailed practices, tips, and guidelines. A sample of points:

- ❑ **Open-ended architecture**—To support evolving or changing designs, and evolutionary delivery, Evo encourages open-ended architectures that encourage easier extension. That is, at predictable variation points, some kind of protection is introduced, such as an interface, data-driven declarations, and so forth.

- ❑ **Safety factor**—The estimated impact of a design should deliver an estimated impact with a defined safety factor, default factor 2 (200% over the target level from the baseline).

- ❑ **Client-driven planning**—If you are uncertain which step to do next, ask your dominant stakeholder.

- ❑ **Whatever adds value**—Rather than a "we are building it" paradigm, focus on "what can I do for my stakeholders next week?" The techniques (such as Planguage and Impact Estimation) are only support to keep this focus, and should not get in the way.

VALUES

Evo's key values include:

- ❑ Learn rapidly by realistic measurement.

- ❏ Deliver real value to stakeholders early, frequently, at every step.

- ❏ Be humble about complex systems: simplify and attack problems one small step at a time

- ❏ Delegate power to the ultimate user, by focusing on end results and not methods and well-intended bureaucracy.

- ❏ Admire, applaud and reward a team based on the flow of measurable results: stakeholder value versus costs.

COMMON MISTAKES AND MISUNDERSTANDINGS

or, How to Fail with Evo

Error: Adoption mistakes—Lack of management support. Lack of training in concepts and methods. Lack of clear quantified management objectives as the basis for evolving towards Evo methods. Lack of clarity about the management objectives of using the method — and how to measure these improvements in practice. Lack of a good successful pilot project to prove it works in your environment. Lack of dramatic motivation to change from older methods.

Error: Lack of focus on results—Self-explanatory.

Error: Giving up or not believing short iterations are possible—Giving up too easily when managers or engineers claim they cannot find small early steps (they need training, motivation and help). Giving up too early and falling back on old habits.

Error: Lack of management encouragement—When a team starts delivering something of value every short iteration, that's often a revolutionary event. Management needs to praise and encourage this result, rather than take it for granted.

Error: Failing to use value/cost priority—Not choosing solutions based on highest value-to-cost.

Error: Customers not involved—Evo is customer and results-driven; they need to participate in providing feedback on the results of evolutionary deliveries, and in steering the next iteration.

Error: No measurements—It is a mistake to avoid regular measurement of the impact of delivered solutions. Frequent numeric measurement is a significant shift for many managers, but central to Evo.

Error: Iterations too long—Evo frontroom iterations should be 2–5% of total project time, with a lower bound of one or two weeks.

Error: Each iteration does *not* end in a delivery—Evo is about evolutionary delivery on a "weekly" basis to real stakeholders for useful results, even when backroom development may take months.

Error: Predictive planning—It is a misunderstanding to create, *at the start of the project*, a believable plan laying out exactly how many iterations there will be for a long project, their lengths, and what will occur in each. This is contrasted with Evo or adaptive planning. The Evo team and customer plans the next iteration, and then planning adapts iteration by iteration, based on measurement and feedback.

SAMPLE PROJECTS

Gilb's view is that any project applying IID and evolutionary delivery is an example of Evo. This of course covers thousands of projects. For an early example, the mid-1970s LAMPS project described on p. 83 is considered an Evo project in Gilb's classification.

PROCESS MIXTURES

None of the other IID methods covered emphasize weekly evolutionary delivery, and related Evo project management measurement.

Evo + Scrum

Most Scrum practices are compatible with Evo. The Scrum meeting, common project room, and demos to external stakeholders at the end of each iteration enhance Evo's feedback goals. The Scrum backlog and progress tracking approaches are also applicable additions. Scrum does not discuss specific specification methods, and thus Evo's Planguage is still applicable.

Evo's measurement emphasis is compatible; indeed, Jeff Sutherland, one of the Scrum creators, takes a strong interest in measurement when applying Scrum.

Scrum's unchanging 30-day iteration length is not consistent with Evo—Evo iterations are usually shorter.

Evo + UP

The UP is especially for software development, and usually for projects involving multiple iterations before production delivery. Consequently, the UP could be applied to Evo backroom development work. However, Evo's evolutionary delivery and project management styles are not exactly in the same spirit as the UP, although both share an interest in early identification and mitigation of risks.

The UP has its own set of workproducts and approach to requirements capture: the Use-Case model (and thus, use cases), and Supplementary Specification for description of functions, features, and non-functional requirements. Evo Planguage elements, such as the Performance Requirement Specification, may be used within the UP Supplementary Specification.

Evo's measurement emphasis is compatible or acceptable with the UP.

The upper bound of UP's 2–6 week iteration length is not consistent with Evo—too long.

Evo + XP

XP values and spirit regarding specifications are not exactly compatible with Evo. XP's value of avoiding written or precise requirements, and preferring oral communication between developers and requirement donors is different than Evo's emphasis that when a specification is required, it be written with clarity and measurable qualities. However, Evo allows a scaling down of precision on small projects; the important Evo point is value to the client, and precision is an optional means to that end.

On the other hand, many XP development practices may be consistently applied with Evo, such as test-driven development, pair programming, and so forth.

XP's emphasis on early results and customer-driven adaptive planning is also consistent with Evo. The XP practice of stand-up meeting, common project room, and whole team together supports Evo's feedback goals.

XP's 1–3 week iteration length is consistent with Evo.

ADOPTION STRATEGIES

As always, coaching by an experienced method expert on the first project is recommended. Evo is results oriented, so not much is sacred in its adoption—other than frequent evolutionary delivery and project management.

Clear, precise, and measurable (though evolutionary) requirements are not that common or enthusiastically developed. One approach to motivate their adoption is to focus early on evolutionary delivery, which of course demands understanding the design ideas, requirements, alternatives, and priorities. Thus, after a few iterations, the participants themselves will better appreciate the value in adopting something like Planguage and greater requirements precision, in order to guide choosing their next step and evaluating the results of the prior one.

Gilb recommends the use of pilot projects to demonstrate the value and viability of Evo.

FACT VERSUS FANTASY

Impact estimation tables are not consistently used by Evo adopters. This may be due to their requiring more analysis and complexity than the priority problem often warrants. As mentioned, a less detailed 0–9 scale for benefit and costs ratios is an Evo alternative.

One-week evolutionary delivery iterations are difficult to sustain; two weeks is easier.

Gilb reports that a significant number of Evo adopters find quantification of their most critical objectives difficult without some coaching.

Evo's PDSA emphasis requires not only estimation and planning, but measuring. Yet, this last step is often dropped under the pressure of work, which of course makes Evo planning less useful.

STRENGTHS VERSUS "OTHER"

Strengths

❏ Early, visible results; frequent delivery to stakeholders.

❏ Measuring the impact of solutions and guiding improvement by measurement data, rather than only by informal guess.

❏ Customer participation and steering.

❏ Worker engagement and satisfaction from seeing their solutions quickly implemented.

❏ Planguage is a simple and compact approach to requirements specification.

❏ Evolutionary and incremental requirements and development, and adaptive behavior.

❏ Emphasizes quality through proven inspection methods and through continual process improvement based on measurement and data.

❏ Practices from other methods (e.g., Scrum or XP) easily included.

Other[6]

❏ Management and requirements overhead of estimating impacts and measuring results.

---

6. Could be viewed as a weakness, strength, or deliberate desirable exclusion depending on point of view.

❏ As with Scrum, minimal guidance within software-specific disciplines, as Evo is a general project management and systems engineering method.

HISTORY

Gilb started some Evo practices in the early 1960s, while consulting (and living) primarily in Europe. In 1976, he wrote about iterative development, evolutionary delivery, and evolutionary project management in his book, *Software Metrics*. This was rather unique in a period dominated by waterfall lifecycle promotion. In the late 1970s, he authored a series of column articles in *Computer Weekly UK* that reiterated and further explored these practices; these articles are arguably the earliest popular press on the subject of IID and adaptive, evolutionary development.

In April 1981, Gilb published "Evolutionary Development" in *ACM Software Engineering Notes*, and in July 1985 published "Evolutionary Delivery versus the 'Waterfall Model'" *ACM Sigsoft Software Requirements Engineering Notes*. These are some of the earliest ACM or IEEE publications related to the subject of IID and adaptive, evolutionary development.

In the 1980s he was also exposed to the work of Deming, and realized that Deming's values and Shewhart's PDSA model captured the intent of Evo.

As mentioned in the introduction, in 1988 Gilb published *Principles of Software Engineering Management*, a milestone early book describing an adaptive, iterative, and evolutionary process, well ahead of its time.

Since then, his early work and Evo have influenced many other methods: XP, Scrum, and the UP all owe debts to Gilb's work. The popular book *Rapid Development* [McConnell96]—which examines many key best practices in software development—cites Gilb's work in 14 sections.

WHAT'S NEXT?

The next chapter examines some method practices in more detail, and introduces other common tips. The final chapter is a FAQ.

RECOMMENDED READINGS

❑ Gilb's 1988 *Principles of Software Engineering Management* is an important step in studying Evo. His 2003 *Competitive Engineering* presents updated refinements, and the details of Planguage; it is the current basis for studying Evo.

❑ *Software Projects: Evolutionary versus Big-bang Delivery*, Felix Redmill, John Wiley & Sons, 1997. Redmill learned Evo from Gilb in the 1980s and managed projects with it. This book describes his experience and lessons learned.

❑ Free online articles and draft books by Gilb—on Evo subjects—are available at his Web site: *www.gilb.com*.

❑ Useful elaboration and refinements for Evo are also available for download from Niels Malotaux at *www.malotaux.nl*.

Supporting or related texts that are recommended include:

❑ *Software Inspection*, by Tom Gilb and Dorothy Graham.

❑ *Out of the Crisis*, by W. Edwards Deming.

❑ *The Deming Management Method*, by W. Edwards Deming and Mary Walton.

❑ *Quality Is Free: The Art of Making Quality Certain*, by Philip Crosby.

PRACTICE TIPS

Prediction is very difficult, especially if it's about the future.
—Niels Bohr

OVERVIEW

❑ Tips for agile or iterative projects, organized into categories such as Project Management and Requirements.

– For example, *Project Management*: Multisite iterative development. *Environment*: Continuous integration. *Test*: Test-driven development.

What practices are applied when working on iterative and agile projects? Many answers are found in the method-specific chapters. This chapter offers other miscellaneous "tips of the trade" and adds detail to some mentioned elsewhere. Regarding the scope and detail: This chapter (and book) is an introduction.

Naturally, many questions arise when first adopting an iterative method, such as:

❑ How does one plan the iterations?

❑ How does continuous integration work?

❑ What does test-driven development look like?

The answers are organized in common discipline categories: *project management*, *environment*, *requirements*, and *test*.

PROJECT MANAGEMENT

This section summarizes some tips related to iteration timing, planning, tasks, tracking, and other project management practices to support iterative or agile development.

There is a trend in some of these tips: The manager is not alone in doing the work of planning, scheduling, estimating, tracking, and so forth. In agile development, it is more of a team sport.

Multiteam or Multisite Early Development

For projects that will be composed of multiple teams, perhaps spread across different locations, consider doing the early iterations at one location, in one common project room, with a small group ideally composed of one or two skilled representatives from each of the subteams. During these iterations, there is an emphasis on requirements analysis and development to discover and build the core architecture of the system—the foundation. Major components, and their collaborations and interfaces are ideally clarified through early programming and testing rather than just speculative design. If UP is your method, this covers the inception and elaboration phase.

In this way, the early project benefits from the close communication, collaboration, common vision, and technical strength of the initial group.

Once the core is built, the representatives return to their respective locations, form larger teams, and the remaining work is done in parallel with multiple subteams. Each representative has developed a clearer picture of the vision and architecture, and can better convey and maintain that for the remainder of the project. Further, each acts as a liaison to the other teams. Also, after having spent some close time with the other subteam leaders, there is

improved communication between the subteams. Figure 11.1 illustrates.

Figure 11.1 multiteam
development

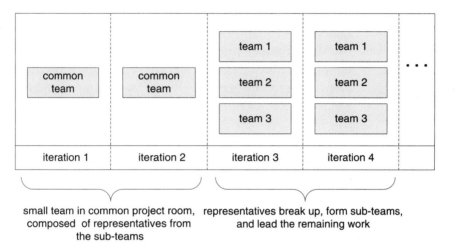

small team in common project room,   representatives break up, form sub-teams,
composed of representatives from   and lead the remaining work
the sub-teams

Difficult Multiteam or Multisite Iteration Planning

It is a worthy goal to have all components, across all subteams or
sites, integrated and tested together to conclude the release of a
common iteration. However, there are times when relaxing this
goal is helpful. For example, consider the example of a multisite
(five sites) research-oriented project spread across 16 time zones,
working on a 3G telephony system that included creation of everything from the 3G handset to the protocol stack [Crocker02].

In this case, due to barriers in time, communication, and the difficult-to-predict research-oriented development, it was seemingly
impossible to get all teams to coordinate and complete all work by
a common iteration end date. For example, one team working on
one layer of the system might need much longer than expected, or

than the other teams, to complete the supporting goals of the iteration.

The successful solution was to establish the rule that at least two of the five teams had to define a common, relatively short iteration with integration between the two (or more) teams, and that no team could go "too long" without participating in a joint iteration. All the subteam project managers and technical leaders would adaptively plan the next iteration. In this way, the product elements were integrated in a series of disjoint iterations. Figure 11.2 illustrates.

Figure 11.2 sub-team iterations

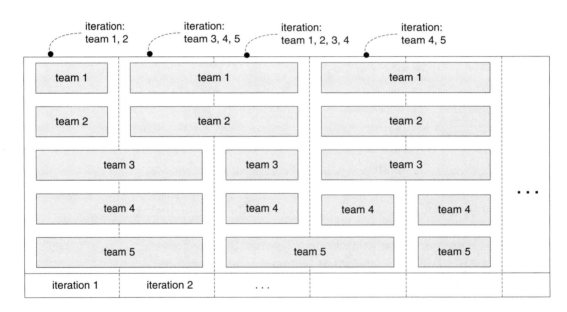

This approach should be the exception rather than the rule. Although helpful for this multisite research-oriented project, the preferred guideline is that all teams work together towards a common goal and integrate on a common iteration end date.

Overlapping or "Pipelining" Activities Across Iterations

Some projects benefit from "pipelining" or overlapping certain activities across iterations, usually requirements analysis and testing [Larman97, JPKP03]. Figure 11.3 illustrates. For example, during iteration N, one or more people are doing requirements analysis for future development in iteration N+1, and a test team is evaluating the release of iteration N–1. In the latter case, defects discovered by the test team are handled in the current iteration if there is planned slack in the iteration schedule for this (and the defect is small), or deferred for a future iteration.

Note that if there is a test team evaluating a prior release (probably for difficult or long-running tests), there should still be plenty of testing for the current release. The release should be as stable and fully tested as possible.

Figure 11.3 pipelining iteration work

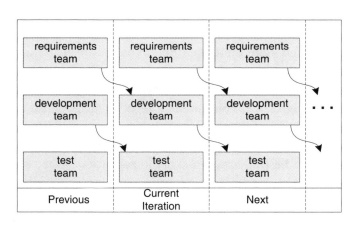

There may be efficiencies with pipelining, but not all projects can or should apply this approach. Furthermore, although the example shows pipelining of both requirements and test, it may of course be applied with only one activity. It is more appropriate for larger projects, those with offsite requirements donors, or those with long, complex testing that must be performed by a separate team. Examples of complex testing includes labor-intensive manual or semi-manual GUI testing, and memory-leak stress testing where the system needs to run for many hours or days to discover subtle leaks.

Pipelining has a seductive aura of efficiency when you look at a chart such as Figure 11.3, but as the agile methods stress, projects and people are not machines or computer processors.[1] There are soft issues that carry potential pitfalls [Kruchten00a].

One pitfall is the slippery slope of overlap and focus. It may succeed for requirements and test, but can be part of a trend to a more general lack of current-iteration focus in other disciplines, such as programming. Working on past or future iteration "stuff" is not in the spirit of "let's work together on the next short step."

Another, related pitfall is a reduction in synergy, cross-discipline insight, "whole team together," "generalists over specialists," "customer close to developers," feedback, and adaptation—all qualities promoted by the agile methods. Pipelining can re-introduce some of the deficiencies of a sequential waterfall model. It requires separation of people by discipline. For example, the developer may no longer be involved in requirements analysis (such as at a requirements workshop), yet research shows this is desirable [KC94]. In a degenerate case, if design work was also pipelined, the programmer would not be the designer. This latter situation is especially inconsistent with agile and adaptive development, where the design emerges from an interplay of some up-front speculation or design thought, combined with programming and testing to prove, disprove, and adapt the evolving system. The programmer and designer must be one and the same, or where design specialization is required—such as in database or UI design—the programmer and designer need to collaborate within the current iteration on

---

1. The term itself was inspired by processor architectures.

common goals. In general, pipelining can reduce interaction and feedback between the disciplines and people; that's undesirable.

In conclusion, it's a double-edged sword.

Rolling Wave Adaptive versus Predictive Planning

One of the big ideas of agile and iterative development is to adapt based on feedback, and this is not only with respect to requirements and design, but also the plan or schedule.

This is the topic of **adaptive planning** versus **predictive planning** [Fowler01]. Adaptive planning in IID methods is a refinement of the well-known **rolling wave planning** concept—more on this later. It implies that there isn't a detailed plan of all the future iterations. There is no fixed plan of how many iterations there will be, how long they are, or what will happen in each. In contrast, predictive planning implies there would be such an iteration-by-iteration plan to the project end.

This does not mean there are no large-grained milestones with dates, or no thinking ahead. In adaptive planning, there *are* milestones with dates, (or at least, there can be) but the path of iterations to those milestones is left flexible or adaptive. And, the milestones themselves may change if in the best interest of the project.

Rolling wave or adaptive planning is a key idea in agile methods. Comments on why this is a good idea—in fact, a better approach than a detailed speculative schedule—will come later, but first an example to help clarify the ideas:

Imagine that after two short exploratory iterations (that include programming and test) into a project, there is enough requirements clarification to be able to say with some certainty that the overall high-level requirements (e.g., use cases and features) are R1, R2, …, R20. Plus, there are rough effort estimates for each, and some understanding of their dependencies. Perhaps R2 must be done before R7, and so forth.

At this point, the customers indicate that they would like to see R1 through R10 by roughly mid-project, and the remainder by the end. The customers ask for an estimate of when R1–R10 can be finished. The customers may be asking for this milestone because of a demo they want to schedule for investors, a trade show, to synchronize with other product development, or simply because they are used to the idea of milestones.

The team does the best it can in estimating R1–R10, and believes it can finish in three months, on July 1, given an estimate of average developer availability. Likewise for R11 to R20, with a completion of September 1. Thus, two milestones have been established, and the team makes a commitment to meet these goals, with an understanding that change is possible later, in light of new insights or priorities. Figure 11.4 illustrates.

Figure 11.4 milestones estimated

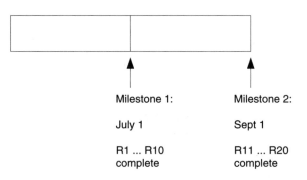

Milestone 1:

July 1

R1 … R10
complete

Milestone 2:

Sept 1

R11 … R20
complete

Note that these milestones are more coarse grained than iterations; there may be many iterations up to the first milestone.

Predictive planning would go further than this, it would speculate a week-by-week or iteration-by-iteration schedule of the path to these milestones. For example, that there will be three iterations before milestone-1, each four weeks long, that R1 and R2 will be done in iteration-1, R3–R5 in iteration-2, and so forth. See Figure 11.5.

Figure 11.5 predictive plan

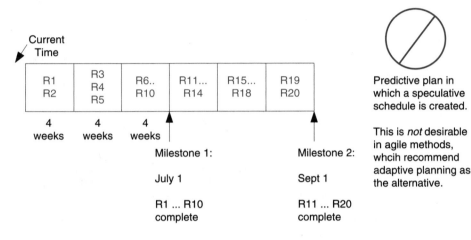

Predictive plan in which a speculative schedule is created.

This is *not* desirable in agile methods, whcih recommend adaptive planning as the alternative.

Rather, in **adaptive planning**—and this is the key point—*we primarily plan in detail for just the next iteration*. This is not an absolute rule. We may see some obvious dependent work to do in the follow-up iteration, or we may know that Jill the database expert will only be available in June, or that the new servers we ordered will arrive July 15. Such presence or absence of resources places obvious constraints on when we schedule certain tasks or requirements. But, all other things being equal, we primarily focus on deciding what to do in the next iteration, and defer making decisions about future iterations, unless obvious or necessary. See Figure 11.6.

Figure 11.6 adaptive plan

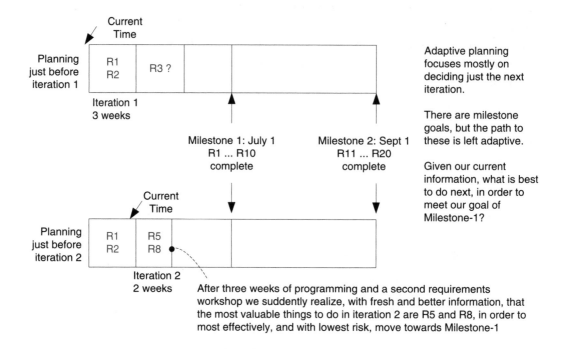

In agile and adaptive planning, the precision is commensurate with the information; the level of detail and commitment to fine-grained scheduling drop as we look further into the future.

Avoiding far-future predictive planning and preferring short-term adaptive planning is not a new or radical idea. It is also called **rolling wave planning** [Githens98], a well-known practice promoted in the PMBOK (Project Management Body of Knowledge) [PMI00], many management courses and texts, and government organizations. That said, there is often a gap between published management recommendations and actual practice or attitudes.

Government oversight agency: *Oh yes, we promote rolling wave planning, as indicated in Standard-773-1. When will the weekly schedule and PERT chart for our new project be finished?*

Regardless, the essence of rolling wave planning is to plan in detail only up to some realistic planning horizon, beyond which things are too speculative. In agile methods, that horizon is the next iteration.

What plan do external stakeholders see? If they want or need to establish milestones, they see a coarse-grained milestone-oriented schedule. A path of iterations to those milestones is not shown.

Finally, to re-emphasize points made before (since this is a common misunderstanding), adaptive planning *does* allow for coarse-grained milestones with dates, and can allow for some distant iteration plans when there are obvious resource constraints.

Benefits of Rolling Wave Adaptive Planning

Why is this useful? Adaptive planning is closer to optimal in terms of working towards milestones; each step can be the most skillful we know how to plan regarding risk, productivity, and effectiveness because each planning step is taken with maximum—and fresh—information. We take a step, and then ask, "Given what we now know, what is the most skillful thing we should do in the next step to work towards our milestone goal?" And repeat.

In contrast, a predictive plan is suboptimal. In fact, it could be close to the worst or most risky possible path to the milestone goal because it is created with the least amount of information, speculating into the far future. The schedule in Figure 11.5 could be a very poor path to the goals; we can't know. It is not wise or useful to believe that five iterations in the future, 17 weeks from today, the best thing we should do is implement requirement R15.

Not only is predictive planning suboptimal with respect to effectiveness and risk, it doesn't account for opportunities. If half-way into the project the marketing manager discovers our competitor is adding the sexy Gromlit feature, a predictive plan does not account for this. Yet, an adaptive plan does; the team can start adding Gromlits the very next iteration. Adaptive plans embrace change and opportunity; predictive plans fight or ignore it.

In addition to supporting adaptation, another key, basic reason for not creating an early detailed schedule is that in evolutionary methods not all the requirement and design details are known near the start of the project. Two weeks after project initiation, you can't plan for use case X in iteration-7 when you don't even know about use case X.

Conclusion

Although rolling wave or adaptive planning has been promoted for years in leading management circles, there are still some inconsistent software project management texts and courses that teach it is ideal to create a detailed predictive schedule or PERT chart of week-by-week activities through to the end of a software project. And, that failing to follow it is a sign of lack of skill on the part of a manager. Ironically, deviating from a speculative plan in response to risks or opportunities is a sensible response, not a failure.

As with the waterfall model, the heart of the problem with predictive planning is that it is misapplied to software projects. It works for mobile phone manufacturing; software is a domain of new product development, not predictable manufacturing.

Planning: Consider Ending on "Wednesday"

If wrapping up an iteration is nontrivial (for example, on larger projects with several subteams), consider making the last Wednesday (or Thursday) rather than Friday the goal date for baselining the release. Although the goal is definitely Wednesday, allow Thursday and Friday as slack days for unanticipated problems.

Thursday and Friday also provide time for group planning of the next iteration, perhaps another requirements workshop, a group iteration assessment or review, a demo to stakeholders, and so forth.

Further, if there is a separate test team that receives the end-of-iteration release (pipeline testing the release of iteration N-1 during iteration N), make Thursday the day when that team expects to start [Blaustein03], again allowing two slack days. This approach decreases the likelihood of working over the weekend to meet a Monday start-of-iteration hard deadline, when everyone is expected to move forward on a new iteration rather than still be working to wrap up the release to hand over to the test team.

Planning: Whole Team Planning Meetings

Agile methods emphasize collaborative planning. An initial release planning meeting and each iteration planning meeting are ideally held with all developers and customers present. If the project is large and composed of subteams, at least include representatives from each subteam.

Planning: Workers Estimate

The agile methods promote the value that the workers doing the work must estimate the work. At the planning meetings, involve the developers in estimation of large-grained requirements that will be allocated to iterations, and also estimation of the related finer-grained tasks. In XP, for example, it is required that the worker who volunteers for a task must be the one who estimates it.

Planning: Improving Estimates with Wideband Delphi

Estimation is a large topic mostly beyond the scope of this introduction. However, in addition to the agile methods practice of workers estimating their tasks, it is worth considering the technique of **Wideband Delphi** for large or valuable projects [Wiegers00]. This is an iterative, adaptive method (hence its inclusion in this chapter) complementary to other estimation methods.[2] The practice is common in successful outsourcing companies whose estimates have low variance to final actuals.

A key point is that Wideband Delphi is used to *complement* an existing estimation method, not replace it. Here are the steps:

1. Kickoff Meeting: Get at least three people (or three pairs) together to estimate. Discuss the source documents and project for which an estimate is to be made. Discuss the units of estimation. End the meeting.

2. Estimation: Then, each person (or pair) creates estimates. This could take minutes or days, depending on the scope. Any specific estimation technique can be used: COCOMO, micro-estimation, etc.

   – Each person/pair creates three estimates, sometimes called the PERT estimates: 1) most likely, 2) optimistic, 3) pessimistic.

3. Meeting: Each estimator gives their estimates to a facilitator, who displays them (see Figure 11.7), with averages. In the purest form of this method, the owners of the estimates are not revealed to the whole group, to reduce the influence of personality or seniority. Finally, each estimator discusses their insights, problems, and assumptions.

---

2. First developed as the Delphi method at RAND Corp in 1948, and refined as Wideband Delphi by Barry Boehm in the early 1970s.

4. Repeat steps 2 and 3 at least once.

   – Note that this is iterative estimation refinement. The point of this step is to provide the feedback to drive adaptation and improvement in the next iteration of estimation.

5. Calculate the final numbers with the following PERT formula, using the averages from the final cycle.

$$Estimate = \frac{Optimistic + Pessimistic + 4MostLikely}{6}$$

$$LikelyDeviation = \frac{Pessimistic - Optimistic}{6}$$

Note that Wideband Delphi sits on top of any other estimation method, improving it through multiple participants, feedback, and iterative refinement.

Figure 11.7 Wideband Delphi sample data

	(person days) Pesimistic	Most Likely	Optimistic
Round 1			
estimates	(900, 1000, 950)	(800, 900, 850)	(700, 800, 800)
averages	950	850	767
Round 2			
estimates	(1000, 1100, 1050)	(900, 950, 875)	(800, 900, 850)
averages	1050	908	850

Planning: Multiple Iteration Planning Meetings

As discussed, agile methods apply adaptive planning; thus, at each iteration (usually near its end), there is an iteration planning meeting for the subsequent iteration, during which it is decided what to do in the next, followed by detailed task generation.

Planning: Agile Task Generation

During each iteration planning meeting, the team generates finer-grained tasks (for example, in the half-day to two-day range) for the iteration requests. XP promotes the approach of either having the team work together to write these on a whiteboard, or each team member brainstorms tasks and writes them on cards, that are grouped and stuck on a wall. In other words, an "agile" approach to a work breakdown structure is performed.

Re-use is worthwhile here; many tasks repeat across iterations and projects. If the final task list is only handwritten on a wall, consider taking a photo of each version, and share these for inspiration at future planning meetings.

Planning: Don't Forget to Budget for Iteration Overhead Tasks

More frequent risk management, iteration demos, iteration planning meetings, a group iteration assessment, a daily Scrum meeting, some average rate of unexpected defects, infrastructure failures, and so on, all consume time, and need to be reflected in the iteration task list. Managers new to iterative development sometimes miss accounting for these overhead tasks.

Planning: People Estimate Their Time Budget Each Iteration

Timeboxing requires a realistic approach to time management. People have to avoid overcommitting, as there is not much slack. So, it is helpful to calculate personal time budgets—also an XP practice. During each iteration planning, people estimate their total "ideal work hours" or uninterrupted attentive time for project tasks for the iteration. This analysis may take five or ten minutes. A common average is around five hours per day—if it is much higher, be skeptical.

Planning: Volunteering

A simple practice related to commitment, motivation, and job satisfaction is to promote volunteering for tasks rather than task assignment by a manager. This approach is part of XP and Scrum.

During the iteration planning meeting, after task generation, people volunteer for enough tasks to get busy. As the days pass and they finish tasks, they volunteer for more. Hold each daily Scrum by the "task list" wall, and the team has the basic information necessary to volunteer.

What if no one volunteers for a particular task? Rather than answer the question prescriptively, it is instructive to learn the agile project management attitude in a method such as Scrum. In Scrum one would respond to this problem by saying, "It isn't the project manager's responsibility to solve this, although she can offer advice or resources in response to a request. We work by self-directed teams, not manager guided. It is the team's collective problem to solve it." This level of self-direction and decentralization of responsibility is a significant value change for some managers or organizations.

Visible Project Plans

Where possible, prefer to show all iteration tasks on a wall or whiteboard. If a daily Scrum meeting is practiced, hold the meeting by this wall. During the meeting, when tasks are reported complete or added, they can be crossed out or written in; likewise with the project blocks or impediments.

Iteration Goals: Risk, Coverage, Criticality, Skills Development

What should be done in the earliest iterations? Rank requests and iterations by risk, coverage, and criticality.

Risk includes both technical complexity and other factors such as uncertainty of effort, poor specification, political problems, the need for a novel UI look and feel, or usability.

Coverage implies that all major parts of the system are at least touched on in early iterations—perhaps a "wide and shallow" implementation across many components. The goal is to discover and stabilize the major software and hardware components, their interfaces, and collaborations. That's an important part of the overall architecture. For example, early use case scenarios may be chosen that require execution (and thus development) across many of the components (e.g., from UI to database). These are called **architecturally significant use cases**.

Criticality refers to functions of high business value; these need at least partial implementations in the earlier iterations, even if not technically risky. This driver may be considered a kind of political or business risk: if the paying customer does not see early evidence of things they care about, their confidence or sense of collaboration with the project team drops. Early inclusion of marketplace-relevant features also makes it easier to demo the product and garner attention.

On some projects, another early driver is skills development—one goal is to help the team master new skills such as adopting an agile method or object technologies. On such projects, skills development is a heavily weighted factor that tends to re-organize the iterations into less risky or simpler requirements in early iterations, motivated by learning rather than risk reduction goals.

Iteration Goals: What to Rank?

Use case scenarios, features, defects, and nonfunctional requirements (e.g., internationalization) can all be ranked with the above criteria of risk, coverage, and so on.

Use cases are often composed of many scenarios. For example, the "Process Sale" use case has one scenario involving paying by credit, and another for paying by cash. Some of these use cases are too complex to implement all scenarios within one reasonably short iteration; thus, they need to be decomposed by scenario for both ranking and scheduling.

Therefore, include all types in a ranking list.

Request	Type	...
Process Sale–pay by credit	scenario	
logging	feature	
Handle Returns	use case	
log-in window not closing	defect	
...	...	

Iteration Goals: How to Rank? Dot Voting

Based on the drivers, requests are ranked. The ranking may be informal and qualitative, generated in a group meeting by members mindful of these drivers. This approach is in the spirit of agile modeling.

Consider using the rapid scoring method of **dot voting**. List the requests on a whiteboard, or display them from a computer projector on a whiteboard. Everyone gets a whiteboard marker pen with which they can make 20 dots (for example). As a group, and in silence (to reduce influence), all approach the board and apply dots beside the items, reflecting the voter's priorities. A voter can assign many dots to one item, or distribute them. On completion, sort and discuss.

That may be sufficient. A slight refinement is to do a second round of silent dot voting to reflect updated insight based on first round voting and discussion. This second round provides the feedback and adaptation by which decisions improve.

The requirements ranking will be done before iteration 1, but then again before iteration 2, and so forth. In this way, the scheduling of iterations adapts to current information and opinion.

Iteration Goals: How to Rank? Quantitative Methods

Group discussion and something like dot voting for request ranking are often sufficient—a collaborative, fast, and fuzzy approach very much in the agile spirit. For the more quantitatively minded, variations on the following have been used. The example values and weights are only suggestive; the point is that numeric values, weights, and weighted sums can be used to reason about priorities.

Request	Type	AS	Risk	Criticality	W. Sum
Process Sale-pay by credit	scenario	3	2	3	15
Logging	feature	2	0	1	5
Handle Returns	use case	1	0	0	2
. . .	. . .	. . .	. . .	. . .	. . .

	Weight	Range
AS: achitecturally significant	2	0-3
Risk: risk, complexity, novelty	3	0-3
Criticality: early high biz value	1	0-3

The exact values should not be taken too seriously, and note that the numbers don't tell the whole story. Even though logging is a low-risk, simple feature, it is architecturally significant because it needs to be integrated throughout the code from the start. It would be awkward and would diminish architectural integrity to add it as an afterthought.

Iteration Goals: Related Iteration Length?

Viewing an iteration like any project, the choices boil down to fixing time and filling it with work, or fixing work and filling it with time. The specific approach varies in some IID methods (such as the XP Planning Game), but general outlines follow.

Iteration Length Chosen First

First, comments on factors that affect iteration length:

- ❑ Most IID methods recommend in the 1–6 week length. Scrum is specific: 30-calendar-day iterations.

- ❑ Smaller teams (such as 10 people) tend towards 1–3 weeks; large projects with sub-teams (such as 200 people) need more time (4–6 weeks) because of the overhead.

- ❑ Early iterations with high rates of discovery and change need more time. Later stable iterations can be shorter.

The steps:

1. Decide the length of the next timeboxed iteration.

2. Estimate total developer "ideal work hour" (focused effort on tasks) availability for the iteration, taking into account the usual overheads and lost days.

3. Choose a high-priority request (feature, use case, defect, and so on). If there is no effort estimate, or if it needs review, a new estimate is created.

4. Repeat step 3 until all available resources for the iteration are consumed.

Requests Chosen First

1. Estimate a per-day average total developer "ideal work hour" (focused effort on tasks) availability, taking into account the usual overheads and lost days. For example, four hours per day per developer, or 100 hours per day if there are 25 developers.

2. Choose a candidate set of requests for the iteration. If there are no effort estimates, or they need review, new estimates are created.

3. Estimate elapsed days: total effort divided by daily availability. Round up to the nearest (five-day) week. For example, 800 hours divided by 100 hours per day leads to a two-week iteration.

4. If the length exceeds desired limits (e.g., three weeks for a small team, six weeks for a massive team), shrink the goals.

Either approach is best done in a collaborative planning effort with all team members, or subteam representatives for large projects.

Iteration Goals: Before the First Development Iteration

I've seen a project team start into iteration one, and quickly falter because the team is impeded waiting for the technical environment to get properly established and debugged: The source control management system, the continuous integration build machine, the application server, project Wiki, and so forth. Strive to have this in place beforehand; it always takes longer than expected.

Iteration Goals: The First Development Iteration

Or, what not to do. Iteration one proceeds slower than expected. So, use generous estimates, and choose small goals among the set of high-ranking requests. Then it is more likely that the team will successfully complete on time with less struggle, building confidence.

If the project also includes skill transfer goals (learning about object technologies, or a new agile method), do not dump a big bucket of new ideas and practices into iteration one. Add them incrementally over two or three iterations. For example, if the team has not used version control before, perhaps leave it and the related continuous integration practice for iteration two, and just emphasize test-first development and daily Scrum meetings in iteration one.

Iteration Goals: Use Cases and Scenarios

If use cases are being employed, it is desirable to fully complete a use case (or many use cases) within one iteration. Planning and scheduling are straightforward, and the growing system has functional cohesion.

This is not always practical. As mentioned in some other tips, use cases are composed of many scenarios (related to "extensions" in Cockburn's popular use case terminology). For example, the Process Sale use case has a scenario involving paying by credit, and another for paying by cash. Some use cases are too complex to implement all scenarios within one reasonably short iteration. Perhaps it would take three months to complete all scenarios of Process Sale—undesirably long for an iteration. Thus, they need to be decomposed by scenario for ranking, scheduling, and tracking. In this case, an iteration should complete the scenarios that it starts; a scenario should not be split across iterations (Figure 11.8).

Figure 11.8 scenarios
across iterations

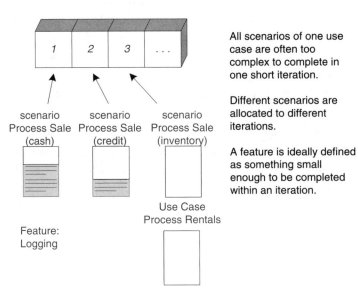

All scenarios of one use
case are often too
complex to complete in
one short iteration.

Different scenarios are
allocated to different
iterations.

A feature is ideally defined
as something small
enough to be completed
within an iteration.

Iteration Goals: Primary and Secondary Requests

By frequently tracking remaining effort estimates, it may eventually appear that not all requests will be completed within the iteration. In timeboxed methods the response is to remove or simplify requests, rather than extend the iteration. What to remove? On projects with a strong customer-driven emphasis (such as XP projects), consider this approach: During the iteration planning meeting with customers, after the requests have been chosen, classify some as secondary that may be deferred. Not only does this support the agile spirit of customer-driven work, it also aids expectation management.

Iteration Goals: Don't Add Requests to an Iteration

An important rule in timeboxed methods is to not allow the addition of new requests once the iteration is underway. The product manager can't come over and ask to squeeze in the sexy Gromlit feature. Gromlits have to wait for the next iteration. Given that an average iteration is two or three weeks, this should not be a hardship. This rule creates an island of sanity and control in a sea of change and chaos.[3] Newly discovered tasks related to existing requests can be added by the team members, but not new requests.

Tracking Iteration Progress

Some methods, such as XP and Scrum, have specific tracking practices discussed in their respective chapters. Some general iterative and agile-oriented principles and practices include:

- ❑ Frequent—often daily—task tracking for each worker is important with timeboxed methods; there isn't much slack in a short iteration.

- ❑ For smaller projects, a visible wall list of tasks is good. Hold the daily Scrum beside it. Cross out tasks when done. As the Xs grow, people see and feel progress.

- ❑ Some projects apply the XP practice of writing task cards that are physically held by the volunteer, or handed off to someone else. When complete, they are handed in to the tracker. Many people report that the physical cards have a positive psychological effect in making the work tangible.

- ❑ Asking people on a daily basis to self-record their remaining estimated task effort is rarely sustained or accurate. The XP practice of a daily tracker is a more sustainable alternative. Someone (other than the manager) visits each person each day (or every few days) and asks and records the remaining estimates on incomplete tasks.

---

3. Ken Schwaber, a Scrum founder, named his Web site www.control-chaos.com to emphasize this point.

❏ Many find a Scrum Sprint Backlog a simple, useful iteration tracking tool. If a daily tracker is asking about progress, they will be the primary person updating this backlog.

Tracking Iteration Progress—What to Track?

Since timeboxing creates a fixed soon-coming deadline, the critical progress data are the *remaining estimated effort on unfinished tasks*. This is the focus of a Scrum Sprint Backlog.

If a project also collects *actual* hours spent on tasks for each worker, consider using a daily tracker to collect this. One immediately relevant use for this data is to share it with the team members during subsequent iteration planning meetings so they can compare their original task estimates with final actuals. This feedback helps people become more accurate estimators—a valuable skill.

Test-driven development is an increasingly popular and valued practice in IID methods, not only in XP. To promote the early creation of more unit tests, some agile projects track (and update on a wall chart) the total number of unit test classes and test methods. The counting can and should be automated with a simple scanning program that runs as part of the continuous integration build process.

Tracking and Planning: XPlanner

If the simple "low-tech, high-touch" tools preferred in agile methods such as a whiteboard task list, paper task cards, or the Sprint Backlog spreadsheet file are found to be insufficient (more likely on larger projects), there are (free) open source software tools emerging to support agile planning and tracking. An example (not an endorsement) is XPlanner, available at www.xplanner.org. It provides support for stories, tasks, time tracking, and metrics.

Earned Value Tracking on IID Projects

Earned value (EV) tracking is a cost and schedule progress measurement method required on many USA government projects. Thus, it must be considered on government projects that want to apply an IID method. The details are beyond the scope of this introduction, but a non-obvious key concept is to measure progress in terms of the *estimates* (or *budgets*), not only in terms of *actuals*. For example, if creating help Web pages for a new system was originally budgeted at 50 person-hours, then when the work is complete, regardless of the actual time spent (for example, 80 hours), the project is said to have "earned" 50 hours of value. A key term in this context is the Budgeted Cost for Work Scheduled (BCWS)—the estimates for future tasks, such as 50 person-hours for the help system.

There are a few practices experimenting with EV tracking on iterative and evolutionary projects, although their true worth is not yet known.

One practice is to re-calculate the BCWS (estimate) values each iteration, as more information arises. This has been called a **rubber baseline**.

Another practice is to apply a simple earned value **recognition rule** to iteration tasks. There are alternative rules, but a common one is that as soon as an iteration task is underway, it earns 50% of its value, in terms of progress tracking. Thus, as soon as the help page work starts, the iteration "earns" 25 hours of progress. Progress remains at 50% until the task is complete.

Ranking Risks

IID methods tend to be risk driven. A fast, useful method to prioritize risks is to estimate their probability *and* impact (in cost, time, or effort). The estimates may be quantitative (which are usually very speculative) or simply qualitative (for example, high-medium-low, based on discussion and group dot voting).

The worst risks requiring proactive actions are naturally those both probable and of high impact.

For example:

Risk	Prob-ability	Impact
Insufficient number and quality of skilled object-oriented developers.	H	H
Demo not ready for the upcoming CEBIT convention in Hamburg.	M	H
…	…	…

Agile modeling promotes the practice of visible models, and that is especially useful for a risk list, with associated actions and status. Display this information using whiteboards or posters on the wall of the project room.

Managing Risks

Many iterative methods are risk driven, which includes not only tackling higher-risk technical elements in early iterations, but also more broadly, identifying and proactively working on all risks.

A key to successfully risk management is *proactive* actions *owned* by individuals, that are *tracked*. Consider keeping owner and status information on the project room's wall display of the risk list (see Table 11.1).

Table 11.1 risk list

Risk	...	Actions	Owner	Status
Insufficient number and quality of skilled object-oriented developers; thus, slow development and poor, buggy design.	...	PROACTIVE - Hire temporary consultants. - Classroom education and mentoring. - Design and program in pairs. REACTIVE - ...	Jill Jill Team	approved in review underway
...	...			

ENVIRONMENT

The project environment includes the physical space and software tools used by the developers. This section includes a few environment tips to support iterative and agile development. Agile methods emphasize the importance of communication or feedback; many of these tips promote it.

Continuous Integration

Part of the XP practices, **continuous integration** (CI) is also useful in other IID methods [FF99]. CI is a refinement and more frequent version of the daily build and smoke test practice popularized at Microsoft. Cycles average 15 to 30 minutes on many Java technology projects. There are at least two open source CI tools: Anthill (www.urbancode.com), and CruiseControl (cruisecontrol.sourceforge.net).

CI is somewhat more than just a frequent build-and-test tool. The details and how it works are explained in Figure 11.9.

Figure 11.9 how
continuous integration
works

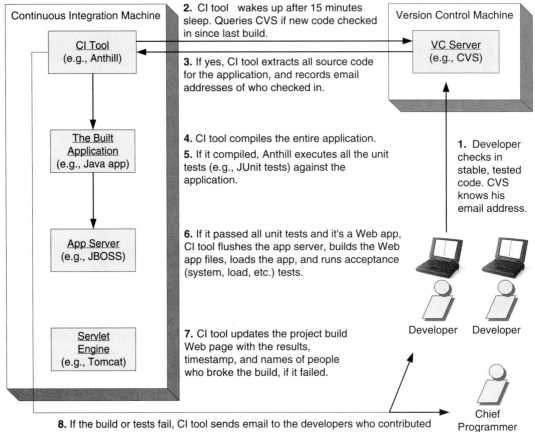

2. CI tool wakes up after 15 minutes sleep. Queries CVS if new code checked in since last build.

3. If yes, CI tool extracts all source code for the application, and records email addresses of who checked in.

4. CI tool compiles the entire application.

5. If it compiled, Anthill executes all the unit tests (e.g., JUnit tests) against the application.

6. If it passed all unit tests and it's a Web app, CI tool flushes the app server, builds the Web app files, loads the app, and runs acceptance (system, load, etc.) tests.

7. CI tool updates the project build Web page with the results, timestamp, and names of people who broke the build, if it failed.

1. Developer checks in stable, tested code. CVS knows his email address.

8. If the build or tests fail, CI tool sends email to the developers who contributed and to the technical leader, indicating who broke the build.

Why bother? If a team practices CI from day one, then the growing application is almost always in a steady state of being integrated and tested. The "drift" from stability is on an extremely small scale. On average, every 15 minutes only a few new components are added. If the build is broken by an addition, it is likely to be a minor infraction. Therefore, the system grows micro-incrementally 15 minutes by 15 minutes, 24/7. There is less need for major end-of-iteration integration across team members or subteams.

What happens if the compile or tests fail? The CI tool sends email to the submitters and chief programmer, and people are expected to react immediately. For example, reverting to a previous version of the components, until the new components are debugged.

What if it takes a very long time to run the tests? Apply the "smoke test" principle promoted by Microsoft: Choose an important set of unit and acceptance tests that can run within 15 or 30 minutes. Run the longer set less frequently, such as four times daily.

Project Wiki Webs

Most people are familiar with blogs or Weblogs, that allow one to easily write and publish to a Web page. The older and more robust version of this idea is **Wiki** Web technology, created by Ward Cunningham (one of the XP founders). XP has the value, "do the simplest thing that could possibly work." In that vein, Cunningham has called Wikis "the simplest online Web database that could possibly work."

Like blogs, Wiki Webs (or Wikis) allow people to edit Web pages using only their browser, but they go farther: They allow one to easily create new pages, and hyperlinks between Wiki pages, using only a browser and special **WikiWords**. Of course, these capabilities are available with myriad tools, but Wikis make the tasks especially simple and fast. Thus, Wikis are a popular tool on agile projects to capture project information, and as a simple knowledge management tool.

Wikis are usually implemented as one or more Perl scripts that you install on an HTTP server. There are many open source Wiki kits. A popular simple version is Usemod (www.usemod.com); a popular elaborate version is Twiki (www.twiki.org)—it includes version control and various fancy features.

You can see how Wikis work and create your own Wiki pages at the original (fascinating) Wiki site: c2.com/cgi/wiki?WelcomeVistors. This site is also the place where the majority of online discussion took place during the mid- and late-1990s on the creation of XP and other agile methods, by their founders. These discussions are still available as Wiki pages.

CASE Tools and Reverse-Engineering

UML-oriented CASE tools support both **forward-engineering** (generation of code from diagrams), and **reverse-engineering** (generation of diagrams from code). If an agile-oriented project uses a CASE tool at all, it is most often simply for the reverse-engineering feature, to support visualization and the more visually-oriented on the team. For example, regeneration of noteworthy (package, class, or sequence) UML diagrams every few days to visualize the growing code base created with a popular IDE such as Eclipse (www.eclipse.org).

When I coach a team through an iteration, we print reverse-engineered UML diagrams zoomed very large on a plotter (if one is available), and stick them on walls. Some developers use the plots during discussions or short design sessions, sketching on them.

It is a misunderstanding to think that agile methods oppose UML diagrams or visual sketching. First, it is only XP that is especially textual-source-code-centric; the other methods are silent on the subject. Second, the XP leaders are not at all opposed to the practices of Agile Modeling, or using a tool to reverse-engineer code to diagrams if the effort is simple and aids communication.

Consider a Plotter

Visualization of information on the walls is promoted in agile methods; large diagrams and font size are important for ease of viewing. Printing large zoomed documents on a laser printer is laborious, as the partial pages have to be puzzle-pieced together. A wide plotter is faster and easier.

Caves and Common Room

The agile methods promote development in a common room rather than separate offices, to increase communication (Figure 11.10). It is a required practice in Scrum and XP. Of course, people also have need for privacy. Ken Auer promotes the "caves and common room" model in which there are also separate private office spaces (floating or dedicated) that developers can use during non-development activities [AM02].

Figure 11.10 agile project common room with walls exposed

Liberate the Walls

Walls are valuable, but not for desks, shelves, or tables. If development is done by teams in common project rooms (a required practice in XP and Scrum), move furniture away from the walls. Expose them to support the agile modeling practices of using many whiteboard spaces, and displaying as much project information (tasks, risk list, vision, and so forth) on the walls as possible. Figure 11.11.

Figure 11.11 floor layout

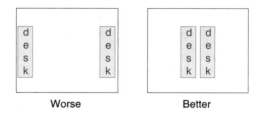

Worse   Better

Cling Sheets or Whiteboard Paint

Agile modeling promotes the use of whiteboard space and free-hand drawing for creative modeling work. In addition to true whiteboards (which may not be available), consider using "cling sheets" or "static cling sheets." These can be purchased at most office supply stores and come in packages like flip-chart paper. They are made of a very thin white flexible plastic material that has a static charge; the sheets cling to most surfaces. Wallpaper them to create a giant whiteboard space. Most important, you can use a whiteboard marker to write and erase on them, as with any whiteboard.

Another alternative is the use of "whiteboard" paint.

Digital Cameras

Agile is about fast, simple, light. Capture hand-sketched whiteboard models or lists with a digital camera. Print, plot, or consider placing the results on a project Wiki.

Figure 11.12 sample room elements

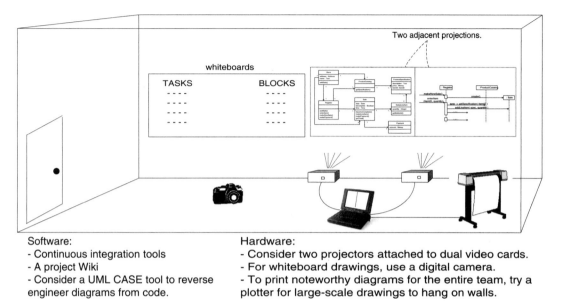

Software:
- Continuous integration tools
- A project Wiki
- Consider a UML CASE tool to reverse engineer diagrams from code.

Hardware:
- Consider two projectors attached to dual video cards.
- For whiteboard drawings, use a digital camera.
- To print noteworthy diagrams for the entire team, try a plotter for large-scale drawings to hang on walls.

REQUIREMENTS

This section introduces tips that support an agile, rapid, evolutionary approach to requirements, in addition to those already covered in other chapters, such as XP's Planning Game and story cards. Note that many of the tips emphasize face-to-face communication and "low-tech high-touch" — common themes in agile methods.

Agile Modeling

Agile Modeling is a set of values and practices consistent and complementary to all the IID methods, and applicable during requirements analysis. See p. 37 for a summary.

Defining and Keeping the Vision

Establishing and reiterating a common vision is frequent advice from agile leaders. It may seem absurd to highlight such an "obvious" idea, but in over 10 years of post-project reviews with hundreds of project members, Standish Group analysts [Johnson02] did not find even two people who stated the same purpose or vision for their project!

Sometimes the military is used as an example of an unhealthy, rigid management system, but modern battlefield leadership is different. Adaptation to unpredictable battle events (as in agile development) is paramount. Therefore, the leadership emphasizes that fighters know the mission goal or vision, rather than concentrating on a fixed plan.

Microsoft values this as well; it is key in the Microsoft Solutions Framework IID method:

> *Use high-level vision statements and outline specifications to get projects going.*

How? Step one is to form a vision, discussed in some of the following tips, such as creating a vision box and product sheet.

Step two is to reinforce it. Jeff Sutherland, a Scrum founder, emphasizes that one of the key communication responsibilities of the Scrum Master during the daily Scrum meeting is to help the team recall a common project vision aligned with the business objectives.

The Product Vision Box

This is a creative, quick practice to craft a common vision, first created and promoted by Bill Shakelford and Jim Highsmith

[Highsmith01], creator of the agile method Adaptive Software Development. The steps are:

1. During day one of the first requirements workshop, break into several small groups. Give each group a box (such as a cereal box).

2. The goal of each group is to create the cover (front and back) of a product box, as though the product were to be sold in a shrink-wrap box.

3. Define and place on the box a name, graphics, a *few* key front-cover selling points for the front, and details (features, operating requirements, and so on) for the back.

4. Each group presents the results.

5. Coalesce the results into a common Moore-style vision statement or common vision box.

A Moore-Style Vision Statement

The vision boxes can be input to a simple, focused vision statement. In Geoffrey Moore's well-known *Crossing the Chasm*, he recommends the following format for a vision statement, which has been widely adopted, including within the UP:

For (target customer)
Who (statement of the need or opportunity)
The (product name) is a (product category)
That (key benefit, compelling reason to buy)
Unlike (primary competitive alternative)
Our product (statement of primary differentiation)

Following the agile modeling practice to display models publicly, this statement goes on the wall—in large font.

Product Sheets

Marketing and requirements experts in product companies promote the early creation of a product data sheet (feature bullets, comparisons, and so forth). It helps clarify the vision and define high-level requirements; plus, the physical limit (one side of one page) forces prioritization and brevity. However, this practice is not only useful for product developers; it helps teams building *internal* systems who want a more agile approach to requirements analysis. As with vision boxes, a complementary tip is to have several teams create them in parallel and coalesce the results.

Evolutionary Requirements Workshops

Although requirements workshops are an old idea (also under the banner of JAD—Joint Application Design—sessions), the iterative and evolutionary approach is to hold *several* of them, one per iteration during the early iterations, interspersed with programming. Keep them short and timeboxed, such as one or two days. In the first workshop, there is an emphasis on defining a vision and scope, and identifying functions and features at a high level (such as just the *names* of use cases and features). However, most nonfunctional requirements (e.g., load, internationalization) need early exploration in detail, as these have a significant architectural impact.

As an example: a project ultimately composed of 20 iterations might hold four requirements workshops across the first four iterations. The goal after four workshops is that 80% or more of the requirements are defined in detail, but in contrast to the waterfall, with the benefit of insight from early programming, evaluation, and feedback. Note also that by the end of the same four iterations, perhaps only 10% of the software is developed.

In the first workshop, for example, the team may discover and *name* 20 use cases (the same applies if features rather than use cases are used). They now have an estimate that the goal of 80% detailed requirements after four workshops will mean that 16 use cases should be written. Yet, in the first workshop they explore and write only two (i.e., 10%) of the highest risk and most architecturally significant in a detailed use case format. Combined with analysis of the product's nonfunctional requirements, that's usually enough to get started with architectural work and early programming.

Figure 11.13 sample completion of artifacts in 5 of 20 iterations.

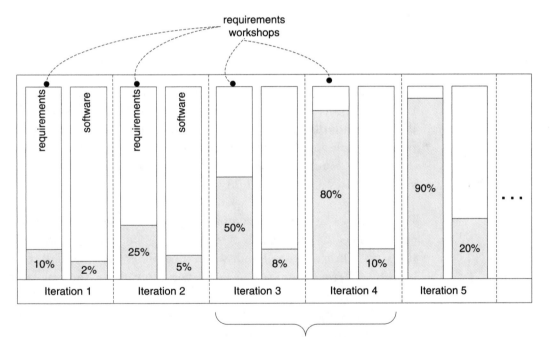

Semi-reliable estimates are more likely starting in this range.

Perhaps the second workshop team discovers three new use cases, eliminates two, and writes 8/21 in detail, refining existing ones, and so on. Figure 11.13 illustrates the process.

Include in each workshop developers who spend time working on the software. It is useful to demo and discuss the results of the most recent iteration. Feedback from building some of the software is crucial to refine and evolve the growing requirements.

This is not the only way to stage evolutionary requirements analysis; pipelining (see p. 251) is another.

The art and science of running a successful workshop is well-covered in *Requirements by Collaboration: Workshops for Defining Needs* by Ellen Gottesdiener.

Tracking Requirements Across Iterations

At the very least, track the lifecycle or status of each request (feature, use case, scenario, bug fix) as they transition through the iterations. XP does status tracking in the simplest way that could possibly work, for example, three piles of cards: "not done," "underway," and "done." Similarly, the Scrum Product Backlog spreadsheet includes a status column.

For use cases that will be completed within one iteration, the use case name is the requirements tracking tag—for example, "Handle Returns." On the other hand, when a complex use case has to be built by different scenarios across several iterations, the trackable requirements tag is a scenario name, not a use case name. If Cockburn's (popular) naming style is used, each scenario has a tag such as "3a" or "4c". Thus, the requirement tracking system can track labels such as "Process Sale-main success" or "Process Sale-3a".

Direct User Involvement in Requirements and Product

Research [KC94] shows that project failure is reduced when there is increased *direct* involvement and links between the *ultimate* clients or users of a new software product and developers. Plus, as an obvious corollary, fewer indirect links via intermediaries and customer proxies (such as business analysts). There are many techniques explicit within IID methods to support this, such as XP's Whole Team Together (Onsite Customer), UP's requirements workshops, and the Scrum demo to users at each iteration. Another popular practice is to send some developers as trainees in the client or target customer setting.

Use Cases are OK

It is a misunderstanding to equate iterative or agile methods with "no detailed written requirements." That value is unique to XP, and is enabled in XP by the presence of onsite customers in the project room who can verbally explain or create the requirements as needed. The other methods, although all are in favor of avoiding excessive documents, allow or support detailed written requirements, created iteratively and interspersed with early programming.

Unless it is an XP project, when written functional requirements are needed, consider use cases (for example, "Provision a Switch"). XP's promotion of feature-oriented "story card" requirements does not mean use cases are unskillful, or wrong for use in other methods. Note, for example, that the well-known agile methodologist Alistair Cockburn (author of *Agile Software Development*) is also an expert in and promoter of use cases, and author of *Writing Effective Use Cases*.

Use cases have the advantage of pulling a set of requirements together—organizing them in the context of scenarios of use. Plus, use case scenarios (e.g., "order, and pay with credit card") make excellent goals for an iteration, because by implementing a scenario you are forced to design and build across many architecturally significant components, from the UI to the database, for example. And, you must early on resolve and test the quality requirements (e.g., reliability, usability) associated with the scenarios. That said, use cases don't fit for all products; sometimes a feature-oriented (e.g., "support EJB 2.0") or combination approach is more relevant.

Note that meaningful use case work is not *drawing* a UML use case diagram, but *writing* detailed use case text. In a workshop this is best done with a projector, so several people can easily view the text.

A popular approach to writing use cases is described in Cockburn's *Writing Effective Use Cases*.

Quantification Is OK

In the name of being more agile, do not succumb to being vague or sloppy about the details of quality requirements, such as load, response times, usability, and so forth. Most of these need quantification and means of measurement to be of much use. Evo places special emphasis on this value. "The UI needs to be usable," "The system should be maintainable," "The system needs to have good performance under high load," and so forth. These statements do not suffice, expressed verbally or in writing.

Agile Manifesto p. 28

On outsourced projects—run with an agile method or otherwise—both the client and service provider need quantified and measurable quality requirements written down in order to avoid messy disputes. Although the Agile Manifesto encourages customer collaboration over contract negotiation, it is a fact of life that misunderstandings about the "...ilities" often lead to severe dissatisfaction—or law suits. I sometimes serve as an expert witness; it happens.

GUIs with Glue

Another practical agile requirements tip is to first prototype UIs and UI navigation (in collaboration with clients) using paper, pen, sticky notes, and so forth, on a wall. This well-known technique goes by many names, but my favorite is Luke Hohmann's "GUIs with glue." Use large sheets of paper to represent Web pages or windows. Place small blue sticky notes on these sheets to represent information and pink sticky notes for UI controls (e.g., a button).

To quickly model navigation between Web pages or windows, consider sketching a UML statechart on a whiteboard, where the states represent the windows or pages, and the transition events represent the UI navigation gestures (for example, clicking a button). See Figure 11.14.

A recommended text on usability engineering is *Don't Make Me Think!* by Steve Krug; many texts and Web sites cover "GUIs with glue" agile flavored UI prototyping.

Brainstorming

Brainstorming is useful and quick during both requirements and joint planning. Most think they know the technique, but surprising few follow its official—and important—rule. It is, simply:

> *When hearing and recording the ideas, no one should comment or laugh.*

The facilitator should record, not react. Keep the ideas flowing.

Figure 11.14 UML
statechart sketch for UI
navigation

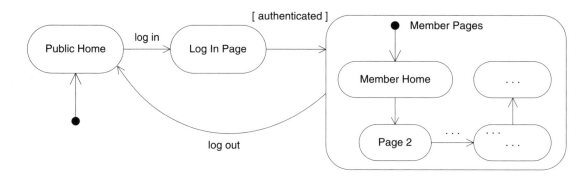

Brainwriting

Brainwriting is a fast adjunct or alternative to brainstorming during a requirements or planning workshop. People are given many index cards or paper scraps. On the topic at hand (e.g., requirements? tasks?), they write a short note on each card as ideas emerge. The cards are collected, and the team does affinity clustering.

Affinity Clustering

Affinity clustering is a rapid technique to dynamically group things—such as brainwriting cards—into cohesive sets. It is usually done by placing the cards randomly on the floor. The team collaborates to organize the cards into the dynamic sets that emerge, such as "database task cards" or "payment feature cards." The results can be posted in groups on walls, or visualized in a mind map.

Mind Maps

Mind maps are another agile-oriented hand-drawing technique to quickly elicit, organize, and expand high-level requirements during a workshop. Deceptively simple, I'm always impressed by how they help the creative discovery process during rapid requirements analysis (Figure 11.15). When facilitating, I sometimes take the output of a brainwriting and affinity clustering session, and mind-map the result. There are several good Web sites; a classic text on the subject is *The Mind Map Book* by the founder, Tony Buzan.

Figure 11.15 sample mind map

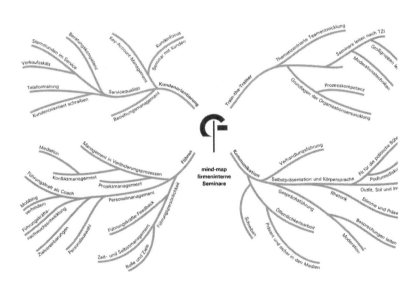

Team Rotation Writing

Another quick, collaborative technique for requirements or planning is **rotation writing**. <N> people sit in a circle, each with a laptop computer. For five or ten minutes, they write on the topic at hand (requirements? tasks?). Then they stop and pass their computer to their neighbor, while they themselves receive another computer. The same approach can be achieved with a wireless network and sharable Wiki pages. Each person starts by reviewing the unfamiliar material, and then enhances it, inspired by the new ideas they see. Rotation continues until each person has worked on each computer document. After the meeting, one person receives all the documents, groups and merges the ideas, which are then later reviewed and refined by the whole team together in a second meeting.

Test

Test-Driven Development

Test-driven development (TDD, that includes the sub-practice of **test-first development**) is a key practice in XP, and is now promoted in several IID methods. An important part of TDD is that there are automated tests for (almost) everything, and most tests (especially unit tests) are written *before* the code to be tested.

This bears repetition: Unit tests are written *before* writing the code to be tested, imagining that the code exists.

Further, the tests simply pass or fail. There is no need for human inspection of specific test results. If you have 2,000 unit tests created in the TDD style, it all boils down to one question "Did they all pass?"

A brief programming example is presented to provide a concrete sense of how this key practice works.

Suppose Jill needs to create a *Money* class (in Java), to support multiple currencies, adding money, and so forth.

Since this is a TDD project, rather than start by writing the *Money* class, she starts by writing the *MoneyTest* class, adding one test method.

```
public class MoneyTest extends TestCase {

public void testSimpleAdd() {
    Money m1 = new Money( 12, "usd" ); // ONE
    Money m2 = new Money( 14, "usd" );
    Money expected = new Money( 26, "usd" );
    Money result = m1.add( m2 ); // TWO
    assertEquals( expected, result ); // THREE
  }
} // end of class
```

Jill *imagines*, at point ONE, that there is a Java constructor in the
Money class that is written and works, and at point TWO, that a
Money.add method is written and works. Notice also at point
THREE that there is an assertion that causes the test to simply
fail or pass; no human inspection of the specific results is required.

Then, Jill programs just enough of the *Money* class to make it pass
the test *testSimpleAdd*, writing the constructor to satisfy point
ONE, and the *add* method to satisfy point TWO:

```
public class Money {

public Money( float value, String currency ) {
// body of method …
}

public Money add( Money other ) {
// body of method …
}
} // end of class
```

The implementation details are not important, but the process is.
Once the code is written, Jill runs the test. If it fails, she debugs
till it passes.

Next, Jill is ready for the *subtract* method. She starts by adding
another test to *MoneyTest*:

```
public class MoneyTest extends TestCase {

public void testSimpleAdd() {
```

```
// ...
}
```

```
public void testSimpleSubtract() { // NEW METHOD
// body of the new test ...
}
```

```
} // end of class
```

Then, she updates *Money* to make it pass this second test.

Test-first development has some practical consequences:

❑ Tests actually get written, which yields a host of benefits. This is obvious, but in many projects that do not practice TDD, tests are just not written.

❑ It is at least a semi-enjoyable way to do testing—that makes it more sustainable. Agile methods tend to emphasize practices that developers (eventually) like—or at least do not dislike—doing. Traditional ("test last") testing is avoided because it is boring or tedious. By writing the tests first, the developer is engaged in thinking through the proper public behavior of the class not yet written. That's interesting and creative. And, she writes the test and then builds something to make it pass. That gives a small feeling of accomplishment.

❑ To expand a point made in the last bullet, by writing the tests first, the developer is engaged in thinking through the proper public behavior of the class not yet written. That thought process—treating the new class as a separate black box with public operations—clarifies in the developer's mind the behavior and design of the class before it is programmed. That thinking tends to improve the design and, as a valuable side benefit, a test written.

continuous integration p. 277

Finally, note that many IID projects also practice continuous integration. All these tests, growing constantly, become part of the continuous integration test process, re-executed on each build cycle.

Fit or Fitnesse for Acceptance Testing

Ward Cunningham, a key figure behind XP, has created a simple, open-source framework and tool to support acceptance testing: Fit. See fit.c2.com. It has become relatively popular in the agile development community. A related tool, Fitnesse, has been developed by Bob Martin and his team at ObjectMentor, early promoters of XP and agile development. See www.fitnesse.org.

FREQUENTLY ASKED QUESTIONS

I have often regretted my answers, never my silence.
—adapted from Xenocrates

These assume an audience relatively new to iterative methods, keeping with the book's theme as an introduction.

QUESTION LIST

QUESTIONS AND ANSWERS

Is there any proof that iterative development is worthwhile, or better in some qualities than the waterfall?

Yes. For the whole story, see the Evidence chapter (p. 63).

For example, will an agile or iterative method make my team more productive?

Yes, there is some evidence, both for productivity and defect reduction (p. 76). However, beware silver-bullet "faster, cheaper" claims made speculatively by various agile method promoters. One must also be mindful of the **Hawthorne Effect** when new methods are introduced: That individual productivity and other behaviors *temporarily* improve when people adopt new methods and know they (or their project results) are being studied.

Sustainable productivity improvements only arise over a long period of effort and change, with long-term initiatives and management support. Gerald Weinberg once cautioned against claiming that anything would make more than a 10% improvement—wise advice.

Perhaps more important than asking about more productivity is asking about *less failure*. Software project failure rates are high, averaging 23% in the USA in 2000. Rather than first searching for the next 2% productivity improvement, it may be a rational higher priority to first focus on preventing some of the lost (estimated for the USA) $50 to $70 billion that is spent each year on cancelled software projects.

Interestingly, investigation by the Standish Group into project failure indicated that this level of failure has not been visible at the CEO and VP levels; not all executives know how bad it is in their software groups. To quote from their 1998 report:

> *For years [software] project failure was simply not discussed. And it certainly was not discussed with the CEO.*

In this context, perhaps the most relevant value of IID is that it is correlated with lower failure rates. And, through the process of early feedback, leads to products more closely aligned with what customers really want.

How do you plan an iterative project?

See tips starting on p. 248.

My customer expects a week-by-week schedule and detailed PERT chart. What should I do?

See "Rolling Wave Adaptive versus Predictive Planning" on p. 253.

One approach is to present a short seminar on IID and client-driven adaptive planning, and propose starting the next project based on this approach. If they are not satisfied after some time period, you will agree to revert to their desire for a predictive plan.

If that isn't possible or doesn't work, another approach is to create the predictive plan they desire, but then run the project with client-driven adaptive planning. At the end of the first iteration, show the customers a demo and update them on progress and new insights. They too will have new insights and priorities based on this feedback. Then invite them to tell you their current priorities and refinement of ideas. Covertly, the project may then slip into adaptive planning as the customer directly sees the benefit of their ability to guide it iteration by iteration.

How to handle fixed-price contracts when applying an IID method?

Also see the follow-on related question and answer: Can IID be applied with contracts (usually fixed-price) in which we are forced to do major up-front requirements analysis? (p. 303)

There are at least two ways to answer this: the ideal, and the usual.

The ideal—which *has* been sold with success by various consulting companies—is to organize the project into two contract phases. Contract phase one corresponds to inception and elaboration (or at least a good part of elaboration) in the UP. See "Fixed-Price Contracts" on p. 18.

Note how this approach reduces the risk for the customer. In phase one they paid for tangible results that moved the project forward, but they didn't commit everything to the project or to one service provider. Also, it is desirable to hire very talented people for this phase one, to create a solid foundation. But it may thus be possible to use less expensive average resources for phase two. Finally, for phase two, the customer will more reliably know the true costs and duration, and will be working with a provider who has a greater chance of remaining both solvent and sane, as the provider accepted the challenge of the project with sufficient initial information to make an informed (rather than desperate) choice.

In summary, this approach balances the risks for the customer and service provider.

As an aside, some consulting companies have run a refinement of this phase one in which one developer from the customer side joined the consulting team. They not only provided insight for the project, but insight to the culture and leaders of the organization. During an end-of-phase demonstration to the customer, the customer-developer herself leads the demonstration created with the consulting team, and thus creates an in-selling effect to help the consulting company win the phase two contract.

The more commonplace answer to the contract question is that service providers are forced to create fixed-price bids without the luxury of the above phase one, and are taking a larger risk. In this case, they bid however they prefer. (Note, as an aside, that the estimation technique of WideBand Delphi can improve their estimates—see p. 260) Yet, running the project iteratively still gives them an advantage: Since iterative development is about tackling the high risks and hard elements in early iterations, they will receive early feedback about how much trouble they are really in, or not! They will discover more quickly if their estimate of the cost or difficulty was low, and be able to take early mitigating actions, such as hiring experienced specialists, looking for preexisting components, early expectation management, and so forth.

Furthermore, by running the project iteratively, they will be showing early visible results of value to the customer. There is an increased chance, through thus winning the confidence of the customer, that they will be able to renegotiate some of the difficult fixed-price contract terms at the suitable strategic moment.

Can IID be applied on projects or contracts (usually fixed-price) in which we are forced to do major up-front requirements analysis?

Yes. even with "the complete requirements" developing via many short iterations has advantages.

To reiterate points from a prior answer, the team receives early feedback about how much trouble they may be in, by building, integrating, and testing early and often (there's nothing like programming to discover what you don't know). This approach drives down the risks, shakes out the requirement bugs, and provides opportunities for reacting sooner rather than later to major problems.

There will be early tangible results for the customer (user, marketing manager, ...), leading to confidence building and quality feedback. If the product needs to be rolled out earlier than planned, there's something available.

And research suggests that developing in short, timeboxed steps is associated with higher productivity and lower defect rates.

What are typical risks and mistakes when adopting an iterative process?

Near the top of the list of mistakes or risks is that the customer or executive management does not understand and accept the change in values and practices, or appreciate how deep and far-reaching the changes need to be. I see this manifest in situations like "Congratulations! We've adopted <iterative process X>. When will the requirements be finished, so we can decide how to design the system?" Or, "It's budget season. Please take a few weeks to identify all the projects for next year, and how much they will cost and how long they will take." Inconsistent culture and expectations derived from waterfall or mass-manufacturing values clash with an iterative and agile approach. As another example, the customer does not actively participate, iteration by iteration. And so on.

The solution includes having an executive and customer champion who understands and can communicate this to their peers, education seminars and learning aides (e.g., this book) for these groups, and "post-partum" project sessions in which the stakeholders share their experiences with other customers and management.

Another common mistake is changing or adding to the goals of an iteration, once underway. In a sea of constant change and chaos, some stability and control is necessary. That comes from leaving the team alone, once they've committed to an iteration. Save the change requests for a future step.

Another problem is using so-called iterative or agile consultants or consulting organizations who don't really comprehend evolutionary, adaptive development. They superimpose waterfall values on top of an iterative process, or try to recast their old waterfall process as an iterative one. Then we get corruptions such as misinterpreting the UP inception phase as requirements, elaboration as design, and so forth. Or, we get promotion of excessive specifications and other documents, instead of early programming. Or, we get predictive planning in which a plan is created listing how many iterations there will be, their durations, and what will occur in each. Or, we get misunderstandings such as "let's iterate over the requirements until they are stable, then we can nail down the design in a series of iterations."

Another risk is attempting to transition to an iterative and agile process without coaching from someone who's been there and done that. I sometimes see well-intentioned local managers championing the adoption of an iterative method, who think they or their staff can lead the adoption without help. And sometimes they can, but a timeboxed, iterative, agile approach is rather different for many teams. Colleagues and I have seen a number of homemade adoption attempts where the adopters didn't appreciate the synergy between the different practices, and they were modifying the newly adopted methods unwisely. For example, claiming to adopt XP by simply eliminating written requirements and writing unit tests occasionally.

Using a coach who isn't steeped in the old local ways and who has the confidence of knowing that the iterative process works is money well spent. And, because we are talking about value changes, it is often more effective that the change agent be from the outside. It seems to be the way of the world that we're never a prophet in our own land, especially regarding software methods.

Another common mistake is overselling or mis-selling the advantages of an iterative, agile method to customers or management. The popular press and a number of agile method books still exhibit the silver-bullet syndrome. The master consultant Gerry Weinberg advised to never promise more than a 10% improvement, not only because greater yields are seldom sustained (and let us not forget the Hawthorne Effect), but more can suggest the *current* management and management practices are really inept, which is seldom true.

On the subject of mis-selling, note that iterative methods are *not* fundamentally for improving productivity or delivery speed or reducing defects, although there is research showing correlations. Rather, they are less ambitiously for reducing the risk of failure and increasing the probability of creating something of value that the stakeholders wanted. Given that recent data shows that 23% of projects fail, this is no small feat. Issues like improved productivity are secondary when one out of four projects simply "goes pear shaped" (as they say so evocatively in the UK), after consuming—on average—$1.2 million USD. Note as a related point that this same failure research indicated that the CIO or CEO has often been "shielded" from these failure rates, and is unaware of the true extent of failure in her development organization.

Big-bang process adoption is another common mistake: Educating many managers and developers in the new method over a short period, and/or applying it on many projects during early adoption. Just like a software project itself, adopt the process iteratively and incrementally, in small steps. Start with pilot projects, and learn from the experience.

Another risk is to try to recast the new process in terms of your current culture's vocabulary and ideas. For example, attempting to adopt the UP but rename the phases and workproducts to old, local names. Or, to make efforts to explain how the new process fits into the ideas and phases of the old one, in a misguided desire to help the new process be successfully adopted. Just surrender to the new; make a clean break from the past.

Some organizations have a small group responsible for process, methods, best practices, and so on. A risky adoption approach is for this group to *speculatively* decide how to apply the new IID process—*armchair methodology*. They try to "enhance" or "refine" it speculatively. Coupled with this problem is the related complication of top-down process advice, which doesn't usually work. For example, if an organization is adopting the UP, it has the concept of tailoring the process to fit the project and organization. A risk is to let this group speculatively create a UP tailoring, an XP tailoring, or whatever. The result will often have little to do with what's really useful in the actual project. Rather, determine how to adopt the new process through experimentation and by the advice of the coach and practitioners on several pilot projects; more bottom-up than top-down.

Some organizations have a separation of software designers and programmers. Maintaining this separation is another mistake when adopting iterative development, although there is still need and value in expert designers such as a chief architect. The programmer must be an active designer, as the design is not fully precast in these methods, but evolves in response to growing insight, test results, refactoring, and so forth.

How to adopt an iterative, agile process within an existing waterfall process culture?

Suggestions include:

- ❏ Have an executive and customer champion who understands and can communicate the ideas to their peers.

- ❏ Define a goal or reason to adopt the method, and a quantitative measure of its success. For example, the number of failed projects per year, or the results on satisfaction surveys for developers, managers or customers. Measure and communicate the results. Don't expect quick or dramatic improvement; process change takes time and skill over a series of projects, and a new method is not a silver bullet that will revolutionize things. The famous (and efficient) Toyota manufacturing system took over 10 years to be fully adopted.

- ❏ Present education seminars and learning aides (e.g., this book) to executive and customer groups.

- ❏ Adopt the method with pilot projects and an incremental approach. Start with one project and a method coach. Drive the adoption from the learning that emerges from these early projects.

- ❏ Don't oversell. Don't claim it will improve productivity and so forth, but propose a pilot as an experiment whose results will guide further steps—in other words, an empirical approach.

❑ A failure on the early projects will—not surprisingly—kill the adoption drive. So, mitigate that risk by using a good method coach. Choose a project big enough to be meaningful but not so big it is dangerous; for example, five or ten people on a six-month project is a good size. Don't introduce too much novelty on the projects, such as many new technologies or unproven third-party components. You don't want the pilots to fail for reasons unrelated to the new method.

❑ Let the participants in the early pilot projects become the new method leaders (or "process engineers") in subsequent projects.

❑ Hold "post-partum" project sessions after these early projects in which the stakeholders share their experiences with other customers and management. This in-selling is more powerful than executive or consultant recommendations.

❑ Results speak louder than theory. Assuming the pilot projects do achieve earlier valuable and visible results with lower risk than the prior waterfall process, record this achievement, and communicate it.

❑ If the waterfall organization is resistant to the idea of short iterations, propose instead that their next 12-month project be run as two 6-month projects or three 4-month projects, in order to "lower the risks and show early results." Capture a record of positive experiences with this change, communicate it, and on the next project, suggest a shorter step: "We improved with two 6-month steps. We think we can do even better with three 4-month steps on the next project."

On the question of what type of pilot project to choose, XP and Scrum have a different answer than the UP. The latter suggests a not-too-risky project, but the former methods (especially Scrum) recommend first adopting it on the most difficult project the organization faces. These method leaders feel confident that their methods, applied correctly, will yield success, and that the crisis of a difficult project provides the right fertile ground to truly abandon the old waterfall habits and seize the new ideas wholeheartedly.

How to control costs if adaptive planning?

Before answering the question directly, there's often an implication in the mind of the questioner: That with predictive planning, costs (and schedule) *is* successfully controlled. But research shows this is not true; indeed, predictive planning has a poor track record for software projects. The root problem is the flawed assumption that software development is predictable manufacturing rather than new product development.

Failure research p. 100

Evo and evolutionary delivery provide one model for the answer. At some point an overall budget or estimate is generated for the project, although it is acknowledged as unreliable. Thereafter, take a small iteration step that represents between 2% and 5% of the budget (or desired duration). Plus, choose a step with a high value-to-cost ratio. Have a quantified goal (or goals) for the iteration, and measure the impact of the step. In the worst case, we have "wasted" a small percentage of the budget on an unsuccessful step. In the best case, we have made a good return on the small investment.

The adaptive plan emphasizes—using the most recent information—maximizing value for a small cost commitment.

How do we measure quality in an iterative process?

The short answer is, the same as in any process, but earlier and more frequently. Yet, there is a distinctive component I want to emphasize. A useful best practice is to *continuously verify quality*, and this implies not only quality of the product, but of the *process*.

A number of agile methods promote some kind of *iteration assessment*, which I usually prefer to call the *beer party* (being Canadian). That is, at the end of each iteration (or the start of the next), get together for a half hour as a group, and ask some questions: what worked well, what didn't, and what are a couple of concrete actions we could take in the next iteration to improve? Maybe Jill spent too many hours explaining the defect tracking system to new joining consultants, and she should take a few hours to write up a Web page summarizing the introduction for the next incoming batch of people. Maybe the evolving set of use cases are useless, and their creation should be stopped, or improved.

The Scrum meeting also provides a way to measure the quality of an iterative process. We see, day by day, how things are going, what's working, and what isn't.

How to coordinate subteams or subcontractors on a large IID project?

One part of the answer involves establishing early personal liaisons between the subteams, and a leader in each with an understanding of the project vision and architecture. See "Multiteam or Multisite Early Development" on p. 248. That section provides the details.

The value of forming these personal relationships with other liaison team members is most significant during later coordination and communication. And, having forged a common, deep understanding of the vision and architecture lowers the risk that the subteams don't understand or create what is needed.

Another part of the answer is to establish cross-team milestones for integration and testing (system, load, etc.) of all components. These are the **macro-iterations** of the project. For example, the project may have a macro-iteration of six weeks; at its completion, all components across all subteams are integrated. Within this macro-iteration the subteams may choose to decompose the time and their own work into shorter **micro-iterations**, such as three two-week iterations.

These macro-iteration milestones provide the heartbeat and mechanism to force regular coordination between the subteams and subcontractors.

Note that very short macro-iterations for large projects with many subteams *may* become awkward or unproductive. The overhead of pulling everything together and testing it takes nontrivial time and resources; a two-week macro-iteration may be too short for completion of sufficient new work, given the overhead of integration and test.

Another proven variation on this macro-iteration approach is to relax the requirement that *all* subteams must integrate, and instead only require that at least *two* of the subteams must integrate. This may allow a shorter macro-iteration, such as two weeks, as the effort of integration and test is lowered. See "Difficult Multiteam or Multisite Iteration Planning" on p. 249.

All of these variations can (and usually should) be combined with the practice of continuous integration—see p. 275.

How to estimate overall effort or duration for an IID project?

One way to answer is, the same as before. Don't assume that scheduling the tasks iteratively will meaningfully change productivity or duration. You may still use parametric estimation models (such as COCOMO II), micro-estimation methods based on work breakdown structures or use cases, and so forth.

That said, some of the IID methods, such as XP, include specific advice on how to estimate. These are introduced in their respective chapters, although study of dedicated method books (listed in the recommended readings sections) is needed for full details.

Wideband Delphi
p. 260

However, I do want to recommend an excellent *iterative* and team-based estimation technique that is complementary to other estimation techniques, Wideband Delphi—see p. 260.

How to estimate the duration of an IID project without having a plan of what will happen week by week?

A total effort (or duration) estimate precedes and is not dependent on detailed task scheduling. Rather, it is primarily a function of the requirements, team size, novelty, and so forth. Of course, scheduling issues can affect an estimated completion date, such as if the project spans the summer months of vacation.

I get this question frequently, and the questioner usually really means to ask, "How to estimate the dates of *intermediate* milestones with an IID method?" Major milestone dates can be estimated based on common effort estimation methods, once the goals for the milestones are decided. As always, the reliability of the estimate is commensurate with the quality of the information and the project's current point on the cone of uncertainty.

If we have use cases, how to schedule them with respect to iterations?

Although it is desirable to fully complete a use case within an iteration—it's a straightforward approach—it isn't always best, because some use cases are so complex (with many scenarios) that it would take an excessively long iteration (such as three months) to complete. Short iterations are almost always preferable for a number of reasons. For details: See "Iteration Goals: Use Cases and Scenarios" on p. 269.

How do we track use case requirements across iterations?

To expand the question, how do we track that some scenarios of a use case have been done, and others haven't?

The answer is dependent on the requirements tracking tool, and the way you write use cases. Let's assume you are using the popular www.usecases.org (Cockburn) format for use cases. In this case, for each use case there is a "main success" scenario and various "extensions" (or "alternatives") with labels such as 3a, 3b, etc.

If you're using a tool like Rational's RequisitePro (which adds macros to Microsoft Word), you can use Word to textually highlight a scenario, and then mark the selected text (e.g., the scenario 3a) as its own requirement in the RequisitePro database, with lifecycle state information such as "approved," "underway," "completed."

If you are using a feature or issue-oriented tracking tool, such as Issuezilla or Bugzilla (which is often used for new requirements, not simply defect tracking), you can record the scenario names as labeled issues, with associated lifecycle state. For example, scenario 3a of the Process Sale use case can have the label "process sale-3a" and the state of "complete" in Bugzilla.

How to persuade our customers (or management) to adopt IID?

Don't propose a definite adoption within the organization. Rather, suggest an experiment, motivated from the data and trends: that IID is associated with lower failure rates and earlier results, that it is now used by many organizations, its use is increasing, and so forth. Some of the data in the Evidence chapter (p. 63) may be helpful.

Then, organize a half-day seminar for the executive team, customers, and other relevant stakeholders. Use a seminar speaker who can present the key ideas and make a persuasive case for the experiment, but avoid overselling the benefits. It is useful to emphasize that IID methods support early visible results and ongoing steering by the customers; of course, customers are interested in this point. It must also be stressed that customers will need to take an active and ongoing role in clarifying the requirements, evaluating results, and providing feedback.

Next, get commitment for the experimental pilot project and find an executive champion. Run the project, capture data on the experience and results, and communicate these. Make a decision to continue, or not.

We want to apply XP, but don't have an onsite customer. What do we do?

See p. 152.

We think we are applying XP, but use fairly detailed written specifications for the iteration rather than an onsite customer. Is that OK?

See p. 156.

What's going to happen with our existing test and QA department if we adopt an IID method?

In a classic waterfall environment, the QA team expects to receive a final system for testing near the end of the project, but may not otherwise be significantly involved in the development. Although a final QA step never hurts, it is not sufficient or efficient—because research shows that it is cheaper to remove defects early rather than late.

With IID methods, there are at least two approaches to working with the QA group. The first is to allocate a QA person (or persons) to the iterative project from the earliest iterations—either full-time or part-time. They are involved, iteration by iteration, in the early creation and execution of tests and other evaluations. They become members of the development team. If the project is running in a common project room, then ideally that's where they work, although there are times this is not possible due to the complexity of the test environment.

Microsoft takes this to the extreme by dedicating more-or-less one tester for each developer, and they collaborate throughout the project. As an aside, Microsoft developers do not usually practice test-first development (see p. 292); it would be very interesting to know if the same number of independent testers would be needed if they did test-first development.

A second approach is to deliver the internal release from each iteration to the QA group for evaluation. While the development team is moving forward with iteration N, the QA team is evaluating the results of iteration N-1. See "Overlapping or "Pipelining" Activities Across Iterations" on p. 251. Their feedback can be handled in the current iteration, or if it is too laborious and there are no slack resources, allocated to the next.

Can a project fail with an IID method?

Certainly, although I like to call IID approaches "fail early" methods, and the waterfall a "fail late" method. A waterfall project can be like the story of the guy who fell off the cliff:

As he was hurtling down, someone yelled, "How are you doing?" The guy replied, "So far, so good!"

In the waterfall, the risks pile up near the end; the project can have the mirage of running smoothly for many months while the less risky and easier work is done. Then, pow!

On an iterative project we discover how much trouble we are in sooner rather than later. We have a better chance to cancel the project before too much is invested, or experiment with solutions.

What new skills are needed for managers and developers?

For managers, perhaps the biggest shift—at least with methods such as XP and Scrum—is to step back and avoid assigning tasks or directing work, not being the taskmaster. Recall that in these methods self-directed teams and volunteering for work is important. The manager's role is to reinforce the project vision and company goals, manage risks, communicate the iteration goals, remove blocks, provide resources, and track progress.

They are also responsible for the new skill of iterative and adaptive planning, which is easier but more frequent than detailed predictive planning.

For developers, they will participate in more project management activities, such as task identification and estimation, each iteration. Especially with XP and Scrum, their biggest shift is perhaps the attitude of "owning" the project and its problems. Recall that in the daily Scrum meeting, it is the team's collective responsibility to spot and fix problems with the project or team members, not the manager's responsibility.

On the technical side, developers require skills in how to set up and do continuous integration, and more frequent and thorough testing than they may have previously been used to.

How to deal with change management in an IID method?

This is specific to the method, although most have in common the following constraint: Once an iteration is underway, no changes are introduced to the iteration. This gives the team a short stable period—some control over the chaos.

Most also have in common the practice of *not* treating change requests informally via talk or email; therein lies a path to project ruin! Rather, changes are captured in a change request (whose form ranges from a simple story card in XP, to an entry in the Bugzilla database), and considered decisions for the requests are made by the key stakeholders during the iteration planning meetings.

Is IID useful for commercial products?

Certainly, and in fact IID methods found early and widespread adoption in the product sector. In many software product companies of Silicon Valley, for example, you will find IID has been commonplace for years.

We have to tell the customer what they will get and what it costs—before starting to build it. Therefore we can't work iteratively, true?

False. There are several ways to answer this. For one, if you are in such a market (still common, for example, with fixed-bid contracts with governments), then do what you must with up-front analysis and estimation. And, the customer might have required a detailed predictive plan; you focus in this plan on identifying what they want in the first and second iteration, and accept that the remaining iterations will be less rigid. Next, start to develop in short iterations, and bring the customer into the evaluation and feedback process. By showing the customer the results of the early iterations quickly, you win confidence. At this point you may say to the customer "Even though we planned <X> for iteration 3, you now have a chance to re-choose according to your latest insight and priorities." And at this point the customer is more likely to view this flexibility and control not as a defect in your skill as a predictive planner, but as a more valuable way. The same practice and psychology applies to the evolution of requirements.

In short, we make a waterfall attempt as desired by the customer, and then run an evolutionary IID project as trust is established, to really benefit the client.

Another perspective is that even if we don't have the degree of requirements evolution we wish, by at least organizing the "frozen" requirements work iteratively, we gain several advantages. As the Evidence chapter shows (p. 63), productivity, defect, and success rates may be improved. And we may still have flexibility over the ordering of the development iterations, to meet our desire to drive down risks early.

Customers don't usually care about fine-grained weekly scheduling. They may want to define a milestone that <X> is completed in two months and <Y> two months later. But, they don't have to see that you organize a two-month phase into four iterations of your choosing.

We can't make a solid architecture if we do not know all the requirements up front, true?

False. What we do need to understand early is the architecturally significant requirements, which is a subset of the total. Plus, architecturally influential factors are mostly nonfunctional quality requirements, such as reliability, security, and so forth, rather than the myriad detailed functional requirements. It is less difficult to learn the former than the latter during early analysis. In addition, if use cases make sense for the project, we can focus in the early phase on understanding the subset of architecturally significant use-case scenarios (which may be 10% of the total set), rather than all use cases.

For example, in the UP, the idea is to analyze something like 10% of the requirements during the inception phase—those that are most architecturally significant. Then, quickly start programming in the elaboration phase, while the majority of the remaining functional requirements are uncovered and evolved—perhaps in a series of requirements workshops—in parallel to programming the core architecture.

Rework (or refactoring) each iteration sounds expensive. Isn't it cheaper to design it correctly up front?

In practice, IID projects infrequently require massive rework; it is more a theoretical than practical concern. This is due to a combination of taking small steps and emphasizing early testing and feedback, so that a solid path is discovered and maintained sooner rather than later.

In addition, modern powerful refactoring tools (in several Java IDEs, for example) make large-scale changes easier and faster.

In any event, complete and near-perfect up-front speculative design or architecture is seldom observed, even when it has been diligently attempted. Decades of failed attempts in waterfall projects demonstrate the difficulty—and expense—of this approach. The reasons are varied: the constant use of new (and unproven) technologies, high complexity, the many degrees of freedom software solutions offer, the unreliability of the requirements on which speculative design decisions are based, and more.

Also, bear in mind that it is only XP which promotes almost no up-front architectural thinking, not the other IID methods. Scrum, UP, Evo (and others) all support some degree of up-front architectural analysis and design, with a balanced interplay of early programming and testing to prove or disprove the ideas.

What use are iterations for short projects of, say, three months duration?

Organizing the development and priorities in two- or three-week timeboxes still helps with achieving early visible progress, and keeping the complexity manageable. Often in these projects, most requirements are semi-reliably known near the start; very good. If your organization has adopted the UP and its concept of the four phases, the distinction of the first three (inception, elaboration, and construction) is not particularly useful on such short projects; rather, simply a series of "development" iterations prioritized by value and risk, followed by a transition phase, is sufficient.

How can we get our management to realize they don't need a final, detailed plan on "day one"?

Through demonstration, analogy, facts and logic.

Demonstration—Create and run an IID pilot project applying the principles of adaptive planning. Have external management and clients drive the choice of work each iteration, and at each post-iteration demo ask "Is the project proceeding as you want?"

Analogy—When we appreciate that building software is new product development or discovery, we can draw analogies from other industry planning practices. It is *normal* to avoid detailed predictive planning at the start of a project in other discovery-dominant domains. For example, examine how new potential oil fields are planned. Or a new type of car, a new bridge, or a new consumer gadget. In each case, there's a significant exploratory phase before reliable plans are expected.

Facts and logic—Perhaps the most relevant fact is an average of 20–40% requirements change on medium to large software projects See "Change Research" on p. 72. Not surprisingly, then, the historical track record of early detailed predictive planning is poor. The problem isn't bad planners, the problem is high degrees of novelty, uncertainty and change. An early and highly speculative fixed plan in that context is not logical; the wrong (mass-manufacturing) model is being applied to a discovery-dominant domain: software development.

Our test environment is very complex and run by another organization. How can we iterate and test?

Before offering some suggestions, note there *are* similar organizations that do this, iteratively. Microsoft is probably the largest example of a company that applies IID in a complex test environment with separate testing groups.

One part of the solution is continuous integration or the more mild *daily build and smoke test* practice. The separate test team adds unit or acceptance tests to the build environment incrementally, as soon as possible.

Another element is pipelining. In this case, when the development team starts iteration N, the test team starts evaluating the just-finished iteration N–1. See "Overlapping or "Pipelining" Activities Across Iterations" on p. 251.

What do we do when time, budget, and scope are all frozen but we still want to apply an iterative or agile method?

The constraints are irrational, but it happens. Spend more time looking for existing (perhaps open source) components or frameworks, contract with specialists who have done something similar and used the reusable components, hire consultants with an existing template system they can modify to your goals, use the technologies most familiar to the team, don't ignore communication (e.g., a daily Scrum) and lots of testing in a misguided rush to save time, and as usual, rank requirements and implement them across the iterations in rank order. When the deadline comes up, at least you'll have the most valuable elements, if not all.

Doesn't iterative development mean that we don't know when we're finished?

It *is* possible to know when we're finished and what "finished" will mean. There are several ways to tackle this dilemma. One approach is to have an initial requirements workshop (part of the Release Planning Game in XP) in which all or most requirements for the release are identified at a high level, such as just the names of use cases or features (XP story cards), with some brief description. This can be the basis for a *rough* scope, effort, and end-date estimate. Of course, as the project progresses, these high-level requirements will evolve into detailed descriptions and may expand, but this does not imply an endless moving target. Rather, it is a temporarily moving target that over time has smaller and smaller pertubations (see the "cone of uncertainty" on p. 18). In early iterations, the fluctuation in the total requirements set is larger, and then it settles. On average, perhaps 20% into the project, a more complete and stable picture emerges.

One can argue that this period of uncertainty is undesirable and that an up-front waterfall requirements approach is thus preferred, but research shows that the requirements change significantly in any event; evolutionary methods admit and embrace this, waterfall-oriented methods deny or resist it.

Another variation, used in the UP (on larger projects especially), is to not expect a definition of "complete" or an end-date until several iterations into the project, at the end of the elaboration phase. This is analogous to exploratory drilling at an oil field. Management doesn't expect reliable answers until after some phase of investigation. In this approach, there are a series of requirement workshops across the early development iterations. By the end of the last workshop (for example, after three workshops across three iterations), the goal is to have discovered all the requirements at a high level (such as the names of use cases) and defined in detail around 80% of the most significant ones. At this point, there is a relatively reliable definition of what "complete" means.

Other variants are build-to-cost (in the 1970s this was known as design-to-cost) or timeboxing the overall project. In the first, "complete" is defined as whatever is finished by the time a fixed budget is consumed. In the latter, "complete" is defined as whatever is finished by a fixed project end date. Both of these strategies may be coupled with evolutionary delivery.

Should I plan the work for all the future iterations to ensure the scope and resources (e.g., people) fit the desired end date?

Laying out a detailed, predictive schedule does not really satisfy this concern, and in fact by doing so and following it, the team is *less* likely to meet the goal. The underlying problem is superimposing a predictable manufacturing model of planning onto new product development projects. Such a plan can give the illusion of satisfying the concern, but since it is highly speculative, assumes low rates of uncertainty and change, and is not feedback driven, it is less skillful than an adaptive planning method.

How do I get feedback when there is little or no user interface?

Primarily from tests and measurements. This question usually comes up for embedded applications, middleware, or servers, where issues such as memory footprint, memory leaks, load, throughput, responsiveness, and so on are important questions. In a well-run IID project, a growing application is evaluated each iteration with respect to these qualities, in the most realistic test environment possible.

Should iteration activities overlap? For example, requirements for the next while testing for the previous?

In general, no. An exception is discussed on p. 251.

How long should iterations be?

See p. 267.

How to handle the design of a database with an iterative process?

Contrary to whatever fears your database experts may hold, it is both possible and effective to apply evolutionary database design and development, especially with the structured application of **database refactorings**—changes to a database schema that improves its design while retaining both its behavioral and informational semantics.

The details are beyond the scope of this introduction. See www.agiledata.org for discussion of agile database development.

Should the customer always be in charge of what gets built each iteration?

Only XP recommends the customers choose the goals of the next iteration, independent of other advisors. Most other IID methods imply or suggest a collaboration between the customers and chief architect. In early iterations especially, the architect is likely to have recommendations on the priority of requests, prompted by their architectural influence or level of technical risk.

How to plan an iteration?

See many of the tips starting on p. 248.

Do I give the results of every iteration to my customer?

No, except for evaluation and feedback, unless your method is Evo (which promotes evolutionary *delivery* each iteration). This is a common confusion with iterative methods. In fact, there may be 10 or 20 iterations before an application is ready for production or commercial release. The "release" of each iteration (except the last) is an *internal* release for testing and baselining the growing system. Some milestone intermediate releases may be made public for alpha testing. That said, one of the advantages of iterative methods is that some internal releases can become—without extraordinary effort—a production release of lesser goals, if circumstances required.

How to do documentation for maintenance, when we want to be agile?

First, define what to document by need, rather than speculation. Is there anyone who has maintained a prior version of the product? What did they previously find useful, or miss?

A few tips:

❏ Put the documentation on a project Web site, such as a Wiki.

❏ Within many systems there are a few key tricky or subtle elements, or themes. Find those, highlight them, and write a short "technical memo" [Larman01] Wiki page for each.

❏ It is usually useful to document different **architectural views**. See [Kruchten95] for details.

❏ **Agile documentation** can be created by splitting the team into pairs, and asking them to document in parallel on different whiteboards. One pair will sketch a logical view of the architecture (perhaps loosely in UML notation) and write some related whiteboard notes, emphasizing the key noteworthy elements in that view. Another pair will sketch a deployment view, another the security view, and so on. A digital picture of each whiteboard is taken, and the pictures inserted on separate Wiki pages, one page for each architectural view. Then, the pairs type in some supporting text on the Wiki page below the picture. Using this approach, I once coached a team that needed only three hours to create the maintenance documentation.

❑ Some insights are worth capturing with a digital movie; it is quick, low effort, and often rich with information. Place the movie file on the project Wiki. For example, consider an interview with the architect structured so that she discusses each architectural view (logical, deployment, …) in turn. They may be situated at a whiteboard (for sketching) while being filmed. Likewise with an experienced maintenance person.

How can I create a work breakdown structure (WBS) without a weekly schedule, or an iteration-by-iteration schedule?

The key point to appreciate is that a WBS is not—or at least should not be—a schedule. It should be a breakdown of work or tasks independent of how or when they are handled.

Some WBSs are organized at the top level by major project phases—a **phase-oriented WBS**. Such a schedule-oriented, predictive planning approach is not consistent with evolutionary development and adaptive planning.

Some WBSs are organized by a decomposition of tasks within major software design elements (subsystem-1 tasks, subsystem-2 tasks)—a **design-oriented WBS**. This is acceptable if the chosen top-level design elements are sufficiently general or high-level to be guaranteed correct (for example, vague elements such as "UI layer"). However, a design-oriented WBS is usually a dangerous approach, since in evolutionary development there should not be fixed, up-front decision on the major design elements—they need to be discovered and evolved during the early exploratory iterations.

A better approach is a **discipline-oriented WBS** whose top-level elements are major project disciplines with activities that occur in parallel throughout the project (test, change management, project management, development, design, environment, requirements analysis). During an iteration planning session, items from this WBS are chosen (i.e., scheduled) for the iteration.

BIBLIOGRAPHY

Ambler00   Ambler, S. 2000. *The Unified Process—Elaboration Phase*. R&D Books.

Ambler02   Ambler, S. 2002. *Agile Modeling*, John Wiley & Sons.

AM02   Auer, K., and Miller, R. 2002. *Extreme Programming Applied: Playing to Win*. Addison-Wesley.

AW02   Augustine, S., and Woodcock, S. 2002. "Agile Project Management: Emergent Order through Visionary Leadership." CC Pace Systems. July 2002.

BDSSS98   Beedle, M., Devos, M., Sharon, Y., Schwaber, K., and Sutherland, J. "SCRUM: A Pattern Language for Hyperproductive Software Development." *Pattern Languages of Program Design* vol. 4. Addison-Wesley.

Beck00   Beck, K. 2000. *Extreme Programming Explained—Embrace Change*. Addison-Wesley.

BEKPSM98   Boehm, B., Egyed, A., Kwan, J., Port, D., Shah, A., and Madachy, R., 1998. "Using the WinWin Spiral Model: A Case Study." *IEEE Computer*, July 1998.

Bertalanfy68   Bertalanfy, Ludwig vog. 1968. *General Systems Theory*. George Braziller Publishers.

Blaustein03   Blaustein, S. 2003. Personal communications, ICSE 2003, Portland, USA.

Booch96   Booch, G., 1996. *Object Solutions: Managing the Object-Oriented Project*. Addison-Wesley.

Boehm81   Boehm, B. 1981. *Software Engineering Economics*. Prentice-Hall.

Boehm85   Boehm, B. 1985. "A Spiral Model of Software Development and Enhancement." *Proceedings of an International Workshop on Software Process and Software Environments*, March 1985.

Boehm96   Boehm, B. 1996. "Anchoring the Software Process." *IEEE Software*. July 1996.

Bowers02   Bowers, P. 2002. "Highpoints From the Agile Software Development Forum." *CrossTalk*: *The Journal of Defense Software Engineering*, Oct. 2002.

BP01   Boehm, B., and Port, D. 2001. "Balancing Discipline and Flexibility with the Spiral Model and MBASE." *CrossTalk*: *The Journal of Defense Software Engineering*, Dec. 2001.

BP88   Boehm, B, and Papaccio, P. 1988. "Understanding and Controlling Software Costs." *IEEE Transactions on Software Engineering*, Oct. 1988.

C3Team98   The C3 Payroll Team, 1998. "Chrysler Goes to Extremes." *Distributed Computing*, Oct. 1998.

CLW01   Cohen, D., Larson, G., and Ware, B. 2001. "Improving Software Investments through Requirements Validation." *IEEE 26th Software Engineering Workshop*.

CM96   Chatzoglou, P., and Macaulay, L. 1996, "Requirements Capture And Analysis: A Survey of Current Practice." *Requirements Engineering Journal* 1(2).

Cockburn01   Cockburn, A. 2001. *Writing Effective Use Cases*. Addison-Wesley.

Cockburn02   Cockburn, A. 2002. *Agile Software Development*. Addison-Wesley.

Coplien94   Coplien, J. 1994. "Borland Software Craftsmanship: A New Look at Process, Quality, and Productivity." *Proceedings of the 5th Annual Borland International Conference*, Orlando, USA.

CP86   Clements, P., and Parnas, D. 1986. "A Rational Design Process: How and why to Fake It." *IEEE Transactions on Software Engineering*. Feb. 1986.

Crocker02   Crocker, R. 2002. Personal communications, JAOO 2002, Aarhus, Denmark.

Deck94   Deck, M. 1994. "Cleanroom Software Engineering: Quality Improvement and Cost Reduction." *Proceedings, 12th Pacific Northwest Software Quality Conference*.

Deming88   Deming, W. E. 1988. *Deming Management Method*. Perigee.

DL99   DeMarco, T., and Lister, T. 1999. *Peopleware*, 2nd edition. Dorset House.

DSB87   Brooks, F., et al. 1987. *Report of the Defense Science Board Task Force on Military Software*, Oct. 1987. USA DoD.

Evans01   Evans, G. 2001. "An Extreme RUP Success." *Software Development Magazine*. Sept, 2001.

Fagan76   Fagan, M. 1976. "Design and Code Inspections to Reduce Errors in Program Development." *IBM Systems Journal*, 15(3).

FDA97   USA Food and Drug Administration. June 1997. *General Principles of Software Validation, Version 1.1*.

FDA02   USA Food and Drug Administration. Jan. 2002. *General Principles of Software Validation; Final Guidance for Industry and FDA Staff*.

FF99   Fowler, M, and Foemmel, M. 1999. "Continuous Integration." Available: www.martinfowler.com/articles/continuousintegration.html.

FH01   Firesmith, D., and Henderson-Sellers, B. 2001. *The OPEN Process Framework: An Introduction*. Addison-Wesley

Firesmith87   Firesmith, D. 1987. "The Management Implications of the Recursive Nature of Object-Oriented Development." *AdaEXPO/SigAda Conference Proceedings*, Boston, USA, Dec. 1987

Fowler01   Fowler, M. 2001. "The New Methodology." Available: www.martinfowler.com/articles/newMethodology.html

GAO98   Government Accounting Office, 1998. *Air Traffic Control: Evolution and Status of FAA's Automation Program*. USA GAO.

GAO99   Government Accounting Office, 1999. *Air Traffic Control: Observation on FAA's Air Traffic Control Modernization Program*. USA GAO.

GB01   Gallagher, B., and Brownsword. L. 2001. *The Rational Unified Process and the Capability Maturity Model–Integrated for Systems and Software Engineering (CMMI)*. Software Engineering Institute.

GG93   Gilb, T., and Graham, D. 1993. *Software Inspection*. Addison-Wesley.

Gilb76   Gilb, T. 1976. *Software Metrics*. Chartwell-Bratt.

Gilb88   Gilb, T. 1988. *Principles of Software Engineering Management*. Addison-Wesley.

Gilb03   Gilb, T. 2003. *Competitive Engineering*. In draft. Available: www.gilb.com.

Githens98   Githens, G. 1998. "Rolling Wave Project Planning." *Proceedings of the 29th Annual Project Management Institute 1998 Seminars and Symposium*.

GNP97   Goldman, S., Nagel, R., and Preiss, K. 1997. *Agile Competitors and Virtual Organizations: Strategies for Enriching the Customer*. John Wiley & Sons.

HC96   Harrison, N, and Coplien, J. 1996. "Patterns of Productive Software Organizations." *Bell Labs Technical Journal*, Summer 1996.

Hetzel84   Hetzel, W. 1984. *The Complete Guide to Software Testing*. QED Information Sciences.

Highsmith00   Highsmith, J. 2000. *Adaptive Software Development: A Collaborative Approach to Managing Complex Systems*. Dorset House.

Highsmith01   Highsmith, J. 2001. "Design the Box." Cutter Consortium's *Agile Project Management E-Mail Advisor*, Aug. 23, 2001.

Highsmith02   Highsmith, J. 2002. *Agile Project Management: Principles and Tools*. Cutter Consortium Executive Report 4(2).

Highsmith02a   Highsmith, J. 2002. *Agile Software Development Ecosystems*. Addison-Wesley.

Humphrey96   Humphrey, W. 1996. *Introduction to the Personal Software Process*. Addison-Wesley.

Jarzombek99   Jarzombek, J. 1999. *The 5th Annual JAWS S3 Proceedings*.

JBR99   Jacobson, I., Booch, G., and Rumbaugh, J. 1999. *The Unified Software Development Process*. Addison-Wesley.

Johnson02   Johnson, J. 2002. Keynote speech, XP 2002, Sardinia, Italy.

Jones95   Jones, C. 1995. *Patterns of Software Failure and Success*. International Thompson Press.

Jones96	Jones, C. 1996. *Patterns of Software Systems Failure and Success*. International Thomson Press.
Jones97	Jones, C. 1997. *Applied Software Measurement*. McGraw Hill.
Jones99	Jones, C. 1999. *Charismatek Countdown: A Software Metrics Newsletter*. Jan. 1999.
Jones00	Jones, C. 2000. *Software Assessments, Benchmarks, and Best Practices*. Addison-Wesley.
JPKP03	Jalote, P., Palit, A., Kurien, P., and Peethamber, V. 2003. *Timeboxing: A Process Model for Iterative Software Development*. Paper in progress.
KC95	Keil, M. and Carmel, E. 1995. "Customer-developer links in software development." *Communications of the ACM*, May 1995.
KK03	Kroll, P, and Kruchten, P. *The Rational Unified Process Made Easy*. Addison-Wesley.
Kruchten95	Kruchten, P. 1995. "The 4+1 View Model of Architecture." *IEEE Software* 12(6).
Kruchten00	Kruchten, P. 2000. *The Rational Unified Process—An Introduction*, 2nd edition. Addison-Wesley.
Kruchten00a	Kruchten, P. 2000. "From Waterfall to Iterative Development — A Challenging Transition for Project Managers," *The Rational Edge*, Dec. 2000.
Larman97	Larman, C. 1997. *Applying UML and Patterns: An Introduction to OOA/D*, 1st edition. Prentice-Hall.
Larman01	Larman, C. 2001. *Applying UML and Patterns: An Introduction to OOA/D and the Unified Process*, 2nd edition. Prentice-Hall.
LB03	Larman, C., and Basili, V. 2003. "Iterative and Incremental Development: A Brief History." *IEEE Computer*, June 2003.
MacCormack01	MacCormack, A. 2001. "Product-Development Practices That Work." *MIT Sloan Management Review*. 42(2).
Malotaux03	Malotaux, N. 2003. *Evolutionary Project Management Methods*. Available: www.malotaux.nl.
Manzo02	Manzo, J. 2002. "Odyssey and Other Code Science Success Stories." *Crosstalk: The Journal of Defense Software Engineering*, Oct. 2002, USA DoD.
Martin91	Martin, J. 1991. *Rapid Application Development*. Macmillan.
McConnell96	McConnell, S. 1996. *Rapid Development*. Microsoft Press.
McConnell98	McConnell, S. 1998. *Software Project Survival Guide*. Microsoft Press.
MJHS90	Mays, R., Jones, C., Holloway, and Studinski, D. 1990. "Experiences with Defect Prevention." *IBM Systems Journal*, 29(1).

MKCC03   MacCormack, A., Kemerer, C., Cusumano, M., and Crandall, B. 2003. "Exploring Trade-offs between Productivity & Quality in the Selection of Software Development Practices." Working draft submitted to *IEEE Software*.

Morales02   Morales, A. 2002. "Going to Extremes." *Software Development*, Jan. 2002.

MVI01   MacCormack, A., Verganti, R., and Iansiti, M. 2001. "Developing Products on Internet Time: The Anatomy of a Flexible Development Process." *Management Science*. Jan. 2001.

OR94   Ogunnaike, B., and Ray, H. 1994. *Process Dynamics, Modeling, and Control.* Oxford University Press.

Parkinson58   Parkinson, N. 1958. *Parkinson's Law: The Pursuit of Progress.* John Murray.

Paulk01   Paulk, M. 2001. "Extreme Programming from a CMM Perspective." *IEEE Software*, Nov 2001.

PF02   Palmer and Felsing. 2002. *A Practical Guide to Feature-Driven Development.* Prentice-Hall.

PKT93   Paine, T., Kruchten, P., and Toth, K. 1993. "Modernizing ATC Through Modern Software Methods," *Proceedings of the Air Traffic Control Association*, Arlington, Virginia.

PMI00   PMI contributors. 2000. *Project Management Body of Knowledge.* Project Management Institute. www.pmi.org

Poppendieck03   Poppendieck, M., and Poppendieck, T. 2003. *Lean Software Development: An Agile Toolkit for Software Development Managers.* Addison-Wesley.

Royce70   Royce, W. 1970. "Managing the Development of Large Software Systems." *Proceedings of IEEE Westcon.*

Russell91   Russell, X. 1991. "Experience with Inspections in Ultralarge-Scale Developments." *IEEE Software*, Jan 1991.

SB02   Schwaber, K., and Beedle, M. 2002. *Agile Software Development with Scrum.* Prentice-Hall.

Schuh01   Schuh, P. 2001. "Recovery, Redemption, and Extreme Programming." *IEEE Software*, Nov. 2001.

Schwaber95   Schwaber, K. 1995. "The Scrum Development Process." *OOPSLA '95 Workshop on Business Object Design and Implementation.* Austin, USA.

SEG68   Sackman, H., Erikson, W., and Grant, E. "Exploratory Experimantal Studies Comparing Online and Offline Programming Performance." *Communications of the ACM*, Jan. 1968.

SEI03   *Capability Maturity Model for Software*, Available: www.sei.cmu.edu/cmm/cmm.html.

Shine03   Corporate Report, 2003. *Agile Methodologies Survey Results*. Shine Technologies Pty Ltd., Victoria, Australia.

SKTYBE92   Sheldon, F., Kavi, K., Tausworth, J., Yu, J., Brettschneider, A., and Everett, W. 1992. "Reliability Measurement from Theory to Practice," *IEEE Software*. July 1992.

Solon02   Solon, R. 2002. "Benchmarking the ROI for Software Process Improvement." *The DoD SoftwareTech News*. Nov. 2002, USA DoD.

Standish00   Jim Johnson, et al. 2000. *ChAOS in the New Millenium*. Published Report. The Standish Group.

Standish94   Jim Johnson, et al. 1994. *Chaos: Charting the Seas of Information Technology*. Published Report. The Standish Group

Standish98   Jim Johnson, et al. 1998. *ChAOS: A Recipe for Success, 1998*. Published Report. The Standish Group.

Stapleton97 Stapleton, J. 1997. *DSDM: Dynamic Systems Development Method*, Addison-Wesley.

Thomas01   Thomas, M. 2001. "IT Projects Sink or Swim." *British Computer Society Review*.

TN86   Takeuchi, H., and Nonaka, I. 1986. "The New New Product Development Game." Harvard Business Review, Jan. 1986.

Turner02   Turner, R. 2002. "A Study of Best Practice Adoption by Defense Acquisition Programs." *Crosstalk: The Journal of Defense Software Engineering*, May 2002, USA DoD.

Wells01   Wells, D. 2001. XP material. Available: www.extremeprogramming.org

Wiegers00   Wiegers, K. 2000. "Stop Promising Miracles." *Software Development*, Feb. 2000.

Wong84   Wong, C. 1984. "A Successful Software Development." *IEEE Transactions of Software Engineering*, 3, 1984.

ZR97   Ziv, H., and Richardson, D. 1997. "The Uncertainty Principle in Software Engineering." *Proceedings of the 19th International Conference on Software Engineering*.

F

failure
iterative 316
failure rates 100
FDA - iterative adoption 91
FDD 38
Feature-Driven Development 38
Firesmith, Don 85
Fit testing framework 295
fixed-price contracts 18, 301, 303
forward-engineering 278
frequently asked questions 297
function points 50

G

GAM-T-17 104
Gilb, Tom 94, 213, 244
goals for iteration 263
GUI modeling 289

H

Hawthorne Effect 299
Highsmith, Jim 29, 38, 282
history
case studies 79
Evo 244
iterative 79
Scrum 135
UP 207
waterfall 102
XP 170
Hunt, Andy 38
hype 34

I

IBM - early iterative practice 82
ideal engineering hours 154
IID 9
impact estimation table 235
incremental delivery 20
incremental development 9
inspection
in Evo 230

integration engineering 82
integration problems 60
inventive projects 3
iteration release 9
iterations 263
day to end 258
definition 9
goals ranking 264
length 267
multiteam or multisite 248, 249
number of 11
pipelining 251
planning 261, 267
planning first 268
ranking goals 266
ranking risks 273, 274
scenarios 269
short projects 320
timeboxed 13
tracking progress 271, 272, 273
use cases 269
iterative 9
adoption trends 22
development 9
failure 316
history 35
planning 12
tips 247

J

Jacobson, Ivar 207
Jeffries, Ron 154, 170
JSP-188 104
JUnit 148

K

knowledge capture on Wikis 277
Kruchten, Philippe 86, 207

L

Larman, Craig 208
Lean Development 38
length of iterations 267

Lister, Tim 39, 98

M

maintenance 326
Malotaux, Niels 218, 245
map maps 291
Martin, James 97
MBASE Spiral Model 22
McConnell, Steve 23
measurement 153
    in XP 152
meeting 259
    in XP 154
    Scrum 118, 120
method
    agile 25
    ceremony 26
    iterative 9
    weight 26, 36
methods
    adoption trends 22
    classification 26
    defined 32
    empirical 32
    prescriptive 32
Microsoft Solutions Framework 22
MIL-498 87
Mills, Harlan 93
MIL-STD-1521B 104
misinformation
    on agile methods 35
mistakes
    Evo 238
    Scrum 127
    UP 194
    when adopting iterative/agile 21
    XP 156
modeling 278, 280
    in XP 153
motivation for iterative or agile 49, 51
multisite 248, 249
multiteam 248, 249, 251, 310

N

NASA - early iterative practice 84
new product development 3
new skills 316

O

Ogannaike, Babatunde 112
onsite customers 147, 156
OPEN Process 22
overtime 150

P

pair programming 149, 158, 159
people over process 30
PeopleWare 98
PERT charts 112, 125, 300
pipelining iterations 251
Planguage 231
planning
    a Sprint 117
    adaptive 12, 17, 253
    client-driven 12
    detailed schedules 300
    estimation 259, 260, 262
    evolutionary 17
    first iteration 268
    iteration goals 263
    iterations 261, 267, 324
    iterations by use cases 269
    iterative 12
    meeting 259
    predictive 17, 253
    predictive plans 324
    ranking goals 264, 265, 266, 270
    ranking risks 273, 274
    risk-driven 12, 273, 274
    rolling wave 253
    scenarios 269
    tasks 262
    use cases 269, 312
    visible plans 263
Planning Game 148
PMBOK 107

Scrum 34, 35, 109
  adoption 132
  and Evo 240
  and UP 201
  and XP 132, 163
  chickens and pigs 119
  classification 110
  common room 120
  daily build 120
  demo 120
  history 135
  meeting 118, 120
  mistakes 127
  practices 116, 117, 125
  problems 133, 134
  Product Backlog 123
  roles 115
  sample projects 130
  Scrum Master 119, 126
  self-directed team 118
  Sprint 117
  Sprint Backlog 124
  Sprint Backlog Graph 125
  Sprint planning 117
  Sprint review 120
  strengths 134
  tracking 125
  values 126
  workproducts 114, 123
Scrum Master 119, 126
Scrum meeting 118, 120
SEI 107
self-directed team 118
Shultz, Scott 97
Sprint 117
  review 120
Sprint Backlog 124, 125
Sprint Backlog Graph 125
standards
  DOD-STD-2167 104
  JSP-188, V-Model, GAM-T-17 104
  MIL-STD-1521B 104
standards-body evidence 87
story cards 148, 151
story example 41

structured analysis and design 99
subcontractors 310
subteams 310
subteams - see multiteam 310
sustainable pace 150
Sutherland, Jeff 113, 135
system metaphor in XP 151

T
task lists 152
tasks
  planning 262
  volunteering 263
team 251
  multisite 248, 249
teams
  as complex adaptive systems 34
test-driven development 148, 292
test-first development 148, 292
testing 292
  acceptance 295
  Fit 295
  in XP 147, 148
Thomas, Dave 38
thought leader evidence 93
timeboxed 13
timeboxing 13
  at Dupont 97
  benefits 54
tips 247
tracking 153, 154, 271, 272, 273, 286, 313
  earned value 273
  in Evo 228
  in Scrum 125
  in XP 152

U
UML 37, 196, 278
Unified Process - see UP 173
UP 173
  adoption 203
  adoption trends 22
  agile vs. heavy 192
  and Evo 201, 240

The Agile Software Development Series

Patterns for Effective Use Cases
0201721848

Agile Software Development
0201699699

Crystal Clear
0201699478

Surviving Object-Oriented Projects
0201498340

Writing Effective Use Cases
0201702258

Configuration Management Principles and Practice
0321117662

Agile Software Development Ecosystems
0201760436

Agile Project Management
0321219775

Agile & Iterative Development
0131111558

Scaling Software Agility
0321458192

Improving Software Organizations
0201758202

Lean Software Development
0321150783

Collaboration Explained
0321268776

Sustainable Software Development
0321286081

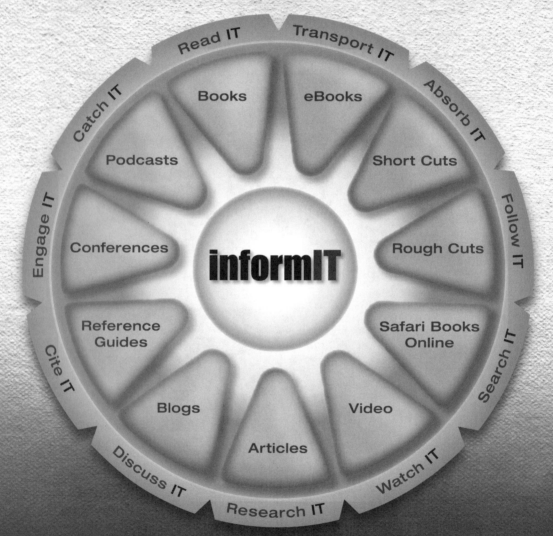